PRAISE FOR *BURKINA FASO*

'A fascinating journey through the turbulent history of Burkina Faso. This book shows how the 2014 uprising was both a remarkable and original episode in the country's long tradition of protests and political inventiveness.'

Marie-Soleil Frère, Université libre de Bruxelles

'Smart, accessible, and essential reading for all who are interested in African politics. It provides new insight into Burkina Faso's fascinating political history, from Sankara to the 2014 uprising.'

Laura Seay, Colby College

'Burkina Faso finds itself at the heart of the current Sahelian crisis, while simultaneously navigating its own revolutionary democratic transition. Harsch's insightful and lively account offers keen insights into the political history of a fascinating – yet unfortunately understudied – country.'

Leonardo A. Villalón, University of Florida

## ABOUT THE AUTHOR

Ernest Harsch is a long-time journalist and academic who specializes in African political and development topics. He worked on African issues for more than twenty years at the United Nations Secretariat in New York, including as managing editor of the UN's quarterly journal *Africa Renewal.* He is a research scholar affiliated with Columbia University's Institute of African Studies and served as an Adjunct Associate Professor at the university's School of International and Public Affairs. In addition to hundreds of newspaper and magazine articles, he has published academic essays on topics including African democratization, social movements, and anti-corruption state reforms. His previous books include *Thomas Sankara: An African Revolutionary* (2014).

# BURKINA FASO

## A History of Power, Protest, and Revolution

ERNEST HARSCH

ZED

*Burkina Faso: A History of Power, Protest, and Revolution*
was first published in 2017 by Zed Books Ltd,
The Foundry, 17 Oval Way, London SE11 5RR, UK.

www.zedbooks.net



Typeset in Adobe Garamond Pro by seagulls.net
Index by Ernest Harsch
Cover design by Kika Sroka-Miller
Cover photo © Panos; 'Young Bella man at the Monday market of Markoye', Burkina Faso



A catalogue record for this book is available from the British Library

ISBN 978-1-78699-136-2 hb
ISBN 978-1-78699-135-5 pb
ISBN 978-1-78699-137-9 pdf
ISBN 978-1-78699-138-6 epub
ISBN 978-1-78699-139-3 mobi

# CONTENTS

# ACKNOWLEDGMENTS

This book has had a long gestation, beginning with visits to Burkina Faso as a journalist in the 1980s and later in pursuit of graduate and post-graduate studies. Over the years, more than two dozen Burkinabè in government, academia, civil society, and the labour movement graciously agreed to be interviewed on record, and their views are cited in the book. Many others also helped in various ways. My greatest appreciation goes to Madnodge Mounoubai, who, though not himself Burkinabè, has been deeply engaged with that country since the 1980s and has frequently given logistical advice, contacts, transcription support, and his own insights. Jean Marie Sawadogo likewise extended essential help during several visits, as an informal guide and with contacts and introductions. Ever since my first trip, Ismael Diallo has been consistently generous with his observations, connections to key informants, and, during the difficult days of the October 1987 coup, the hospitality of his own home. For their informal observations, I would like to thank Moussa Diallo, the late Pascal Zagré, and the late Etienne Zongo. Numerous editors have permitted me to share my thinking about Burkina Faso through their publications, most notably Margaret Novicki at *Africa Report*, Salim Lone at the UN's *Africa Recovery*, and Masimba Tafirenyika at its successor *Africa Renewal*. Gillian Berchowitz, editor-in-chief of Ohio University Press, presided over my previous book on Burkina Faso, a biography of Thomas Sankara, and shared valuable ideas for framing this one. In academia, Pierre Englebert repeatedly provided invaluable observations and contacts. I would additionally like to thank the New School for Social Research for its Chiune Sugihara Dissertation Fellowship, which helped defray some of my graduate research costs. I am especially grateful to the late Charles Tilly, at both the New School and Columbia University, who pushed me to ask difficult questions, maintain a comparative perspective, and better highlight the wider significance of the upheavals in Burkina Faso. If this book can make a small contribution towards understanding the dynamics of such a little-studied country, it is largely thanks to these numerous collaborators. And as always, I am beyond grateful to my wife, Eloise Linger, for her support in so many different ways.

# ACRONYMS

| | |
|---|---|
| ADF | Alliance pour la démocratie et la fédération, Alliance for Democracy and Federation |
| ADF-RDA | Alliance pour la démocratie et la fédération–Rassemblement démocratique africain, Alliance for Democracy and Federation–African Democratic Rally |
| AJB | Association des journalistes du Burkina, Burkina Journalists' Association |
| AMP | Alliance des partis et formations politiques de la mouvance présidentielle, Alliance of Parties and Political Formations of the Presidential Current |
| ANEB | Association nationale des étudiants burkinabè, National Association of Burkinabè Students |
| ASCE-LC | Autorité supérieure de contrôle de l'Etat et de lutte contre la corruption, High Authority for State Control and the Struggle against Corruption |
| CAR | Collectif anti-référendum, Anti-Referendum Collective; in 2015 renamed Citoyen africain pour la renaissance, African Citizen for the Renaissance |
| CCRP | Conseil consultatif sur les réformes politiques, Advisory Council on Political Reforms |
| CCVC | Coalition nationale contre la vie chère, National Coalition against the High Cost of Living |
| CDP | Congrès pour la démocratie et le progrès, Congress for Democracy and Progress |
| CDRs | Comités de défense de la révolution, Committees for the Defence of the Revolution |
| CENI | Commission électorale nationale indépendante, Independent National Electoral Commission |
| CFA | Communauté financière d'Afrique, Africa Financial Community; 1960–94: 50 CFA francs = 1 French franc; 1994–99: CFA100 = F1; subsequently CFA656 = €1. |

| | |
|---|---|
| CFD | Coordination des forces démocratiques, Coordination of Democratic Forces |
| CFOP | Chef de file de l'opposition politique, Leader of the Political Opposition |
| CGD | Centre pour la gouvernance démocratique, Centre for Democratic Governance |
| CGTB | Confédération générale du travail du Burkina, General Labour Confederation of Burkina |
| CMRPN | Comité militaire de redressement pour le progrès national, Military Committee for the Enhancement of National Progress |
| CNPP/PSD | Convention nationale des patriotes progressistes/Parti social-démocrate, National Convention of Progressive Patriots/Social Democratic Party |
| CNR | Conseil national de la révolution, National Council of the Revolution |
| CNT | Conseil national de la transition, National Council of the Transition |
| CNTB | Confédération nationale des travailleurs burkinabè, National Confederation of Burkinabè Workers |
| CODMPP | Collectif d'organisations démocratiques de masse et de partis politiques, Collective of Democratic Mass Organizations and Political Parties |
| Cofedec | Collectif des femmes pour la défense de la constitution, Women's Collective to Defend the Constitution |
| CRs | Comités révolutionnaires, Revolutionary Committees |
| CRS | Compagnie républicaine de sécurité, Republican Security Company |
| CSM | Conseil supérieur de la magistrature, High Council of the Judiciary |
| CSP | Conseil du salut du peuple, People's Salvation Council |
| CSV/CSB | Confédération syndicale voltaïque/burkinabè, Voltaic/Burkinabè Union Confederation |
| FEDAP-BC | Fédération associative pour la paix et le progrès avec Blaise Compaoré, Associative Federation for Peace and Progress with Blaise Compaoré |
| Focal | Forum des citoyens et citoyennes pour l'alternance, Citizens' Forum on Alternance |

| | |
|---|---|
| FRC | Front de résistance citoyenne, Citizens' Resistance Front |
| GCB | Groupe communiste burkinabè, Burkinabè Communist Group |
| Lipad | Ligue patriotique pour le développement, Patriotic Development League |
| M21 | Mouvement 21 avril, 21 April Movement |
| MBDC | Mouvement burkinabè pour le développement et le civisme, Burkinabè Movement for Development and Citizenship |
| MBDHP | Mouvement burkinabè des droits de l'homme et des peuples, Burkinabè Movement for Human and Peoples' Rights |
| MDV | Mouvement démocratique voltaïque, Voltaic Democratic Movement |
| MLN | Mouvement de libération nationale, National Liberation Movement |
| MPP | Mouvement du peuple pour le progrès, People's Movement for Progress |
| ODP/MT | Organisation pour la démocratie populaire/Mouvement du travail, Organization for Popular Democracy/Movement of Labour |
| Ofnacer | Office national des céréales, National Grain Office |
| OMR | Organisation militaire révolutionnaire, Revolutionary Military Organization |
| ONSL | Organisation nationale des syndicats libres, National Organization of Free Trade Unions |
| PAI | Parti africain de l'indépendance, African Independence Party |
| PCRV | Parti communiste révolutionnaire voltaïque, Voltaic Revolutionary Communist Party |
| PDP/PS | Parti pour la démocratie et le progrès/Parti socialiste, Party for Democracy and Progress/Socialist Party |
| PPD | Programme populaire de développement, People's Development Programme |
| RDA | Rassemblement démocratique africain, African Democratic Rally |
| Ren-lac | Réseau national de lutte anti-corruption, National Network to Combat Corruption |
| RSP | Régiment de la sécurité presidentielle, Presidential Security Regiment |
| SAMAB | Syndicat autonome des magistrats burkinabè, Autonomous Union of Burkinabè Magistrates |

| | |
|---|---|
| SBM | Syndicat burkinabè des magistrats, Burkinabè Union of Magistrates |
| SEP | Société des éditeurs de la presse privée, Association of Private Press Editors |
| SGN | Secrétariat général national des CDRs, National General Secretariat of the CDRs |
| SMB | Syndicat des magistrats du Burkina, Magistrates' Union of Burkina |
| SNEAHV | Syndicat national des enseignants africains de Haute-Volta, National Teachers' Union of Upper Volta |
| Sofitex | Société des fibres et textiles, Fibre and Textile Company |
| SUVESS | Syndicat unique voltaïque des enseignants du secondaire et du supérieur, United Voltaic Union of Secondary and Higher Education Teachers |
| TGIs | Tribunaux de grande instance, Courts of Major Jurisdiction |
| TPCs | Tribunaux populaires de conciliation, People's Conciliation Tribunals |
| TPRs | Tribunaux populaires de la révolution, People's Revolutionary Tribunals |
| UAS | Unité d'action syndicale, Unity of Union Action |
| UCB | Union communiste burkinabè, Burkinabè Communist Union |
| UFB | Union des femmes du Burkina, Women's Union of Burkina |
| UFGN | Union de fédérations des groupements naam, Union of Federations of Naam Groups |
| ULC | Union de lutte communiste, Union of Communist Struggle |
| ULCR | Union de lutte communiste-reconstruite, Union of Communist Struggle-Reconstructed |
| UNIR/PS | Union pour la renaissance/Parti sankariste, Union for the Renaissance/Sankarist Party |
| UNPCB | Union nationale des producteurs de coton du Burkina, National Union of Cotton Producers of Burkina |
| UPC | Union pour le progrès et le changement, Union for Progress and Change |
| USTV/USTB | Union syndicale des travailleurs voltaïque/burkinabè, Voltaic/Burkinabè Workers Union Federation |

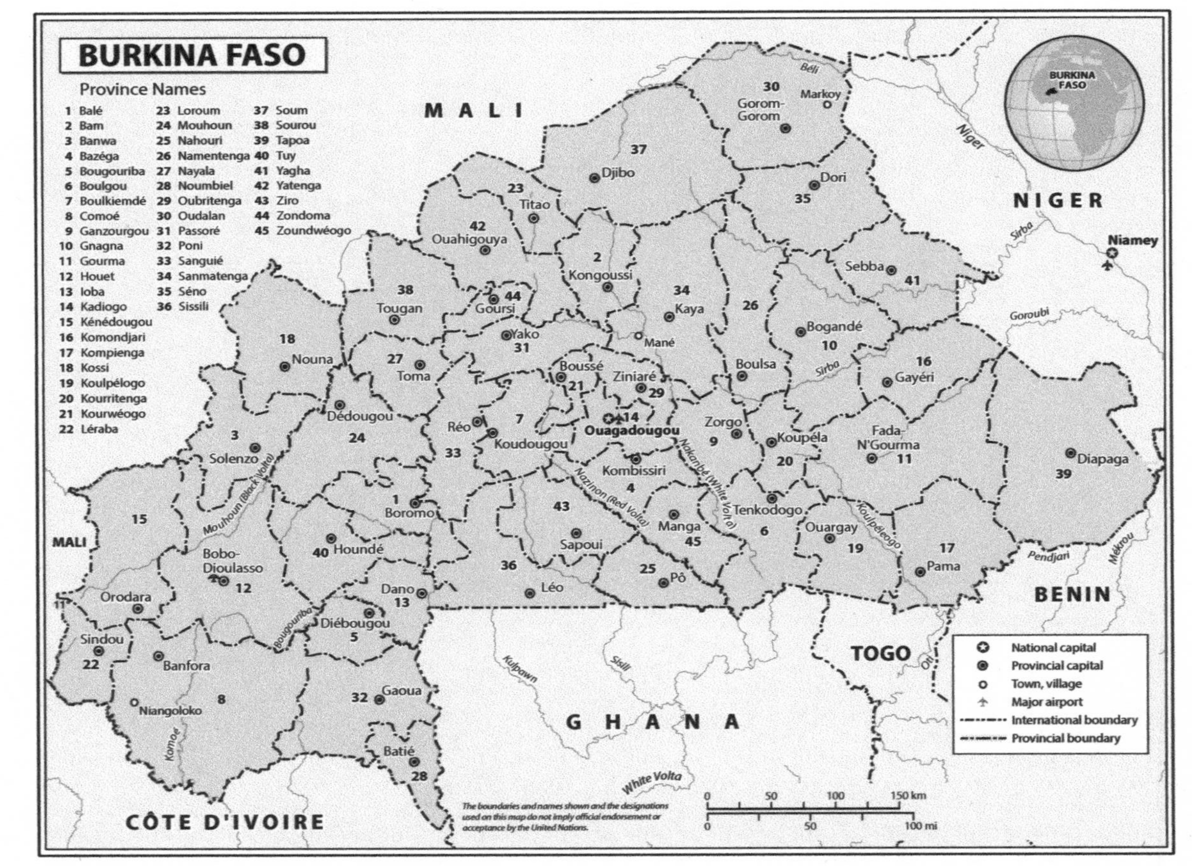

BURKINA FASO
Province Names
1 Balé
2 Bam
3 Banwa
4 Bazéga
5 Bougouriba
6 Boulgou
7 Boulkiemdé
8 Comoé
9 Ganzourgou
10 Gnagna
11 Gourma
12 Houet
13 Ioba
14 Kadiogo
15 Kénédougou
16 Komondjari
17 Kompienga
18 Kossi
19 Koulpélogo
20 Kourritenga
21 Kourwéogo
22 Léraba
23 Loroum
24 Mouhoun
25 Nahouri
26 Namentenga
27 Nayala
28 Noumbiel
29 Oubritenga
30 Oudalan
31 Passoré
32 Poni
33 Sanguié
34 Sanmatenga
35 Séno
36 Sissili
37 Soum
38 Sourou
39 Tapoa
40 Tuy
41 Yagha
42 Yatenga
43 Ziro
44 Zondoma
45 Zoundwéogo
MALI
NIGER
BENIN
TOGO
GHANA
CÔTE D'IVOIRE
MALI
BURKINA FASO
Niamey
Niger
Sirba
Goroubi
Béli
Markoy
Gorom-Gorom
Dori
Djibo
Titao
Ouahigouya
Kongoussi
Kaya
Sebba
Bogandé
Gayéri
Tougan
Goursi
Yako
Mané
Nouna
Toma
Boussé
Ziniaré
Boulsa
Dédougou
Réo
Koudougou
Ouagadougou
Zorgo
Koupéla
Fada-N'Gourma
Diapaga
Solenzo
Kombissiri
Nakambé (White Volta)
Nazinon (Red Volta)
Mouhoun (Black Volta)
Boromo
Tenkodogo
Manga
Ouargay
Koulpélogo
Sapoui
Houndé
Bobo-Dioulasso
Léo
Pô
Pama
Pendjari
Mékrou
Dano
Orodara
Diébougou
Bougouriba
Sindou
Banfora
Niangoloko
Komoé
Gaoua
Batié
Kulpawn
Sissili
Oti
White Volta
National capital
Provincial capital
Town, village
Major airport
International boundary
Provincial boundary
0 50 100 150 km
0 50 100 mi
The boundaries and names shown and the designations used on this map do not imply official endorsement or acceptance by the United Nations.

# 1
# INSURGENT CITIZENS AND THE STATE

For more than a quarter-century Burkina Faso's legislature sat prominently at the heart of the capital, Ouagadougou, a representation of dominance by the country's ruling elites. But now the walls of the former National Assembly are soot-blackened, its windows shattered, and the skeleton of a fire-gutted vehicle sits just inside the main gate. The charred ruins were left by angry demonstrators who sacked and burned the building in a popular insurrection that ousted an autocratic president, Blaise Compaoré, during the last two days of October 2014. Although elections were held a year later, the new legislators met elsewhere in temporary quarters, with no plans to restore the former seat of parliament. Rather, they chose to transform it into a museum and monument, a lasting reminder to future generations that the insurgent action of ordinary citizens—their "transformative violence," as the official museum agreement termed it—can oblige rulers to respect "the sovereign people's will, democracy, and freedom."[1]

Like many others, the people of Burkina Faso embrace their historical symbols. Almost a century before the October 2014 insurrection, in 1915–16, there was an anti-colonial uprising by the peoples of the west, bloodily suppressed by French forces. There was also a January 1966 outpouring in Ouagadougou that brought down the nation's first president, followed by an August 1983 takeover by a revolutionary alliance led by Thomas Sankara. The contemporary name of the country, Burkina Faso (formerly Upper Volta), and its people, Burkinabè, date from that revolutionary era. Many local political thinkers and activists cite this heritage of revolt in explaining the Burkinabè people's readiness to challenge oppressive authority.

Powerholders and those contesting power usually use different, competing representations. State officials generally employ those that uphold order, project power, promote a myth of omnipotence, or instil fear in potential challengers.

These worked for Compaoré for twenty-seven years, one of the longest reigns in contemporary Africa. Domestically, he dominated the political scene with a combination of coercion, corruption, and periodic electoral displays that usually delivered vote margins of 80 percent or more. He also depended on powerful backers in France, the United States, and the major international financial institutions.

Yet people's fear of the state eventually eroded. It took many months for popular contention to build up, but when the end came, it came suddenly. Some activists likened the Compaoré regime to a baobab tree: long-lived, with a very broad, solid trunk, but beneath the soil a root system that was rather shallow. When the tree toppled over, exposing its underlying weakness, an ecstatic citizenry could at last celebrate the possibility of a more democratic future.

The tremors extended beyond Burkina Faso's borders. Other African countries also had recently been experiencing widespread agitation spurred by persistent poverty, corruption, social exclusion, profiteering, or elections that offered few real choices. But it was still rare (other than in the exceptional cases of Egypt and Tunisia in 2011–11) for popular mobilization to actually bring down an entrenched autocracy. Just as activists across the continent and elsewhere in the world closely followed the Arab Spring revolts for encouragement and to draw possible lessons for their own struggles, they were inspired by the achievement of the Burkinabè people. That example was all the more attractive in that it was able to avoid the kind of democratic reversal or civil war that afflicted Egypt and most other Arab Spring countries. When Compaoré's former presidential guard tried to stage a military coup in September 2015, Burkinabè again poured into the streets to defeat the putschists, and then went on to hold genuinely democratic elections two months later.

Among other questions, this book explores *how* the people of Burkina Faso got to that point. The acumen, determination, and flexibility of activist networks and their ability to mobilize ever larger numbers of citizens were important in preparing the way to the insurrection. So were the blunders of Compaoré, who appeared oblivious to the growing power of the streets and effectively provoked the uprising by trying to hang onto his position in blatant defiance of the constitution. But there were other factors as well, including Burkina Faso's particular history of rebellion. Less obviously, some likewise lay in the way the state and its institutions grew and developed over time and how that process influenced the changing forms and expressions of citizen action.

## BETWEEN COERCION AND LEGITIMACY

On a continent of many weak and fragile states, the one in Burkina Faso was in certain respects especially feeble. Unlike some, it did not collapse or descend into civil war or debilitating ethnic conflict. But the size of the Burkinabè state was exceptionally limited, whether measured by the ratio of civil servants to population, the resources in its treasury, or the reach of state institutions beyond the capital and a few other main towns. Although the bureaucracy was not overly corrupt, it was lethargic, inefficient, and unmotivated. Before the 1980s most citizens had only the most sporadic contact with any state agent, even a tax collector. Public schools and health facilities were available almost exclusively to city dwellers, and not even all of them.

The greatest weakness was in state authority. Many citizens, if they thought about the state at all, did not regard it as particularly legitimate. They did not see themselves as owing allegiance to or being served by those who occupied government offices, presided over courtrooms, or rode around in military vehicles. As in most African countries, the basic problem derived from the state's colonial origins. The territories incorporated into then Upper Volta were conquered by French expeditionary forces and the institutions founded to manage the local population were crafted by the colonial office in Paris, to serve the economic and political interests of the metropole. Since Upper Volta was far inland and had little known natural wealth at the time, those French interests were in fact limited, lending a certain ambivalence to the colonial enterprise. First created as a separate colony in 1919, Upper Volta was broken up in 1932 and its components attached to three neighbouring colonies, and then reconstituted yet again in 1947. For local Voltaic employees of the colonial state, this territorial uncertainty made it harder to conceive a shared proto-national "imagined community" that could aspire to independent statehood.[2]

Yet it did become independent in 1960, largely because of changing French policies, rather than any great domestic pressure. The new state's shallow roots among the people it governed contributed to a series of pathologies typical of many former colonial territories. Its external sovereignty was heavily constrained by the many French administrators still staffing the civil service and technical ministries, large and regular French financial contributions to the state budget, and multiple political ties with France and its closest regional allies, such as the government in neighbouring Côte d'Ivoire. Within the country, the state's limited reach and authority led it to perpetuate the colonial-era policy of "indirect rule":

relying on traditional chiefs to ensure the compliance of their subjects in the countryside, where the state administration was largely absent. What loyalty there was to the political authorities in Ouagadougou came from extensive systems of patronage in which scarce resources were doled out selectively to favoured clients. The weakness of central state and political institutions also meant that political leadership often became personalized. Much of the country's post-colonial history was dominated by just a few figures, whatever the political complexion of the government: Sangoulé Lamizana, Thomas Sankara, Blaise Compaoré.

Finally, the state's limited *legitimate* authority meant that officeholders relied excessively on *coercive* authority, that is, the power of their police, soldiers, courts, and prisons. The distinction was first drawn by some of the earliest scholars of state formation, but continues to be employed by contemporary analysts of African states.[3] Essentially, legitimate authority rests on commonly shared beliefs or social contracts that give citizens confidence that state officials will make decisions in their long-term interests. When such confidence exists, people obey government instructions not only out of fear or because of immediate material benefits, but because they think those directives are in some fashion just and socially beneficial. But when legitimacy is lacking, outright compulsion may be the only way to get people to comply.

The coercive tilt of state authority was evident in most African countries following independence, expressed dramatically in a succession of military coups and single-party regimes. They ensured a momentary order, but permitted little free expression. Upper Volta was thus typical, experiencing its first military takeover in 1966. For nearly half a century after that, every head of state had his origins in the armed forces, a trend that only ended with the first post-Compaoré elections of November 2015. Although they may sometimes be long-lasting, states that depend largely on coercion are inherently fragile. With weak social foundations, they are rigid, find it hard to adapt to changing circumstances, and may crack under the pressures of economic crisis.

Sometimes rifts at the political centre provide openings for reformers keen to modernize the state and widen the social bases of state authority. Such a process began in Upper Volta in the early 1980s. The next three decades were marked by two dominant and contrasting examples of resolute state-building, each with a different approach to social engagement and the challenges of authority: the brief revolutionary regime of Thomas Sankara (1983–87) and the long reign of Blaise Compaoré (1987–2014).

The Sankara government attempted to strengthen the state by reducing corruption, extending its institutions deeper into the countryside, bypassing traditional chiefs in favour of direct interaction with citizens, and asserting greater state sovereignty in international affairs. Although it was quite coercive against recalcitrant elements of the old political and social elites, it simultaneously created locally elected popular committees and encouraged mobilization by previously marginalized sectors of the population: youth, women, workers, urban poor, and, above all, rural folk. In a conscious effort at *nation*-building, the revolutionary government also promoted a new national identity, one that was both proudly African and encompassed all the country's diverse ethnic groups. That revolutionary project succeeded in altering the contours of the state and of social and political life, but was itself unable to survive the hostile reaction of domestic conservatism and imperial alarm in Paris and other Western capitals.[4]

Compaoré, once a close ally of Sankara, staged a military coup that killed his predecessor. He pursued a more conservative direction in economic and social policy and relied heavily on coercion, with critics subjected to imprisonment, torture, exile, and death. After several years, domestic and foreign pressures obliged the authorities to adopt the formal trappings of representative democratic institutions. But that search for electoral legitimacy fell short. Instead of a competitive party system, Compaoré fashioned a dominant party-state that marginalized effective opposition and regularly manufactured huge pro-government vote margins. Meanwhile, the regime reverted to some of the standard features of pre-revolutionary Upper Volta: a renewed reliance on rural traditional chiefs, rampant corruption that enriched those closest to power, a patronage machine that tied the state bureaucracy to the ruling party, the co-optation of potential challengers, and a resumption of close political ties with France and other Western powers. Compaoré's system was "semi-authoritarian," argued Burkinabè scholar Augustin Loada. Those desiring change either grew disillusioned with the seeming impossibility of real reform or concluded that violence was necessary to break the impasse. Loada cited one activist's reaction to a series of minor government concessions in the 1990s, "If we didn't burn or break things, much would never have changed in this country."[5]

Although tainted by an autocratic executive, state institutions as such continued to grow in size, geographical reach, and function. In the process, sectors of the state became more modernized, with some officeholders acquiring a professional outlook and creating pockets of resistance to corruption and the arbitrary use of power. In turn, such contention within the state widened openings for the emergence of new notions of citizen action, as ordinary Burkinabè became better organized across the country.

## CITIZEN AWAKENING

Despite official representations, the state in Africa and elsewhere is not usually a solid entity acting with a common purpose. Its institutions function with varying degrees of effectiveness and capacity, and while usually following the lead of the central authorities, sometimes act autonomously or at cross-purposes. Nor is the state immune from social influences. State institutions and agents interact with members of society in many official and unofficial ways: ensuring compliance with laws, levying taxes, providing public services, soliciting bribes, and so on.[6] Members of various social groups function both inside and outside state institutions. States may help mould societies, but are themselves shaped by social pressures and processes.[7]

Citizenship lies at the heart of state–society relations. The concept defines citizens' obligations and rights, in exchange for state protection and other benefits. The particular balance between duties and rights and that between what is expected of the state and of its citizens vary considerably. Sometimes those understandings are enshrined in a written constitution, sometimes hammered out more informally in practice. Economic and social inequalities often impede the ability of poorer citizens to exercise their rights, while venal and autocratic rulers may not fulfil their expected obligations. The struggle for full and effective citizenship is thus a constant one.

In colonial Upper Volta, only resident French nationals and a tiny handful of educated and culturally assimilated Africans were accorded the rights of (French) citizenship. For everyone else, the accent fell heavily on obligations: to pay oppressive "head" taxes, grow cotton, perform compulsory labour, and serve in the French army. Shortly before independence a restricted right to vote was introduced, to elect representatives to France's West African territorial assembly. That franchise widened after independence. But in practice voters had little choice, since an increasingly repressive government had banned most formal political opposition, while in rural areas traditional chiefs simply ordered their subjects to cast ballots for the ruling party. As in other African countries, independence did not bring full citizenship to rural residents, but effectively left them consigned to the status of subjects in an ongoing system of indirect rule.[8]

Little changed until the revolutionary era of the 1980s. Sankara and his colleagues never contemplated representative elections to a national legislature, and in fact outlawed the established political parties of the old elites. Yet inspired by notions of participatory democracy, they encouraged the creation of popular Committees for the Defence of the Revolution (CDRs). Operating in urban neighbourhoods, workplaces, and rural villages, they not only had mass memberships but also elected their officeholders openly. In rural areas, villagers for the first time were able to act beyond the influence of traditional chiefs, making the committees especially popular among youths, women, ethnic minorities, and lower social castes. Many years later, despite the abusive reputation of some CDRs and the later reintroduction of elected representative institutions, the efforts of the Sankara era to solicit active involvement by ordinary citizens was widely seen as positive. "To this day, Burkina Faso largely defines itself on the basis of the democratic principles born during the revolution," declared a commentary in the official state-owned daily on the thirty-third anniversary of Sankara's seizure of power.[9]

Such views persisted partly in reaction to people's experience with the Compaoré regime. The constitution permitted formally open elections, multiple parties, and a wide range of basic political and human rights, including those of assembly, expression, and the press. But those freedoms were frequently violated as the ruling party blocked the emergence of strong opposition parties, rural chiefs again pressured their subjects on the authorities' behalf, and student protesters, trade unionists, outspoken journalists, and others were occasionally shot or imprisoned. Nevertheless, official constitutional guarantees, public pressures, and rifts among the elites hindered the regime's ability to stifle independent thought and expression. Those limitations in turn provided "political opportunities" for regime challengers.[10] As a result, a vibrant civil society numbering many hundreds of organizations developed and became more outspoken, the independent press grew considerably, and as the authorities moved more recklessly to try to perpetuate Compaoré's hold on power, opposition parties and activist networks were able to mobilize large numbers of ordinary people to defend their constitution and resist a government seen as increasingly autocratic and corrupt.

As mass opposition became more transgressive, the government sometimes tried to identify citizenship with "civility," that is, obedience to laws, peaceful conduct, and respect for the authority of elders and officeholders. Many

Burkinabè, however, asserted a different kind of citizenship, one of active engagement that challenged the constraints of the official political system. As some scholars have emphasized, "to be a 'citizen' might be said to overlap with the rise not only of civil and political organizations but also of protest movements," a form of "insurgent citizenship" in which people blocked from official channels of representation nevertheless create alternative ways to fight for their rights.[11]

Among activists in Burkina Faso, this struggle for citizenship was often a conscious endeavour. One of the main civil associations at the head of the insurrectionary movement in October 2014 was Balai citoyen (Citizens' Broom). Another, a coalition of activist groups, called itself the Front de résistance citoyenne (Citizens' Resistance Front) and its supporters carried banners reading, "We are citizens. We will never be subjects."[12]

# 2
# UNEASY COLONIAL ROOTS

Contemporary interactions between the state and its citizens in Burkina Faso partly follow pathways marked out decades earlier. Although with different dynamics, the post-independence state owes much to the French colonial institutions of Haute-Volta (Upper Volta). Those demarcated both the centre of political power and its territorial scope.

Upper Volta's pre-colonial societies spanned a wide spectrum (see Figure 2.1). These ranged from relatively decentralized groupings governed by lineage elders and local chiefdoms covering modest populations and expanses of territory to a more centralized and hierarchical kingdom, the Mossi empire, which ruled over a sizeable population, engaged in conquest, and extracted tribute from subjugated peoples. Very roughly, the degree of "stateness" correlated with two elements: the local economy's ability to produce surpluses beyond the bare necessities of familial or clan survival, and the exigencies of warfare and military defence, factors of "capital" and "coercion" that have shaped state-making processes elsewhere.[1] The former, by permitting the accumulation of some wealth, enabled the emergence of specialized occupations such as warriors, priests, and chiefs. In the pre-colonial period, economic and social prospects depended largely on population density, labour availability, soil fertility, and links to external trade routes and markets. Prior forms of social organization also mattered, as traditional mechanisms of wealth redistribution and communal solidarity constrained stratification, although war, conquest, migration, and spreading market relations tended to erode such traditional controls.

Many chiefs, despite autocratic tendencies, had limited authority. Some were selected by councils of elders and could be removed for transgressions. Others had to share authority with priests or "land chiefs" (usually representing the earliest resident populations). Most were obliged to redistribute wealth and ensure the well-being of the community as a whole. If a chief egregiously violated traditional norms, villagers could sometimes simply relocate elsewhere en masse or perhaps support a rival claimant's challenge. While such checks sometimes made it risky for incumbents to ignore their socially defined duties, that did not make pre-colonial societies either democratic or socially just. Women, social juniors, commoners, immigrants, war captives, and slaves—the big majority in many such societies—had little or no voice.

Among the peoples at the more decentralized end of the spectrum were a number straddling the border of present-day Burkina Faso and Ghana and known variously as Lobi, Dagara, Birifor, and Oulé, among others. They had no chiefs and therefore no defined territorial organization. The main social unit was a small farming group of related families, which combined only for purposes of military defence or to decide property inheritance.[2]

Not far removed from the Lobi and Dagara in terms of social organization were the Gourounsi. They recognized land chiefs who decided on land allocations and performed religious rituals. Most Gourounsi also acknowledged

***Figure 2.1: Main ethnic groups in Burkina Faso***

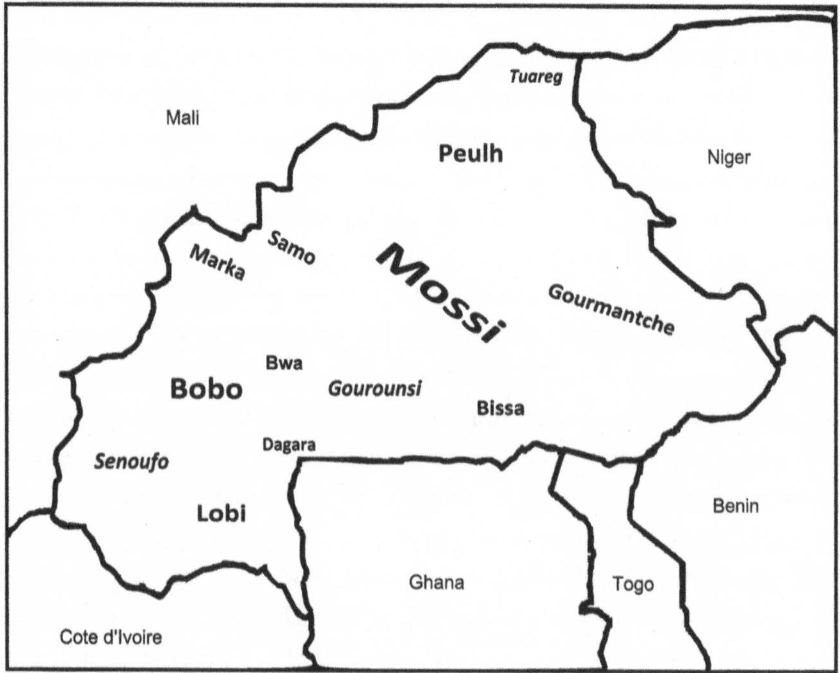


© Ernest Harsch

village chiefs, responsible for organizing war parties in conflicts with neighbouring villages or attacks by non-Gourounsi. By the nineteenth century, a number of higher-level chiefs also had arisen.[3] Some of these chiefs abused their authority by acquiring disproportionate shares of land, and villagers made distinctions between chiefs who "ate big" and those who "ate small." Oral histories recount tales of "hungry" chiefs who provoked social resistance and met violent ends.[4]

Scattered across the western regions, but also in many other parts of West Africa, were the Dioula. Engaged heavily in itinerant trade, they were less rooted to specific areas than most local ethnic groups, but were linked together by their Islamic faith and commercial networks, often establishing decentralized towns in non-Muslim societies.[5]

In the nineteenth century a number of highly stratified states were established by conquest or war. The most significant was Liptako, established around 1810 with the defeat of the Gourmantché by the semi-nomadic Peulh (as West Africa's Fulani are locally known). Liptako was a theocratic Islamic emirate that included free Peulh, subordinate castes, subjugated peoples, and slaves. The emir named canton chiefs directly but generally only confirmed village chiefs selected by local elders.[6]

In the centre was the Mossi kingdom. Oral traditions cite a common origin with the Dagomba and Mamprusi of northern Ghana, and it is believed that the Mossi themselves arose after groups of mounted warriors moved northward and intermarried with local peoples. The initial conquerors and their descendants formed the royal lineages, while large numbers of originally non-Mossi and ex-slaves gradually assimilated into Mossi society and culture.[7] Some early accounts dated the formation of centralized Mossi polities as far back as the eleventh century, but more recent scholarship suggests a few centuries later.[8] Gradually, the Mossi royal lineages, descended from the original conquerors, imposed chiefdoms over a wide area of the central plateau region. This empire was ruled from Wagadugu (Ouagadougou) by a central monarch called the Mogho Naaba. Until the French takeover at the end of the nineteenth century, the Mossi empire fought off attacks from neighbouring powers and resisted wholesale conversion to either Islam or Christianity, inhibiting external influences and helping preserve its culture and social coherence.

The Mossi were governed by a hierarchical chieftaincy system. There were, in fact, two kinds of chiefs.[9] The most powerful were political chiefs, chosen from among an aristocracy of royal lineages, the *nakomce*. Only they were deemed to hold the *naam* (power), and once named held office for life.[10] Those political and administrative chiefs formed a pyramid of authority from the local village and district *naaba*, to nearly a score of *naaba* governing principalities, up to the Mogho Naaba in Ouagadougou, who reigned as the monarch of all Mossi. But that central authority had limits. Many principalities exercised varying degrees of autonomy, with Yatenga often proving particularly troublesome.[11] Below the national hierarchy, at the village level, there were also land chiefs, often coming from lower-ranking lineages indigenous to the area.[12] While the *naaba* were officials of a centralized Mossi state, the land chiefs were leading members of village communities. Many villagers resented the presence of nobles, whom they viewed as exploiters. The willingness of the central aristocracy to acknowledge local land chiefs contributed to the long-term stability of the Mossi political system, in part by imposing limits on the extraction of revenue from subjects. As one scholar emphasized, "A district chief had to be temperate in his demands upon his villagers."[13]

## COLONIAL CONQUEST AND STATE-MAKING

The Mossi empire remained virtually unknown to France or other European powers until late in the nineteenth century. In 1888 the first French representative set out from Senegal to convince Mossi rulers to place themselves under French protection, but was expelled from Ouagadougou by a justifiably suspicious Mogho Naaba Wobgho. Unable to sway the empire's central authorities, the French found a more opportune opening in the strife-torn north-western principality of Yatenga, backing first one contender, then another, leading in 1895 to Yatenga's proclamation as a "protectorate" of France.[14]

The following year, a large force under Lieutenant Voulet marched from Yatenga to Ouagadougou. Lacking time to organize the city's defences, the Mogho Naaba withdrew, permitting Voulet to enter without immediate resistance. When the Mogho Naaba's forces then tried to retake Ouagadougou, they suffered heavy losses and Voulet ordered much of the city to be burned. Unable to capture Wobgho, Voulet enthroned his brother, who in exchange signed a treaty placing "the Mossi and all the territories that legitimately depend on it" (Mossi or non-Mossi vassal states) under the "exclusive protection and absolute sovereignty of France."[15] More French attacks eventually broke the continued resistance of Wobgho's forces, pushing him across the border into neighbouring Gold Coast (a British colony now known as Ghana), where he died in exile in 1904.[16]

Although the new French rulers had subdued the Mossi territories by the end of the century, it took several more years to conquer the Bobo, Samo, Lobi, Gourounsi, Gourmantché, Tuareg, and other peoples. But even then the territory still was not entirely pacified. In 1915–16 a major revolt erupted among the Bwa, Marka, and other peoples of the west. While the French mobilized thousands of troops from throughout West Africa to suppress the rebellion, the insurgents' initial victories attracted wide participation across ethnic and religious lines. The colonial authorities, who estimated the rebel force at some 90,000, expressed amazement not only at the popular scope of the revolt, but also the level of coordination among such disparate peoples. Only additional reinforcements, artillery, the obliteration of a score of villages, and the slaughter of about 30,000 insurgents and their supporters enabled the colonial forces to reassert control.[17]

Throughout this period, the region was ruled as part of a larger French West African colony known at different times as Soudan or Haut-Sénégal et Niger. Only in 1919 was it formally established as a separate colony, called Haute-Volta (Upper Volta). Imposed through conquest, the new French-run colonial state continued to rest on force and the threat of force, whatever its ideological justifications about bringing civilization, economic development, and social progress. Among the peoples of Upper Volta, this was later remembered simply as "the time of force."[18] Yet force alone could not suffice. This was not a colony of large-scale European settlement, since the inhospitable climate and prevalence of debilitating diseases dissuaded many Europeans from seeking to live there. Nor was the colonial office keen to bear the cost of maintaining large military garrisons. So once the initial resistance had been suppressed, the authorities shifted as much as possible to civil administration.

New state institutions were introduced at both the central and local levels, with senior positions filled by Europeans and junior posts by Africans who had learned to speak, and perhaps read and write, French. These institutions—to collect taxes, count and categorize the population, build and maintain roads, recruit labour, draft laws and regulations, police, provide sanitation and basic health services, and carry out other routine tasks—were often modelled on those of the metropole. Although colonial administrators sometimes accommodated local concerns, they were ultimately accountable to their ministries back home. The very nature of the colonial state thus severely limited the possibility of local support and cooperation.

Some French administrators initially asserted that chiefs should be little more than colonial auxiliaries, in line with the general belief that the French role in sub-Saharan Africa was to sweep away "feudal" structures and replace them with modern, bureaucratic state institutions. On the ground these were represented by the *commandant de cercle*, the "circle" being the main administrative unit in most of French West Africa. Such officials wielded not only executive authority, but in practice also legislated and carried out judicial functions. Given those multiple roles, the Burkinabè historian Joseph Ki-Zerbo later characterized the circle commandant to be, simultaneously:

> judge, financier, public works engineer, police and security agent, military commander, manager of the public granaries, school inspector, sanitation agent or recruiter, etc. Quite simply, he commanded everything and everyone. And the distance [from the capital] helped him even more to become a veritable "god of the bush."[19]

In short, as a leading French administrator put it, local commandants were expected to function "as a chief."[20]

To directly assist local officials and staff administrative offices, African civil servants were required: interpreters to communicate colonial directives, clerks, messengers, drivers, guards, and record-keepers of various kinds. The authorities established a number of training institutions for such support personnel, but otherwise saw little reason to establish schools, ensuring the lowest school-attendance rate in all of French West Africa.[21]

African employees of the colonial state often used their positions to extort money, goods, or services from local residents. Such conduct did not overly bother the colonial authorities. In the Lobi areas, the *porsandés*, who were both administrative agents and canton guards, were scarcely paid and as a result carried out some of the worst exactions.[22] Permitting African staff to misuse their positions helped them supplement their salaries at little direct cost to the colonial treasury, while simultaneously cementing their loyalty. The colonial administration thus functioned as much along patronage lines as according to bureaucratic norms—and helped instil practices that carried over into the independence era.

## INDIRECT RULE

Scholars of colonial rule in Africa have often highlighted broad differences in how French and British authorities approached local chieftaincies. In their general policy statements, leading British administrators tended to favour "indirect rule," that is, leaving some local authority in the hands of indigenous chiefs. By contrast, French administrators were inclined towards greater direct intervention, using either French personnel or Africans working under their direct supervision. As noted by Salfo-Albert Balima, one of Upper Volta's pioneering historians, even in the Mossi areas, where a structured pre-colonial state system existed, the French "started out by destroying it. Certainly, their very republican convictions sat uneasily with the spectacle of feudal standards in the twentieth century. But how to demolish in a day centuries of customs and practices…?"[23]

The French colonial ideologists eventually had to confront reality. Bypassing chiefs was not always possible. In the most populous territory in French West Africa there were few educated Africans to serve the state and the number of French administrators was tiny: only about fifty in 1929, with each head of a sub-division theoretically responsible for a population of between 400,000 and 450,000.[24] As one French official commented, "We occupy the country, but we don't administer it."[25]

So despite their earlier inclinations, the authorities soon turned to the chiefs. André de Beauminy, a French administrator in Ouagadougou, described the change in approach:

> Not without reason, we followed the rule of regarding the great black chiefs as exploiters of their peoples, and this caused us to introduce and to maintain a policy aimed at reducing their authority. Later on we were compelled to abandon this policy … During the past few years we have restored power and prestige to the Mogho Naba and to his vassals, the Mossi chiefs … The rulers are now helping us to restore, on a newer and sounder basis, a political edifice which had once appeared to be on the point of collapse.[26]

For French commandants, the process of governing through chiefs was easiest in the former Mossi empire, where a "veritable feudal organization exists," as one administrative report gratefully noted.[27] With an effective hierarchy in place, directives could be transmitted from the colonial administrators through the

Mogho Naaba or his vassals downward to the village level. Although the colony's residents came from many different ethnic groups, those close ties between the colonial authorities and the Mossi chiefs gave a pronounced Mossi cast to the administration, stirring some resentment among non-Mossi elites.[28]

The French faced greater problems where strong chieftaincies had not previously existed. In the west, they arbitrarily grouped villages into broader administrative units, called cantons, and then simply appointed some individual as chief. Initially, the authorities turned to ethnic "strangers," installing Dioula merchants as chiefs over the Lobi of the south-west and Peulh over the Bwa and Samo, until suitable indigenous figures could be trained. But such externally imposed personalities enjoyed limited credibility. Koudougou's inhabitants were "rebellious and individualistic" by nature, the circle's commandant complained in 1930. "The Gourounsi peasant is always ready to ask his chief: 'Who made you king?'"[29]

Some chiefs took advantage of their position to divert revenues for their personal benefit, especially now that colonial rule had eliminated many of the old community checks on chiefs' behaviour. The judicial system was especially prone to abuses, with chiefs permitted to pocket court fines and some able to keep their own prisons. Since chiefs also retained a portion of the colonial taxes imposed on household heads, they often overestimated how many subjects they had in order to boost their own share of the taxes collected. Most resented were the massive colonial conscriptions of Africans, with chiefs as the main recruiters. Under the French legal code for colonial subjects known as the *indigénat*, labour and military service were compulsory and refusal was punishable by fine or imprisonment. The French authorities annually ordered tens of thousands to build roads, bridges, and administrative or private buildings in Upper Volta. Many others were dispatched to the plantations of Côte d'Ivoire or the construction sites of the Senegal-Soudan and Côte d'Ivoire–Upper Volta railway lines. Even without leaving their own areas, many villagers were obliged to grow cotton. The resulting withdrawal of labour time from normal food production took a heavy toll in hunger in the countryside.[30] During World War I, France conscripted more than 200,000 troops from its sub-Saharan colonies, of whom more than 150,000 saw combat on various European fronts. A significant proportion came from Upper Volta.

Taxation, forced cotton cultivation, and labour and military conscription were all highly unpopular, contributing to the intensity of the 1915–16 revolt in the west. They helped stoke unrest for years after. Major French military sweeps were needed to put down agitation in areas inhabited by the Lobi in the 1930s, with a few sub-divisions remaining under direct military administration well into the 1940s. Then again in 1953 artillery barrages were unleashed on a Lobi village that organized a boycott of colonial taxes.[31]

There were hardly any recorded instances of overt resistance in Mossi areas. But even there chiefs faced constant popular pressure. A circle commandant in Ouahigouya reported in the early 1930s that Mossi were evading taxes and labour demands by leaving their villages to live among Peulh. In the Mossi villages themselves, the commandant detected "insubordination," as villagers "are increasingly freeing themselves from dependence on their chiefs. They don't want to obey or recognize their authority."[32]

Economically, the French always regarded Upper Volta as marginal. It had few exploitable resources other than its labour. So to cut administrative costs and make Voltaic workers even more available to neighbouring French-ruled territories, Paris decided to suppress the colony entirely in 1932. The biggest area, in both territory and population, was incorporated directly into Côte d'Ivoire, under the designation Haute Côte d'Ivoire. The circles of Ouahigouya and a small part of Dédougou became part of Soudan (Mali), while Gourma and Liptako were attached to Niger.

Mossi chiefs were shocked. The change not only placed them in a more subordinate position to the colonial administration in the distant Ivorian capital, Abidjan, but also dismembered the old Mossi empire by cutting off Ouahigouya, the core of the once-powerful Yatenga. Despite the perceived betrayal, the chiefs continued to collect taxes and recruit labour for their colonial authorities, hoping to convince the French that their loyalty should be rewarded with a reconstitution of the former colony. During World War II, the Mogho Naaba fortuitously declared his support for Charles de Gaulle's anti-Nazi resistance forces. But only in September 1947 did the restored French republican authorities decide to reconstitute Upper Volta as an "overseas territory," within its old colonial borders. By that time, their motivation had little to do with rewarding the Mossi chiefs' loyalty. Rather, it was to counter the rise of post-war anti-colonialism by playing off the politically conservative Mossi chiefs against radical nationalists in Côte d'Ivoire.

## DECOLONIZATION

In the wake of World War II, nationalist movements swept through much of the colonial world. Across Africa there was agitation by workers, ex-servicemen, export-crop producers, associations of urbanized "youngmen," and other sectors in both British and French colonies.[33] In Upper Volta, French administrators, African politicians, chiefs, intellectuals, and trade union leaders alike took note of the dramatic developments across the colony's southern border, where the Gold Coast gained independence as Ghana in 1957. But in the absence of large-scale popular mobilization in Upper Volta itself, few among its tiny educated African elite could imagine cutting strings with France. Political life nevertheless began to stir, prompted by France's elimination in 1945–46 of forced labour and the oppressive *indigénat* legal statutes, while allowing some freedom of assembly and the press. The colonies, now renamed "territories," were accorded new assemblies elected on a restricted franchise, with some say over budgets, public works, and other matters.[34]

Since Upper Volta did not then exist as a distinct entity, its politics were strongly influenced by the regional context. While the conservative Mossi aristocracy focused on restoring Upper Volta's old borders, a number of more progressive Voltaic nationalists became active in the Rassemblement démocratique africain (RDA), a regional party centred in Côte d'Ivoire. The initial militancy of the RDA, then closely allied with the French Communist Party, worried both the French authorities and the Mossi chiefs. When RDA leader Félix Houphouët-Boigny approached the Mogho Naaba to support his candidacy for the French Constituent Assembly in 1945, the latter spurned him. Houphouët-Boigny won anyway, and played a key role in helping draft some of the changes in colonial policy. The chiefs then sent representatives to Paris, seizing on the government's concern about the radicalism of the "communist" RDA, to win support for Upper Volta's restoration.

When restoration came, the French authorities did not revert completely to their previous reliance on the Mossi chiefs. The chiefs retained authority at the local level, but the administration also introduced new institutions such as a territorial assembly. That obliged the Mogho Naaba and his counsellors to enter the arena of party politics. With the first assembly election in June 1948 restricted to less than 5 percent of the adult population, a party formed by the chiefs easily secured an overwhelming majority. The RDA, hampered by electoral manipulation and outright police harassment and detentions, was thrown onto the defensive in both Upper Volta and Côte d'Ivoire.

By the mid-1950s, however, the RDA was on the rebound. As elections became more inclusive, it was able to demonstrate growing electoral strength, both in Côte d'Ivoire and in the non-Mossi regions of western Upper Volta. The RDA meanwhile had become more palatable to the French authorities as Houphouët-Boigny greatly tempered its earlier radicalism. The Mossi aristocracy similarly found the RDA less dangerous, and when the chiefs' faction-ridden party started to break apart, new alliances developed between some of its components and the local RDA, bringing together elements of the traditional hierarchy (mainly Mossi) with representatives of the tiny elite of teachers and civil servants (both Mossi and non-Mossi). In 1956 an expanded RDA, locally called the Parti démocratique unifié, won dominance in the territorial assembly.

None of the Upper Volta formations were mass parties, nor did they have any clear ideology. Although the steady expansion of suffrage forced them to appeal to villagers and urban poor, their campaigns were highly personalized. Candidates approached chiefs, prominent merchants, and religious leaders, gave them gifts, and then moved on, assured that those "grand electors" would deliver their clients' votes. Given the high salaries and perks that came with elected office, the competition was stiff and frequently electoral fraud and sometimes violence decided the outcome.[35]

The RDA's central leader in Upper Volta was Ouezzin Coulibaly. Although a Bobo from the west, he had served as a deputy of Côte d'Ivoire to the French National Assembly before returning to Upper Volta. His speeches suggested concern for the territory's economic development and for establishing a political system led by educated functionaries and professionals, of all ethnic groups. In that sense, Coulibaly was one of the first prominent Voltaic *nationalists*, as distinct from traditionalist politicians favouring the Mossi aristocracy. Yet like other party leaders, Coulibaly did not speak of independence from France, an option that was not then as clear an alternative as it later appeared, given the prospects for further expansion of African citizenship rights under continued French rule.[36]

In 1958, de Gaulle himself posed the question of independence by calling a referendum across all the French colonies in West and Central Africa to approve his conception of a Franco-African Community. The Community would provide for limited local autonomy, with continued French control of defence, foreign policy, courts, higher education, external transport and communications, monetary affairs, and economic policy. Any territory voting "no," he declared, would go its own way. Almost all the dominant parties throughout the region campaigned for a "yes" vote. Ultimately only Guinea rejected the

Community proposal, and as a result became immediately independent. In Upper Volta, the RDA favoured de Gaulle's proposal, as did the Mouvement démocratique voltaïque (MDV), which otherwise was distinguished by radical opposition to the Mossi chiefs, French administrators, and Catholic Church hierarchy. Only the Mouvement de libération nationale (MLN) and the Parti africain de l'indépendance (PAI) called for a "no" vote, that is, for independence. Both were narrowly rooted in the academic community, having just recently been formed in several of the colonies, including Upper Volta, by professors and radical student activists.[37] The final official tally was 91 percent in favour of continued French affiliation.

Although the chiefs had supported that outcome, they remained uneasy about the changing political situation. Just a few weeks after the referendum, the territorial assembly was scheduled to choose a successor to Coulibaly, who had died after an illness. Mogho Naaba Kougri, an inexperienced twenty-seven-year-old who had just ascended to the throne after his father's death, sought to influence the outcome by proposing a "government of union and public safety" under a constitutional monarchy. The legislators refused to comply. Then the Mossi aristocracy mounted a show of force outside the assembly by some 3,000 armed warriors, who only dispersed under threat of French military action.[38] The Mogho Naaba's move backfired, stirring popular anti-chief sentiments.

In late October the RDA confirmed Maurice Yaméogo as head of government, a position he had held on an interim basis since Coulibaly's death. A former clerk in the colonial administration, Yaméogo had only recently become a central figure in the RDA. A Mossi commoner with a solid political base in his hometown of Koudougou, he was well-placed to take advantage of the Mogho Naaba's blunder. He was no radical, however. His administration ordered police to harass the two explicitly pro-independence parties, the MLN and PAI. Through repression, threats, and bribery, most opposition deputies soon were either driven out of the assembly or absorbed into the RDA, which itself was purged of many potential challengers to Yaméogo's dominance. Some parties were banned outright.

Unexpectedly for Yaméogo, the prospect of outright independence advanced when de Gaulle unilaterally announced in December 1959 that the territories within the Franco-African Community could accede to independence without losing French assistance. Although Yaméogo then started proclaiming the virtues of state sovereignty, he was determined to control the process as tightly as possible. In late June, a little more than a month before the scheduled date for Upper Volta's independence (5 August 1960), six prominent opposition figures sent a letter to Yaméogo proposing a "national union" government to help build the new state. Yaméogo responded by ordering their arrest. Five were soon picked up, while the sixth managed to flee abroad.[39]

Yaméogo epitomized a narrow strata of Voltaic society: the stewards, civil servants, and functionaries who had staffed the lower grades of the colonial administration and now had a chance to step upwards a rung or two. Ahmadou Dicko, a leader of the MLN, captured the contempt with which pro-independence activists viewed this group:

> Throughout the era of the *indigénat* and forced labour, the African functionary—symbolized by the clerk, the interpreter, and the canton guard—was the occupier's most zealous auxiliary ... And now he—whose gods always were the commandant, the governor and the governor-general—sees the possibility that his wildest dreams may be answered, that he has a chance to take the place of the commandant, to take the place of the governor, to take the place of the governor-general, to become, at the same time, rich and "esteemed."[40]

Or as Nazi Boni, the opposition politician who had evaded arrest a few weeks earlier by fleeing abroad, laconically observed, independence was formally proclaimed by "those who had been its fiercest enemies, who today, as yesterday, are ready to sabotage it. It's a paradox of life. It's a human comedy."[41]

# 3
# MINISTRIES OF PLUNDER

Although colonial rule had a low-key end, once independence came the new government enjoyed an initial stock of political capital. Even some sceptics were willing to give the politician occupying the national executive the benefit of the doubt—for a time. However, unlike some of the other "founding fathers" of Africa's new states, Maurice Yaméogo exhibited little inclination to seriously tackle colonialism's political, social, and economic legacies.

Consistent with his misgivings about independence, Yaméogo held onto the French umbilical cord. Although his government did not permit French military bases, many French officers were seconded to the new Voltaic army as "technical advisers."[1] For at least another decade-and-a-half, many state services were run by foreign technical assistants, mainly French. The French government, moreover, regularly topped up the national budget in exchange for Upper Volta's continued membership in the franc monetary zone (CFA),[2] which facilitated the continued dominance of local business by French interests.

Political and economic ties with Côte d'Ivoire also remained close, especially since the ruling parties in both countries were offshoots of the same former regional party and upwards of a million Voltaic migrants worked in Côte d'Ivoire and sent substantial remittances back home. Meanwhile, Yaméogo made sporadic efforts to establish some pan-African credentials. He flirted briefly with Ghana's Kwame Nkrumah shortly after independence. While closer pan-African ties were a central part of Nkrumah's foreign agenda, on Yaméogo's side they were a feint to frighten his patrons into providing more assistance. Then, during a 1965 visit to Washington to seek military aid, Yaméogo flipped, presenting his regime as an anti-communist bastion against Nkrumah. His subsequent speeches were peppered with diatribes against communist "subversion" and the danger of a "Chinese invasion."[3]

On the domestic front, Yaméogo expressed little vision for nation- or state-building and made only minor modifications to the state structures inherited from the colonial authorities. As before, the two linchpins of rural administration were the canton and village chiefs and the *commandants de cercle*. Because of his own political conflicts with the top echelons of the Mossi chieftaincy just before independence, Yaméogo placed somewhat more emphasis on the role of state-appointed officials and local leaders of the ruling RDA. In part, Yaméogo saw the chiefs as potential competitors with those local party representatives. He often denounced "feudal" attitudes and practices, prohibited chiefs from wearing royal regalia and attire in public, decreed that no chiefs could be replaced upon their deaths, and towards the end of his government declared that any chiefs fulfilling administrative functions, such as the canton chiefs, should be directly elected by adult suffrage.[4] Combined with draft legislation to regulate polygamy, child marriage, and bride prices, such edicts stirred alarm among chiefs. But ultimately they had little practical effect. The system of parallel court jurisdictions remained untouched, so that alongside the state courts run by commandants and appointed magistrates, there still were traditional courts run by chiefs. Nor were the decrees trimming the other powers and prerogatives of chiefs ever seriously implemented. As Yaméogo himself acknowledged, central state directives often simply "evaporated" before they reached the villages.[5]

In the cities, the state bureaucracy was a somewhat more tangible force. Hundreds of new civil servants were hired and a new school of national administration trained scores of senior officials, mainly in Ouagadougou and Bobo-Dioulasso.[6] But greater numbers did not mean improved efficiency. One government circular complained that "almost all" administrative agents exhibited an "alarming" lack of professional conduct, with frequent absences, long delays in dealing with files, and a tendency to fill office hours with personal affairs.[7] Some civil servants stole or embezzled funds. Because of diversions, dubious contracts, and other lapses, many financial allocations from the reserve bank and the state investment fund simply melted away.[8]

A few errant personnel were punished as Yaméogo from time to time lashed out against favouritism, nepotism, "theft, the organized pillage of the state, corruption, and rottenness."[9] Anti-corruption measures failed to dent the extravagant lifestyles of Yaméogo and his colleagues, but they *were* used as weapons against those who crossed Yaméogo politically. One case was that of Maxime Ouédraogo, a former union organizer who became minister of labour. In 1963 he was arrested on charges of theft from a state marketing enterprise. Whatever the veracity of the accusations, it was no coincidence that Ouédraogo was one of the most popular political figures in Ouagadougou, and thus a potential political rival.[10] Ouédraogo soon had company in prison from other former union leaders, ex-ministers, and party officials. The detentions reflected a steady tightening of Yaméogo's political control. The RDA, already the sole legal party, sought to extend its reach by creating allied women's and youth wings. The trade unions were subjected to a combination of co-optation and repression. Official political life, always confined to a tiny elite, shrank even more.

In hindsight, however repressive and corrupt Yaméogo's rule, it was also inept, in that his arbitrary purges and spurning of key constituencies left it exceptionally vulnerable. When Frédéric Guirma, one of his ambassadors, later wrote a biography of the president, he chose a title suggesting an instructional manual: "How to Lose Power."[11]

In 1964 Yaméogo further antagonized the unions with an abortive effort to cut their international affiliations and force them into a new RDA-linked union federation, while simultaneously introducing severe economic austerity, including cuts in employees' family allowances. He may have regarded the risk as minimal, since the sphere of formal labour was quite small. At the time of independence there were only an estimated 25,000 salaried employees nationally.[12] But as a particularly well-organized sector of the population, the unions proved to be disproportionately influential.

Throughout 1965 Yaméogo also alienated important sectors of the Voltaic elites, as popular anger simultaneously mounted over his policies and style of rule. With any possible opposition candidate barred from running, Yaméogo claimed re-election in October 1965 with 99.98 percent of the vote, followed the next month by legislative elections in which the RDA slate, again unopposed, won 99.97 percent. In both polls, voter turnout was extremely low. Then in December the new budget featured a 20 percent across-the-board cut in salaries. Seemingly oblivious to the reaction this stirred, Yaméogo that same month went on a lavish honeymoon to Brazil and the United States with a new wife. Following an earlier divorce and an end to government subsidies to Catholic schools, the spectacle of the honeymoon further irritated the Catholic hierarchy. It also heightened public resentment over corruption and such ostentatious symbols as a new party headquarters and a second presidential palace in Koudougou. To cap it all, Yaméogo announced a dual-nationality agreement with Ivorian President Houphouët-Boigny. While of potential benefit to Voltaic migrants living in Côte d'Ivoire, the agreement provoked a nationalist reaction, fuelled by long-standing resentment over Ivorian high-handedness.[13]

The first large-scale response to Yaméogo's year-end initiatives came from labour. Virtually all unions came together in a joint committee to demand lower taxes and the reversal of the 20 percent wage cut. The government did not budge. On 31 December, while union leaders were meeting to discuss further action, police dispersed them with tear gas, but not before the committee decided to call a general strike for 3 January 1966. Top union leaders went into hiding, but about 100 others were arrested on the orders of the president's cousin, Interior Minister Dénis Yaméogo. The Catholic cardinal and the Mogho Naaba tried to cool things by urging Yaméogo to make some concessions, but he refused.

Meanwhile, about 500 union messengers spread word about the general strike, as student activists prepared their own mass demonstrations. Some Mossi chiefs let it be known that they approved the strike. On the morning of 3 January hardly any employees reported for work. Students from secondary schools and the teacher training college marched to the central square, just opposite army headquarters, where they were joined by workers, street vendors, unemployed youths, and many others. Estimates of the size of the crowd have varied, ranging from 25,000 to upwards of 100,000, but historians agree that it was the largest single protest the country had yet seen. Demonstrators raised various slogans: against the wage cuts and corruption and for "Bread, water, democracy." Some, referring to Yaméogo's 99.98 percent election score, carried signs reading, "We, the 0.02%." Many soldiers, confronting the huge crowd, made their sympathies known (their own salaries had also been cut). When Yaméogo ordered the army commander, Lieutenant Colonel Sangoulé Lamizana, to have his troops disperse the demonstrators with gunfire, the colonel refused, a stance shared by most senior officers. As the day wore on and the soldiers' refusal to fire became evident, many demonstrators started chanting "Army to power!" That evening Yaméogo announced that the 20 percent wage cut would be rescinded. But it was too late. Demonstrators continued to demand his departure. A few hours later Yaméogo formally resigned and transferred power to Lamizana.[14]

## OFFICERS AT THE HELM

Compared with its predecessor and with some military regimes in neighbouring countries, the military government of Sangoulé Lamizana appeared far less toxic.

Only a handful of dissidents were ever jailed. Troublesome trade unionists were offered high-paid positions to buy their silence or, if that failed, were transferred to isolated postings. Student activists frequently received government scholarships to leave the country and study abroad. Although Lamizana was in power for nearly a decade and a half, he did not accumulate much visible wealth. By the turn of the century, he was still living in a house much more modest than those of many Ouagadougou politicians and nouveaux riches, his advice as a respected elder statesman occasionally solicited. Yet under his government, Upper Volta remained in virtual stasis, as poor and underdeveloped as when it was under colonial rule, still economically dependent and politically beholden to Paris, with public life confined to a tiny urban elite and the rural chieftaincy. There was occasional talk of political and social reform, but little action.

When Lamizana first took the helm after the January 1966 insurrection, he hinted at impending changes, including efforts to instil discipline and integrity in the state administration. Indeed, the very takeover of government affairs by the military, untainted by the corruption and patronage of civilian politicians, was welcomed as a step towards honest government, as were the dissolution of the National Assembly and prohibition of political activities. The civil service minister promised reforms to revitalize the administration and eliminate "state decadence, waste, abuses, favouritism, routinism, chaos, and inertia."[15]

The unions, invigorated by their success in helping oust Yaméogo, put constant pressure on the new government to bring the former president and his allies to justice. The teachers' Syndicat national des enseignants africains de Haute-Volta (SNEAHV) demanded that the authorities freeze the bank accounts of all former officials, investigate the incomes and properties of Yaméogo and his allies, try all believed to have stolen funds, and confiscate illegally acquired assets. The Union syndicale des travailleurs voltaïque (USTV), one of the central union federations, urged an investigative commission previously set up by Lamizana to speed up its work.[16] It took well over a year, but eventually the government ordered the confiscation of various buildings and other properties belonging to Yaméogo and eight other top officials. In 1969 the former president was found guilty of corruption by a special court and sentenced to five years' hard labour, although Lamizana ordered his release a little more than a year later.[17]

Though modest in scope and severity, such anti-corruption efforts made it possible for Lamizana to do something his predecessor could not: impose stringent economic austerity. During the first year of military rule, the Finance Ministry, under Quartermaster First Class Marc Tiémoko Garango, sought to balance the books by getting rid of hundreds of state employees, reducing salaries by 10 percent, and imposing "patriotic contributions" equivalent to a half-month's pay. The measures, in some respects more severe than what Yaméogo had tried to implement, were unpopular and contributed to trade union bitterness that would erupt later on. But for the time being the avoidance of ostentatious displays of wealth and waste by government officials, along with cuts in ministers' own housing and utility subsidies, enabled Lamizana to carry through his austerity programme. Within five years the government succeeded in clearing its debt arrears, strengthening tax collection, and saving enough money to permit moderately greater outlays for both public salaries and new investments.[18]

While of some consequence in the cities, many of those policies did not significantly affect the bulk of Upper Volta's people, who still lived in isolated villages beyond the reach of most state institutions. There, traditional chiefs remained the most immediate force in people's day-to-day lives. Although somewhat harassed and forsaken under the previous government, the chiefs sensed that Lamizana was open to reviving their authority. In 1968 nearly 170 chiefs from around the country met in Ouagadougou at the palace of Mogho Naaba Kougri. They reconstituted a moribund association of chiefs and appealed to the government to restore all their previous privileges. Lamizana himself accepted the Mogho Naaba's petition and a few months later bestowed on the emperor one of the highest national honours. That October the chiefs held a national congress at which the Mogho Naaba pledged that the chiefs would do nothing to undermine governmental authority.[19]

For a government with limited resources and personnel, the chiefs served a useful function as indirect local agents of the central state. But for a number of organized social groups, the restoration of unbridled chiefly authority was a step backwards. The most prominent women's federation complained that the customary courts upheld practices that severely limited women's rights.[20] In 1968, when the resurgence of chiefly power was first becoming more pronounced, a congress of the national students' association devoted most of its sessions to the plight of the country's rural majority, identifying "feudal" chiefs as a hindrance to villagers' advancement. The students also criticized the local circle commandants appointed by the state as "monarchs over the subjugated natives."[21]

The students' terminology was scarcely an exaggeration. Some rural state officials and their superiors in Ouagadougou explicitly assumed the aura of traditional chiefs. As a minister of the interior, Lieutenant Colonel Gabriel Somé Yorian, advised his prefects:

> In your capacity as representatives of the central government, it falls on you to direct the affairs of your region. You should demonstrate a spirit of availability and courtesy towards your collaborators, without however forgetting: he who loves well, punishes well. In short, you must be chiefs, in the full meaning of the word.[22]

## POLITICIANS BACK AT THE TROUGH

Meanwhile, party politicians began suggesting a return to civilian government. They never had been excluded entirely; indeed, several served as ministers in Lamizana's various cabinets, although as individuals, not party representatives. But the politicians kept up steady pressure for a bigger role. As early as 1968, some trade unions linked with the old parties publicly called for a new constitution. "Return to a civilian regime," proclaimed some of the banners at that year's May Day marches.[23]

That November, Lamizana authorized political parties to function openly again. Yet it took another year for him to set up a constitutional committee to draft a new national charter. It was a carefully controlled undertaking. All fifty members were appointed, including five officers, four political party representatives, five union leaders, a number of figures from professional and other associations, and twenty "rural" members, many of them chiefs. Although the committee's overall composition was conservative, Lamizana took no chances and accorded it only advisory powers. In the end, it produced a draft that elicited vigorous protests from the party leaders. Lamizana relented somewhat and used his discretionary powers to amend the text to accommodate some party concerns.[24]

The draft nevertheless retained a considerable role for the military. Although it provided for an elected National Assembly with legislative authority and budgetary oversight, it stipulated that the army would not only ensure national order and defence, but could pursue "any action of national construction," a formulation broad enough to justify military involvement in many areas of public life. Moreover, transitional provisions in effect for four years specified that one-third of government ministers would be military officers and, most importantly, that the presidency would not be elected, but occupied by "the most senior military personality of the highest rank": in other words, Lamizana, who had been promoted to general two years earlier.[25] The party leaders were willing to live with that and campaigned for approval of the draft by public referendum. Not all unions rallied behind the new constitution, however. The SNEAHV teachers' union, still one of the most outspoken, called for an outright "no" vote to reject both the "confusion of the political parties" and the army's efforts to elevate itself into a "privileged class."[26] Few others saw it that way. In June 1970 the constitution was adopted by an overwhelming 98.6 percent of voters, with a relatively high turnout of 75 percent of the eligible electorate.[27]

Several months later, in December 1970, voters again went to the polls to elect deputies to the new National Assembly. The overwhelmingly dominant force was the old RDA, which had retained a solid national political machine. It held thirty-seven of the fifty-seven assembly seats and one of its central leaders, Gérard Kango Ouédraogo, was named prime minister. Two other parties secured more than a dozen seats, while the MLN of Professor Joseph Ki-Zerbo, which presented itself as pan-Africanist and social democratic, got six.[28] The parties (with the partial exception of the MLN) were organized primarily along the patronage lines that prevailed in the 1950s and 1960s.[29]

By February 1971 a cabinet of ten civilians and five military officers was in place. This Second Republic exhibited strong lines of continuity with the first, except that it perpetuated the military hierarchy's substantial role in political and state affairs. Yet civilian politicians had been given enough scope to claim credit (or take the blame) for the new government's performance. Economic policy more or less reflected the same combination of selective state intervention and openness to commercial market interests. Few alterations of any kind were made in overall state organization or procedures. There was some discussion about the problems of the judiciary, but no significant reforms were initiated and no one seriously challenged maintenance of the chiefs' customary tribunals.[30]

Meanwhile, a severe famine began to expose more sharply the social inequities and bureaucratic lethargy of Upper Volta's established order. Although the country had already experienced several poor harvests in the late 1960s, conditions worsened markedly in 1972–73, a time of drought and starvation throughout the West African Sahel. As in neighbouring Mali and Niger, food became scarce in Upper Volta's northern region. Hundreds of thousands were driven to the edge of starvation and an unknown number perished. Herds of cattle and other livestock were decimated. Masses of people migrated southwards in search of food and water. Entire villages simply disappeared from the map. As shortages drove up market prices for grain, water, and other basic necessities nationally, many people in the cities and the more fertile southern and western regions also felt the impact. Later oral history accounts by Sahelian villagers recalled that time as the most traumatic of their lives.[31]

The RDA government of Prime Minister Ouédraogo was very slow to respond, detached as it was from the difficulties of country folk, especially the semi-nomadic Peulh and Tuareg livestock herders who were among the famine's first victims. It did not officially acknowledge that full-scale famine existed until February 1973. Aside from appealing for international relief, the government maintained that there was little it could do beyond temporarily suspending the colonial-era "head" and livestock taxes in the most severely affected regions. The administration's official grain marketing structures were so weak and underfinanced that commercial merchants and private transport owners were able to seize on the scarcities to realize exceptional profits, often hoarding grain to drive prices up even further. Popular anger turned most immediately against the merchants. Some contemporary analysts, however, suggested that the government's failure to control profiteering was not simply because it lacked the ability. "When one knows the relations between the governing RDA and this class of merchants, then it is hardly surprising that the government's actions have had no effect on national markets," commented a non-governmental relief group.[32]

Some state officials were directly involved in profiteering. As early as 1971–72, both civilian and military personnel were implicated in embezzling aid funds or stealing relief shipments for resale on the black market. Only a few lower-level figures were sentenced to short prison terms. Outrage swept the country. With the US Watergate scandal making international headlines, local critics quickly adapted the label: "Sahelgate," or, more popularly, "Watergrain."[33]

At a time of growing uncertainty, marked by threats of famine and exposures of dishonest conduct by officials and merchants, social unrest rose once again. In late 1971 and early 1972, secondary school students in Bobo-Dioulasso and Banfora boycotted classes and demonstrated, prompting severe police intervention. In January 1972, on the sixth anniversary of the 1966 insurrection against Yaméogo, three labour federations and nearly a dozen autonomous unions demanded that the government raise the minimum wage, ease taxes, eliminate fraudulent practices by parliamentary deputies, and stop trying to revive the "feudal" system in the countryside. Judging that the government was ignoring their demands, the unions later threatened a general strike, and by the end of the year had won a 10 percent wage increase. The teachers' unions remained dissatisfied and carried out a series of illegal strikes throughout much of 1973. Prime Minister Ouédraogo characterized the strikes as "insurrectional" and complained that people in general were unfairly blaming the government for everything.[34] His sense of being under siege was compounded by growing dissent within his own party: by January 1974 an RDA faction linked to the president of the National Assembly had grown strong enough to contemplate forcing the prime minister's removal or resignation.[35]

Fearing the consequences of a possible governmental rift at a time of growing public discontent, Lamizana used the civilian politicians' factional squabbles to justify unilateral action. On 8 February, with the army's full backing, he simply suspended the constitution, dissolved the National Assembly, and banned party activities, abruptly ending the experiment of the Second Republic. Some analysts suggested that motivations internal to the military may also have been a factor, either to shield senior officers involved in the RDA's corruption scandals or to forestall action by more junior officers.[36] In any case, a new cycle of direct rule by military decree commenced. Even more than after Lamizana's original takeover in 1966, the armed forces took a predominant role in the state administration. In the cabinet Lamizana soon appointed, eleven were military officers and only four were civilians. By July 1974 the country's regions were reorganized into ten departments, all headed by military prefects, with officers also heading some sub-prefectures.[37] A national consultative council was appointed with a number of civilian members, but it was purely advisory, and in any case was headed by a military commander (its first secretary was another officer, Lieutenant Jean-Baptiste Lingani, later to become a key figure in the revolutionary government of 1983–87).[38] The military's share of the national budget increased significantly, reaching 31 percent of total expenditures in 1975, compared with 17 percent at the start of the decade.[39]

The civilian politicians' perception of exclusion was aggravated when Lamizana unveiled plans to build a single national party of his own, the Mouvement national pour le renouveau, along the lines of similar military-sponsored parties elsewhere in Africa. Although officially launched in November 1975, Lamizana's party was still-born. Upper Volta's politicians rejected the notion outright, favouring a new constitution and political system that gave party leaders key roles. Their cause was facilitated by continued labour unrest. Still feeling the effects of Garango's austerity policies and the additional burden of a "patriotic" tax imposed during Upper Volta's brief border war with Mali in 1975, organized workers pressed for a 30 percent pay hike, trials of those implicated in the theft of drought relief, and action against the director-general of the social security agency, who was believed to have embezzled CFA260 million. Some unions also backed the calls for a return to constitutional rule, in part fearing that if Lamizana were successful in imposing his party, he would then try to subordinate the labour movement as well. Many of these demands were presented at a huge demonstration in Ouagadougou organized by the unions and political parties a day after Lamizana's party was officially launched. In December 1975, the four main labour federations, with support from student organizations, called a two-day general strike that largely paralysed the country.[40] Many years later, union leaders recalled that strike as another instance in which popular action managed to block a move towards authoritarianism and preserve some space for democratic expression.[41]

## "LIES AND DECEIT"

In face of such stiff opposition and the erosion of his own credibility, Lamizana backtracked quickly. By January 1976 he had abandoned efforts to build his party, dismissed Garango, granted a 25 percent increase in the minimum wage, and named a new "national union" cabinet that featured substantially more civilians. A cabinet reshuffle a year later brought in yet more civilian figures. The parties engaged in behind-the-scenes jockeying for influence, with the first cabinet reflecting some distinct inroads by Ki-Zerbo's MLN and the second leaning more towards the RDA. Overall, the politicians saw Lamizana's willingness to work with them as a first step towards constitutional rule, as the president himself began promising by early 1977. Meanwhile, social unrest continued to keep some pressure on the government, mainly in the form of student demonstrations and teachers' strikes (one of the teachers' unions was politically linked to the MLN, and many believed its actions were influenced by the party's exclusion from the second cabinet).[42]

By October 1977, another draft constitution had been produced, and was approved by referendum the following month. Like the constitution of 1970, it provided for an elected National Assembly. But the new charter also stipulated direct election of the president, without the previous constitution's transitional provisions entrenching a formal military role. At the time, it was one of the most liberal constitutions in Africa, enshrining numerous democratic and civil rights, although it sought to minimize competition among political parties by restricting their number to three.[43]

That limitation did not apply to the parliamentary elections themselves, held at the end of April 1978. Seven parties fielded candidates, of which five secured enough votes to gain seats. Subsequently, the two parties that won no seats were dissolved, while the two parties with the lowest parliamentary representation were obliged to merge with one or another of the three larger parties. The greatest number of seats was won by the old RDA, led by Gérard Kango Ouédraogo, followed by a split-off party of those loyal to former president Yaméogo, with Ki-Zerbo's party (now called the Union progressiste voltaïque) coming in third. Lamizana himself stood for election in the presidential poll two weeks later.[44] Although not himself a member of the RDA, he secured the RDA's formal support, along with the backing of four of the other parties, as well as of the Mogho Naaba, who ordered his subordinate chiefs to deliver votes for Lamizana. Standing against the general were Macaire Ouédraogo from Yaméogo's party, Joseph Ouédraogo representing a faction of the RDA that had refused to go along with the party's endorsement of Lamizana, and Ki-Zerbo. On a very low turnout of 35 percent, Lamizana obtained 42 percent of the vote. Since he fell short of an absolute majority, he was thrown into a run-off two weeks later against the second-place candidate, Macaire Ouédraogo. In that round he won 56 percent of the vote, thus retaining the presidency. On a continent where incumbent presidents often rigged elections to generate crushing majorities, some local analysts credited Lamizana with being a relatively "honest man."[45]

Nevertheless, among ordinary citizens the election did not generate great enthusiasm and expectations of the government remained low. Joseph Conombo, Lamizana's prime minister, acknowledged that people viewed politics as a "game of lies and deceit."[46] A subsequent commission on administrative reform confirmed that the bureaucracy was marked by "great malaise," state enterprises were created in an anarchic manner, officers granted themselves "exorbitant" salaries and benefits, and there was "an ever growing tendency towards embezzlement in all sectors."[47]

Unlike in 1970–74, public scorn was no longer directed mainly at civilian officials. When soldiers appeared in their red berets at soccer matches and other public events, crowds often chanted "Red berets, American sorghum," alluding to the diversions of US food relief.[48] Kollin Noaga's 1977 satire *Haro! Camarade commandante* depicted a typical military commander who spent eight times more on his household than for the purchase of emergency grain stocks.[49] The French agronomist, René Dumont, recounting a return visit to Ouagadougou, was struck by the greater number of new cars and motorcycles, the increased presence of soldiers, police, and French and US expatriates, and the many spacious villas in an area of the capital known as the "Bois de Boulogne," after Paris' ritzy suburb.[50] For workers, such visible displays of wealth made austerity policies all the harder to swallow. "How can we have confidence in people who refuse to satisfy the workers' legitimate demands on the pretext that there is hardly any money in the treasury, when they themselves fill their pockets?" asked Soumane Touré, secretary-general of the Confédération syndicale voltaïque (CSV), a union federation formed just a few years earlier.[51] Lamizana himself, in his 1980 New Year's address, denounced the "treason of the elites" who cared little for the good of the country but instead worshipped "the religion of power and money."[52]

Such admonishments aside, the government's general stance remained lax. Although an effective political survivor, Lamizana had demonstrated, after nearly a decade and a half in power, that he could neither instil dynamism and discipline into the public administration nor check the profligate practices of Upper Volta's elites. Those shortcomings probably were of less concern to some of his military colleagues than his failure to ensure social and political stability. Since the start of the 1970s, none of the swings in governmental form had succeeded in pacifying or suppressing the activism of the militant student and labour movements, and the Third Republic was no exception. Following earlier actions by health workers, the teachers launched prolonged strikes in September 1980, escalating by late October and early November into a broader confrontation as the four union federations organized two general strikes in support of the teachers.[53]

## COLONELS' "DISCIPLINE"

On 25 November 1980, a group of military officers led by Colonel Saye Zerbo staged another coup, citing, among other reasons for their action, an "erosion of state authority." Adopting the rather unwieldy name of the Comité militaire de redressement pour le progrès national (CMRPN), they deposed Lamizana's government, detained the former president and many other officials, scrapped the constitution, dissolved the National Assembly, suspended parties, and prohibited all political activities. Zerbo, a veteran of French military campaigns in Indochina, repeatedly accused the Lamizana government of having gone "soft." He vowed to bring discipline to the state administration and "fight all forms of corruption and embezzlement."[54] Towards that end the CMRPN set up commissions to consider reforms of the civil service and investigate the properties and practices of the detained officials of the Third Republic.

Reflecting the extent to which Lamizana's hybrid military–RDA government had lost public credibility, the coup initially elicited effusive declarations of support. Cardinal Paul Zoungrana, head of the Catholic Church, proclaimed the coup "a blessing of God," while the Imam of Ouagadougou and the Mogho Naaba indicated their approval in somewhat more restrained terms. The teachers' unions, granted a number of their demands, publicly declared their willingness to work with the new government, as did several of the union federations.[55]

It was not long before the CMRPN's relations with key social and political sectors soured. Citing reckless public spending during the last years of the Lamizana regime, renewed drought, and the doubling of the oil import bill, Zerbo unveiled another austerity programme, dashing the unions' hopes that their economic grievances would receive a more sympathetic hearing. The regime's arguments about the need to reduce budgetary expenditures and rationalize the public sector were not without foundation. But the problems had less to do with the salary bill than the way public resources had been managed. There was little coordination or supervision of spending by government ministries and departments, and service directors enjoyed wide discretionary spending powers. In 1981 alone, about CFA6 billion could not be properly accounted for. In addition there were scores of public enterprises with considerable financial autonomy that allowed leading officials to grant themselves high salaries and benefits, embezzle funds, hire friends and relatives, illegally sell off company vehicles and equipment, and engage in fraudulent marketing practices. Some enterprises were headed by simple incompetents who had obtained their positions through personal connections.[56] Such practices, noted one press commentator, helped feed public perceptions of enterprise directors as fat, rolling in money, smoking cigars, drinking whisky or rum, and baptizing their children in champagne.[57]

The CMRPN responded by holding trials of a few officials or lower-ranking state personnel, usually after exposure of outright theft. It appointed several commissions to look into the functioning of state enterprises and the civil service more generally. Very little came of those inquiries. The commission on state enterprises drafted a report that was never published, apparently because it incriminated a number of powerful figures.[58] Nor were the investigations of the Third Republic officials ever released.

In early 1982 a series of scandals surfaced and drew wide attention, thanks to coverage in both the state media and private press. Michel Kpooda, a former official of the publicly owned Banque internationale des Volta, the second largest bank in the country, appeared to have embezzled more than CFA500 million (nearly equivalent to the bank's initial capital stock), acting in collusion with a former police officer and a businessman from Mali.[59] A Ministry of Finance service director was exposed for taking payments from several merchants in exchange for forged documents authorizing wheat imports.[60] Two senior postal officials were found guilty of embezzling CFA8.7 million.[61] Meanwhile, a commission on rental housing in Ouagadougou and other urban centres reported that rents had risen far beyond the reach of ordinary workers and civil servants, thanks to real estate speculation by private merchants and "newly rich" state officials and army officers.[62]

These affairs received rare coverage in the state media during a brief period from November 1981 through April 1982 when a young military officer, Captain Thomas Sankara, served as the government's secretary of information. He encouraged journalists to report the truth, and their exposures furthered public perceptions that corruption was worsening and high-level officials were deeply implicated.

As before, the unions were the most vocal in pressing for a crackdown on corruption, with the teachers' SNEAHV in particular denouncing continued "fraud and waste" and warning of "popular indignation" over the government's silence on the work of its commissions.[63] By that point, however, the unions' concerns over corruption had become overshadowed by a bigger worry: their very right to function. By February–March 1981 a number of unions, including the teachers and the CSV federation, had indicated that they no longer had much confidence in the Zerbo regime. The CSV, led by supporters of the Marxist PAI, not only pressed workers' economic grievances, but also openly backed the calls of the radical students' movement for the release of detained student activists, even though the federation's secretary-general, Soumane Touré, still sat on the commission investigating officials' assets.[64]

Zerbo's reaction was the most heavy-handed of any government since independence. Claiming "subversion" and the "irresponsible exercise of the right to strike," the military council in November 1981 formally suspended the right to strike, which Zerbo maintained was a "luxury" in Upper Volta's difficult economic circumstances. The blanket ban was lifted a few months later, but procedural restrictions were so stringent that in practice strikes remained illegal.[65] Less than a month after its original imposition, the strike ban was openly defied by a train drivers' work stoppage. More seriously, the CSV called for a general strike in December 1981 against the "fascist military dictatorship" and Soumane Touré defiantly resigned from the assets commission. The junta then decreed the CSV's dissolution and ordered Touré's arrest. Although Touré managed to evade capture for some time, other leaders of the federation and the PAI were picked up.[66]

The three other union federations failed to come to the CSV's support, and did not even challenge the strike ban until the following May.[67] But the more militant wing of the union movement had already become strong enough—and had important links with student activists, left-wing political groupings, and even sectors of the military itself—that it did not fold in the face of the repression. In January 1982 teachers, in open defiance of the strike ban, organized a walkout that paralysed the school system for weeks. Then in April the CSV called a general strike in defence of labour rights. Although it was not well-supported, the regime's subsequent crackdown, featuring trials of many union activists, kept the political atmosphere in a state of high tension for months. That the circumstances were particularly volatile was further demonstrated in July when large crowds in Bobo-Dioulasso, incensed by seizures of goods by the customs police, sacked the service's local warehouses.[68]

The Zerbo regime's authoritarian stance did not have the desired effect and served mainly to polarize the country. In conjunction with the colonels' failure to go after high-level profiteers and embezzlers, their attacks on the labour movement were widely interpreted as an effort by a segment of the elites to safeguard the prevailing political and social order. But it was not only workers, students, and other poorer strata of the population that thought the grievances against the CMRPN were justified. So did a layer of more junior officers. The discipline of the armed forces hierarchy, already frayed during the deposing of Lamizana, now deteriorated further—and would bring about the downfall of Zerbo's military council before it reached its second anniversary.

# 4
# FROM CRISIS TO REVOLUTION

After just two decades of national independence, official rhetoric about unity and sacrifice had lost its allure, giving way to widespread disenchantment and cynicism. The political and social elites appeared to many as gluttonous self-seekers, eager for the smallest personal advantage or patronage resource, ready to accommodate the former colonial power in exchange for military and financial support, uncommitted to their own professed goals of development and national progress, and disdainful of "the people" they claimed to lead and represent. To ordinary citizens, the notion of public service seemed a cruel joke, and politics little more than an inaccessible game for the wealthy and powerful.

By the early 1980s such popular disillusionment had become prevalent in Upper Volta. The alternation of civilian and military rule changed little of substance, suggesting to many that the problem was not so much institutional as systemic. Neither military nor civilian elites seemed to offer a genuine alternative to the basic pattern of exclusionary, predacious rule.

The absence of a palatable choice among the dominant "big men," combined with an erosion of overall economic and social conditions, made wide sectors of society receptive to radical proposals and set the stage for the emergence of new political actors. Left-wing and militantly nationalist groupings began to coalesce, most openly among students and intellectuals, to some extent within the labour movement, and, not least, within portions of the military itself. Of those in uniform, junior and non-commissioned officers were especially open to such ideas. Younger and often from humbler social strata than the senior officers, they shared many of the attitudes of disillusionment and disgruntlement of their civilian peers. They were also relatively well-educated and politicized, some entering the military after direct contact with the anti-imperialist and revolutionary ideas of the student movements. Ironically, some also gained exposure to left-wing theory in military academies. As several officers from Upper Volta noted, it was not unusual for officer training programmes to introduce the writings of Ho Chi Minh, Che Guevara, or Algerian revolutionary leaders as part of their counter-insurgency courses.[1]

These junior officers shared the contempt of their senior commanders for civilian politicians and parliamentary institutions, considering them inherently corrupt, indecisive, and inefficient. They basically accepted the ethos of the military's "developmental" role: that as one of the few well-organized institutions in society, it had a duty to promote economic development, social advancement, and the construction of a coherent and effective state. But experience had convinced many that the top military hierarchy was simply incapable of carrying out such tasks. In their eyes, it had become another bulwark of the neo-colonial order. So their anger was directed most immediately against their superior officers.

Yet given the failure of earlier reform campaigns, some also came to understand that action from within the military alone would not be likely to bring lasting, fundamental change, and that they had to ally themselves with other societal forces. Over months of political conflict these junior officers were drawn into revolutionary coalitions that included leaders of organized left-wing parties, academics, student activists, trade unionists, and other civilians. Although these were real, if unstable, alliances, those who came from the military remained the dominant actors, in large part because of the arms and organization at their command, but also because of the political credibility that figures like Captain Sankara enjoyed among wider sectors of the public.

## THE CONSEIL DU SALUT DU PEUPLE

By 1982, the military junta headed by Colonel Zerbo, the CMRPN, was confronting a growing crisis. In comparison with the previous governments of General Lamizana, it was seen by many people as less inclusive, more corrupt, and, above all, more repressive. The CMRPN's direct confrontations with the trade unions, arrests of students, and suspension of numerous democratic and labour rights exemplified the widening gulf between the ruling officers and the best-organized sectors of society.

Those wider tensions accelerated the rifts within the military itself, especially between the clique of officers around Zerbo and an increasingly influential current of younger officers who shared many of the radical ideas of the student movement, some unionists, and the clandestine left. As early as April 1982, those radical officers directly and dramatically challenged the CMRPN's political authority when Sankara resigned his cabinet-level position as secretary of information, citing "differences of opinion" and publicly proclaiming, "Woe to those who would gag their people."[2] In response, the CMRPN stripped Sankara of his rank and arrested him, along with two close colleagues, Captain Henri Zongo and Captain Blaise Compaoré. But there were other factions in the military as well, and they too contemplated moving against Zerbo.

On 7 November 1982 military units occupied key locations in Ouagadougou and elsewhere and overthrew the CMRPN, with five reported deaths, including that of the interior minister. Colonel Zerbo and other dignitaries were taken into custody. The first proclamation of the new Conseil du salut du peuple (CSP) justified the overthrow by citing Zerbo's "adventurist policies," waste, "corruption and illegal and spectacular enrichment," "unjustified repression" of workers and students, and suspension of basic civil liberties. It lifted the sackings and suspensions that had been imposed on strikers.[3]

While generally expressing relief over Zerbo's removal, most residents of the capital showed little enthusiasm for the coup. In fact, few had any real idea what was going on or who was behind the takeover. At first, the only name publicly associated with the new regime was Commander Jean-Baptiste Ouédraogo, a virtually unknown officer in the military's medical service, who was proclaimed president of the CSP. Without more solid details, all sorts of rumours spread, including that Sankara was behind the coup, fuelled by the CSP's decision immediately after the takeover to lift the arrest warrant against Sankara, Zongo, and Compaoré and restore their ranks.[4]

In reality, two other military factions initiated the action against Zerbo. One was led by Commander Gabriel Somé Yorian, a politically conservative officer who had served as a minister in every government since 1971. He was perceived as close to Upper Volta's first president, Maurice Yaméogo, with many suspecting that his move against Zerbo was designed to clear the way for Yaméogo's return to office. The other faction, also relatively conservative, was led by Commander Fidèle Guébré, who backed a different political contender, retired General Marc Garango, the powerful finance minister under Lamizana. Since these two factions were sharply divided, they agreed on Jean-Baptiste Ouédraogo as a compromise figurehead president.[5]

Acknowledging the relative popularity of Sankara and his radical colleagues among the lower ranks of the military and the general public, the coup plotters apparently had solicited their participation in Zerbo's removal. Yet Sankara refused to take an active role, arguing that the elaboration of a political platform was, in his eyes, an essential precondition. But agreement on a common political platform would have been hard to imagine between the conservative officers and those around Sankara. A number of the latter had direct, if still secret, contacts with several of the country's left-wing revolutionary groupings. Sankara himself, while undergoing paratrooper training in Paris in the early 1970s, met with members of Voltaic communist groupings and read Marxist writings picked up at left-wing bookshops. When he returned to Upper Volta in 1974, he also maintained contacts with leaders of the numerous clandestine Marxist groups: the Ligue patriotique pour le développement (Lipad), which was affiliated with the Soviet-oriented PAI; the Union de lutte communiste (ULC), which leaned politically towards China; and the Parti communiste révolutionnaire voltaïque (PCRV), which was aligned with Albania. One of Sankara's friends was Soumane Touré, a leader of Lipad and the secretary-general of the CSV, the labour federation that had been most in conflict with the Zerbo regime. Commander Jean-Baptiste Lingani, another of the radical officers, was secretly a member of the PAI.[6]

Although this radical current did not play an active role in the coup itself, its strength was such that it came to wield considerable influence within the military and in national politics during the first months of the CSP. When the council's composition was finally announced on 26 November, following the election of representatives by military units around the country, some of their names figured prominently. Lingani became secretary-general of the CSP and Compaoré was a member. A list of cabinet ministers included several who belonged to either Lipad or the ULC.[7] As a whole, the composition of the CSP reflected a shift away from the senior commanders. Mainly comprising junior officers, it also included a corporal and a sergeant, but no officers above the rank of battalion commander. Subsequently, twenty-one senior officers, including the country's only two active service generals, were forcibly retired from the military or placed on the reserve list.[8]

A political amalgam, the CSP was unstable and faction-ridden from the start. The policy pronouncements of its different members were often contradictory and inconsistent. The countervailing pressures were evident in the CSP's initial actions. The council moved from prison to house arrest a number of prominent party leaders who had been held under Zerbo and proclaimed that it would hand power over to an elected civilian regime after two years.[9] The two initiatives seemed to lend credence to a view that some CSP leaders were trying to facilitate a return to power of Yaméogo or other old-guard politicians. President Ouédraogo appeared to be part of that camp.[10]

However, other CSP figures, usually but not always from the more radical wing, emphasized bringing the corrupt officials of previous regimes to justice. The mandate of the special courts set up by the CMRPN was extended to cover investigations of officials of all previous governments, including the CMRPN itself. The trial of Michel Kpooda and ten other businessmen and bank officials for embezzlement began within a week of the coup, after previous delays.[11] But since the CSP insisted on pursuing the established judicial system's intricate and cumbersome procedures, neither that trial nor investigations of other officials suspected of corruption moved beyond a snail's pace. None were completed while the CSP was still in office.

Meanwhile, CSP officials pledged to shake up the state bureaucracy and civil service. In early December, the benefits enjoyed by the head of state, cabinet ministers, department directors, and other high officials were reduced by 25 percent or more. In a New Year's address, President Ouédraogo declared that the public administration should become more dynamic and no longer serve as a "source of jobs for those with political and family connections." He promised that "practices of active or passive corruption will be energetically fought."[12]

By that point, the pendulum was swinging further in the direction of the CSP's radical wing. Sankara, though not a member of the council, was sent to speak on its behalf to a congress of the secondary and university teachers' union, the Syndicat unique voltaïque des enseignants du secondaire et du supérieur (SUVESS), one of the most militant in the country. Stating that the army was facing "the same contradictions as the Voltaic people" as a whole, Sankara affirmed that "struggles for liberty" were gaining support within the military barracks and vowed that the CSP would support union rights. While professing that the government would permit the unions to select their own leaderships, he was also highly critical of the union movement's lethargy and collusion between some unions and the "forces that oppress the masses."[13] While fiery pronouncements had become almost routine for trade union leaders, noted an independent press commentary, it was "the first time an officer of the Voltaic armed forces had made such engaged statements in public."[14]

On 10 January 1983 Sankara was named prime minister by an extraordinary assembly of the CSP, making him officially the number two to President Ouédraogo. While his formal policy-making powers were limited, it provided a platform from which Sankara could press for more far-reaching reforms and win greater support from the general public. That aim was evident when he took the oath of office on 1 February. He emphasized that government members were there to serve the people, "not to serve themselves." The people wanted freedom, he said, but "this freedom should not be confused with the freedom of a few to exploit the rest through illicit profits, speculation, embezzlement, or theft." Upper Volta also needed to break free of any exploitative external dependency, he said.[15]

Largely at the initiative of the radical officers, direct contacts between the CSP and the trade unions picked up, and the council lifted the CMRPN's blanket ban on strikes.[16] Not all union federations had been in open conflict with the previous regime, and a few were even politically aligned with the CMRPN; so while they generally welcomed the CSP's more open stance towards the unions, most kept a wary distance. However, the CSV, which had suffered the most under Zerbo, was openly sympathetic to the new government, especially since several members of Lipad, the political grouping with which it was aligned, were either in the cabinet or the CSP itself. But this did not prevent the union federation from continuing to speak out. Its customary May Day grievances listed a variety of economic demands and called for "a complete clean-up of the administrative apparatus" and the "Voltaization" of senior staff in state enterprises (where French nationals often filled key positions).[17]

On the latter issue, CSV-affiliated unionists at the Bravolta brewery had already taken action. Citing long-standing disputes over discriminatory overtime and layoff threats, as well as the poor management and "insensitivity" of the French-born director, the Bravolta workers physically evicted him from the enterprise and his company residence. Before acting, the local union leaders, with the approval of CSV leader Soumane Touré, had presented their case directly to Prime Minister Sankara and told him of their plans to oust the director. Sankara seemed to give his tacit approval.[18]

Like other sectors of the social elites, traditional chiefs were not sure what to make of the CSP. Following the death in December 1982 of Mogho Naaba Kougri, his son ascended to the throne a few weeks later, taking the name Naaba Baôngo. He and his councillors subsequently met with the president, prime minister, and other government officials. Echoing the indirect-rule language of the French colonial era, President Ouédraogo told the chiefs that they should act as the "ears and voice of the central government among our toiling masses ... This is the image of the chieftaincy, as an auxiliary of the state administration, that we henceforth intend to pursue."[19] Not long after, Sankara took a sterner line, criticizing chiefs as "forces of obscuritanism who, under a spiritual and traditional cover, exploit the people." The state electricity company then cut off power to the Mogho Naaba's palace because neither he nor his father had ever paid the electricity bills.[20]

In a series of "information missions" across the countryside, cabinet ministers and other CSP representatives soon learned that chiefs were not the only ones able to speak up about rural issues. Villagers raised recurrent problems such as shortages of water, food deficits, high taxes, chieftaincy disputes, cattle theft, and the lack of schools, health care, and other social services. In the Centre-West region, according to a local media report:

> the charge that the rural world has no political initiative was stripped of its foundations. The proof is that in many regions the peasants insisted that the civil service be reformed. Even more, in Yako they demanded that a national control commission be established for "rotten" functionaries. They also criticized the way the government utilized taxes, and even insisted on an effective decentralization of the state apparatus.[21]

In Mané, villagers applauded loudly when Lieutenant Dihré Laye of the CSP declared:

> When we know that the peasant often is forced to sell even his own food to pay his taxes, it is inconceivable that those charged with managing public resources illegally enrich themselves. Henceforth, such conduct will be considered a crime, and will be punished as such.[22]

Villagers frequently asked the CSP representatives what would happen when the council handed over to a civilian government in two years' time. Would the old politicians come back into power? They also asked whether the CSP was "red," a question to which some representatives visiting the Centre-East region replied: "We're cleaning up the state coffers. If that's red, then we are."[23] But more conservative officials were clearly embarrassed by such questions. Seeming to identify ideology with a foreign policy stance, Commander Guébré responded to a query about whether the CSP's ideology was communist by stating that the council was simply "Voltaic," that it was interested only in national concerns.[24]

Sankara meanwhile demonstrated that some government leaders did keenly follow foreign policy issues. In February, much to the unease of France, other Western powers, and some immediate neighbours such as President Félix Houphouët-Boigny in Côte d'Ivoire, Sankara paid a state visit to Libya. Then, in April, Muammar al-Qaddafi briefly stopped over in Ouagadougou to return the visit. In between the two meetings with Qaddafi, Sankara travelled to North Korea and represented Upper Volta at a summit meeting of the Non-Aligned Movement in New Delhi. There he actively sought out various Third World revolutionary leaders, including Fidel Castro of Cuba, Samora Machel of Mozambique, and Maurice Bishop of Grenada. In his speech to the summit, Sankara openly aligned himself with the more radical wing of the Non-Aligned Movement, including by supporting rebel forces in El Salvador and the Nicaraguan government against the US.[25]

The depth of the political divisions within the CSP became glaringly evident after Sankara's return from New Delhi. On 26 March a mass public rally was held in an open square in Ouagadougou, to explain the CSP's views on recent events that had raised political tensions, including the ostensible discovery of a coup plot aimed at restoring the CMRPN and the arrest of several former politicians on charges of corruption, subversion, and engaging in illegal political activities.[26] The rally was intended to present the public with the image of a CSP solidly united against its domestic opponents, and therefore featured the three top officials: Commander Lingani as secretary-general of the CSP, Prime Minister Sankara, and President Ouédraogo. Lingani gave only a short introduction before turning the podium over to Sankara. The prime minister began with a broadside against virtually all sectors of Upper Volta's old social and political elites: bureaucrats, businessmen, party politicians, religious and traditional leaders, and corrupt officers. He denounced "imperialism" and defended Upper Volta's sovereign right to maintain political ties with any other government that it wished. The next speaker, President Ouédraogo, who lacked the prime minister's command of public oration, appeared to have been upstaged. He tried to subtly distance himself from the tenor of Sankara's remarks, insisting that the CSP was nationalist, without "any ideology or model of society," and emphasizing that its main goal was to hand over to a civilian government.[27] But not much of the crowd had actually stayed around to listen to him, drifting away in a visible demonstration of which wing of the CSP enjoyed the most popular support. On 14 May a similar scenario played out in Bobo-Dioulasso. Sankara received very enthusiastic applause at a rally of youth organizations, but when Ouédraogo took the podium, he was greeted at first with silence, then as he was speaking the crowd dispersed, amidst chants of "Sankara! Sankara!"[28] The two rallies, together with other signs of growing public support for the radical officers, appears to have convinced the conservative officers in the CSP that their attempt at co-optation was seriously backfiring.

## POWER IN THE BALANCE

Before dawn on 17 May, armoured units detained Sankara and Lingani and took up strategic positions around the capital. At Camp Guillaume in central Ouagadougou, however, Captain Henri Zongo rallied a number of troops and vowed to resist the coup-in-progress. With superior forces arrayed against them, Zongo and his men negotiated their return to barracks.[29] Amidst the chaos that day, Captain Compaoré managed to evade arrest and escaped to Pô, where the troops of Sankara's old paracommando training base had refused to recognize the authorities in Ouagadougou.[30]

In a radio address later that day, President Ouédraogo announced that the CSP had decided to "remove from its ranks all those who were working to turn it from its initial path through behaviour, declarations, and acts that were as demagogic as they were irresponsible."[31] He directly accused the PAI/Lipad of using Sankara and Lingani to advance its project for a communist society.[32] Ouédraogo soon acknowledged, however, that the CSP as a body had taken no actual decision to remove Sankara and Lingani. This came from him, some military commanders, and "certain influential persons in the CSP." In fact, he proclaimed the outright dissolution of the leading organs of the CSP: the general assembly, permanent secretariat, and control commission.[33] Meanwhile, Colonel Somé Yorian, one of the presumed authors of the coup, was named secretary-general of national defence.[34] When the new cabinet list was released a few days later, the names of all who had belonged to left-wing parties or who were otherwise politically associated with Sankara were missing.[35]

Did a small circle of officers decide, by themselves, to depose the prime minister and remove the other radicals? Some were deeply conservative, feared the kind of fundamental changes that Sankara and his colleagues proposed, and therefore had solid reasons for acting. But many observers of the 17 May coup believed that the French government also had a role. The evidence was largely circumstantial: Guy Penne, the influential adviser on African affairs to French President François Mitterrand, arrived in Ouagadougou the evening of 16 May and left the next afternoon, while the coup was under way, and after agreeing to provide the new government with more financial aid. Given France's highly interventionist policy towards its former African colonies, suggesting or approving a coup to get rid of potentially destabilizing radicals would not be implausible.

Whoever took the final decision to oust Sankara, Lingani, and the others, the move did not go as planned. Protests erupted almost immediately, prompted to some extent by the perceptions of French involvement. Over 20–21 May, large and sometimes violent demonstrations rocked Ouagadougou, involving high-school students, youths from poor neighbourhoods, and some trade unionists. Protesters cried, "Free Sankara!" and chanted anti-imperialist slogans, particularly against France. Pro-government forces managed to organize a support march in favour of President Ouédraogo on 22 May, but many participants were heckled or pelted with stones by groups of youths. Seeing the hand of Lipad and other political groups and unions behind the anti-coup demonstrations, the military ordered the arrest of a number of prominent figures, including Ibrahima Koné, the former CSP minister of youth and sports, Soumane Touré of the CSV union federation, and Etienne Traoré, head of the SUVESS teachers' union.[36]

Whatever their ideological differences, most of the left-wing political groups were drawn together in rejection of the "reactionary coup" of 17 May. They encouraged the formation of clandestine committees of civilians to oppose the government and fight for the radicals' return. Tracts circulated in the barracks denouncing President Ouédraogo and his backers. Most seriously for the authorities, the garrison in Pô remained under the control of Captain Compaoré, standing as a direct challenge to the political authority of the government and encouraging both civilian and military supporters in Ouagadougou and elsewhere in the country.

The Ouédraogo government—commonly known as the "CSP-II"—was under considerable pressure, and from opposing sides. The protests in the streets prompted the president to free Sankara and Lingani from their place of detention in Dori and instead put them under house arrest in Ouagadougou. He also freed many of the civilian politicians and members of the Zerbo regime who had been detained under the "CSP-I" and restored Yaméogo's civil rights.[37] Seeing an opening, those politicians pressed the military to move ahead with the process of preparing for renewed civilian rule. In response, President Ouédraogo reiterated his pledge to step aside within two years.[38]

Yet the various political moves of the CSP-II betrayed an air of unreality. Aside from the old political parties and some sectors of the social elites, it had little evident public base. Attempts to organize more support marches fizzled out. The military command did not enjoy enough solid loyalty from its own troops to risk an open assault on the Pô garrison. So for a period of about two months, Upper Volta remained in a state of limbo, politically divided between competing camps.

The "Sankarist" camp gradually consolidated its strength. From the paracommando base in Pô, Sankara's supporters extended their control to the town itself, and then over many neighbouring villages. In Ouagadougou, the clandestine committees stepped up their preparations and even cut electrical power to the capital to test their coordination. Messengers shuttled back and forth between the oppositionists in Ouagadougou and Pô, and some students and other youths travelled from the capital to Pô for military training. The government felt obliged to open negotiations with the Pô rebels, in the process permitting Sankara himself to make a brief trip to the town. That simply permitted the rebel forces in Ouagadougou and Pô to coordinate their actions and plans even more closely.[39] Meanwhile, the Pô rebels established clandestine contacts with the Jerry Rawlings government in Ghana (the border is just twenty kilometres to the south). Sankara later revealed that Rawlings "dared to support us with all his military, political, and diplomatic strength" during that period.[40]

According to some accounts, the forces in Pô obtained information that Colonel Somé Yorian was preparing to push President Ouédraogo aside and assassinate Sankara, Lingani, and Zongo in an effort to break the stalemate. So they decided to strike first. On the afternoon of 4 August 1983, commandos from Pô headed for the capital, leaving the Pô garrison under the guard of armed civilians. They travelled quickly in trucks commandeered from a Canadian construction firm, slipped into the capital, and took up positions around key locations: the presidency, radio station, security and gendarme headquarters, and the armoured group at Camp Guillaume. The clandestine civilian groups played a central supporting role, as guides and by again cutting the city's power. At 9:30 pm, in a closely coordinated operation, the commandos seized all their main targets, facing very little resistance. Meanwhile, junior officers led takeovers at the air base and the artillery camp. By 10:00 pm Sankara was on the radio to proclaim the overthrow of the government. Hardly any blood was shed in the takeover, although a few days later both Colonel Somé Yorian and Colonel Guébré were killed, supposedly shot while trying to escape.[41]

## THE CONSEIL NATIONAL DE LA RÉVOLUTION

In his initial address to the nation on the evening of 4 August—broadcast over the radio several times during the night in French, Mooré, and Gourounsi—Sankara announced the formation of the Conseil national de la révolution (CNR, National Council of the Revolution). In the first of many such signals, he emphasized that the new state entity would seek to take action not only on its own initiative, but in conjunction with wider sectors of the citizenry, "the people." He urged supporters to immediately form committees for the defence of the revolution "everywhere, in order to fully participate in the CNR's great patriotic struggle and to prevent our enemies here and abroad from doing our people harm."[42]

The precise structure and composition of the CNR itself were never publicly revealed, ostensibly for security reasons. But in interviews and later accounts by some of its members, its general contours emerged. In comparison with the CSP, which was a strictly military affair, the CNR included both military and civilian members, although the former were far more numerous, continuing a preponderant military role in the country's political life.[43] The "four historic leaders" of the 4 August takeover (Sankara, Lingani, Zongo, and Compaoré) were publicly known to be members. Valère Somé, himself a member of the CNR, mentioned several other military figures who took part in the council's deliberations.[44] In addition, Sankara revealed that representatives of most left-wing groups were in the council as well.[45] In the first cabinet named after the CNR's seizure of power, there were five ministers known to belong to Lipad, three to Valère Somé's Union de lutte communiste-reconstruite (ULCR, as the core ULC had reconstituted itself), as well as a few other civilians from smaller groups, plus some "sincere patriots" not affiliated with any organization.[46]

By explicitly proclaiming their government to be revolutionary, Sankara and his colleagues made it clear that their goal was to initiate far-reaching economic, social, and political changes, and not simply reform the inherited structures. Unlike the previous government, the CNR set no deadline for returning to constitutional rule. It was openly hostile to the established political parties (which it banned outright) and viewed elected parliamentary institutions as inherently biased in favour of the social elites. In Africa at the time—before the democratization wave of the early 1990s—this absence of elected representative institutions was not regarded within the country or in neighbouring states as a major shortcoming. It later would be, including by many of the surviving leaders who had been politically aligned with Sankara. The CNR did speak of democratic mechanisms, however, although largely in the language of "popular democracy," reflected in part through the new revolutionary defence committees elected in urban neighbourhoods, villages, workplaces, schools, and state institutions.

The CNR's critique of the established system was sweeping. It called into question the entire post-colonial era, in terms that drew liberally from both Marxism and dependency theory. There was little difference between colonial domination and "neo-colonial society," Sankara emphasized in the CNR's main programmatic declaration, known as the political orientation speech, except that "Voltaic nationals were to take over as agents for foreign domination and exploitation," while some new social classes were formed and the alignment of others shifted to some degree.[47]

CNR leaders did not speak solely in terms of class or fighting external domination. They also emphasized the importance of combating corruption. The notion of integrity was in fact woven directly into the new national identity the CNR sought to instil. On the first anniversary of the 4 August takeover the council renamed the country "Burkina Faso," which roughly translates as "land of the upright people."

# 5
# REFASHIONING THE STATE

The "supreme task" of the revolution in Burkina Faso, said President Sankara, "will be the total conversion of the entire state machinery with its laws, administration, courts, police, and army."[1] History, according to an official media commentary, demonstrated that "revolutionaries cannot content themselves with simply taking over and managing the existing state apparatus." By dismissing functionaries and military personnel who were "incapable of following the rhythm" of the revolution, the governing CNR would unleash a sweeping campaign against "nepotism, laxity, poor management, absenteeism, indifference, and mediocrity."[2]

In its four years in power, the CNR was able to point in the direction of a new kind of state, even if it could not follow through on all aspects of its ambitious vision. But by shaking up the foundations of the old order and exposing its fundamental flaws, the revolutionaries nevertheless accomplished more to strengthen state–society relations than had been done in the previous quarter century.

One hurdle, at the very outset, was that there was simply little existing state to reform, compared with many other African countries at the time. The problem was not so much to rebuild the state administration, as to *build* it, in some respects virtually from scratch. As of 1987, there were only 29,700 civil servants in Burkina Faso, or 3.5 for every 1,000 residents, one of the lowest rates anywhere in Africa. Neighbouring Ghana, by comparison, had 22.1 per 1,000.[3]

Size was not the only factor. On the positive side, the administration inherited by the CNR had never decayed as dramatically as had those in some of its other neighbours. Pre-revolutionary Upper Volta had its share of corrupt and incompetent officials, but high-level malpractices had not spread very much downwards into the middle and lower rungs of the civil service and military. In the West African region, Voltaic civil servants enjoyed an image of relative honesty.

That did not mean the bureaucracy was efficient. Even local personnel were not attuned to the concerns of ordinary citizens. The administrative system was highly centralized, and only top officials had the authority to make decisions, so that even habitual procedures dragged on interminably. Management was extremely lax, and absenteeism and tardiness were legendary—one of the surest ways to arouse civil servants' ire was to suggest that bars be closed during normal office hours. Not only high officials but also regular salaried personnel often used their positions to advance their economic and social standing: receipt of a wide range of benefits and allowances, favoured access to state loans to enable a spouse or other relative to open a small business, preference in acquiring subsidized houses or residential lots that could then be rented out, and so on. To the ordinary villager, the state seemed a distant, urban entity, staffed by privileged personnel who rarely set foot in the countryside. And when they did, it was mainly to impose some obligation, without offering tangible benefits in return.

## LOCALIZATION OF THE STATE

Because of the CNR's goals of dramatically expanding the state's territorial authority and shifting its actions and focus more towards the countryside, the reordering of local state institutions was an especially high priority. Without more state presence at the local level, other reforms would have entailed little more than readjusting political life for the tiny urban minority.

Since earlier regimes had opted to govern the countryside indirectly, through traditional chiefs and other local notables, they saw little need for much of an administrative apparatus outside the cities. The first post-independence government created just four departments in 1963 to manage all rural affairs. Much smaller "rural collectivities" were also established to encompass a number of neighbouring villages, but without funds or staff they existed mainly on paper. In 1970, the number of departments was doubled to eight, a figure that finally rose to eleven in 1979.[4] Even then, they were responsible for too much territory to have real influence outside the main towns. Most development projects were financed and managed by foreign donor agencies, which thus tended to make the most important decisions affecting local people. Since the colonial-era "head" tax was still being collected on behalf of the central government by traditional chiefs, not even the tax man was seen in the villages.

In November 1983, three months after the CNR seized power, it created four different types of territorial division: the village, commune, department, and province. At the highest level, the provinces replaced the eleven old departments, but with smaller boundaries determined partly by population density to ensure better administrative coverage. At first, the number of provinces was set at twenty-five.[5] Then in August 1984 five more were carved out to yield a total of thirty,[6] a number that remained in effect until the late 1990s. That reconfiguration of the administrative map symbolized the new policy of extending the state's reach and influence to the most remote areas.

While most high positions were appointed directly by the central government, the CDRs played the greatest direct role at the lower levels. That meant shifting effective political and administrative authority from traditional chiefs to the defence committees. In December 1983 the chiefs lost the state stipends they had received since the days of colonial rule as well as any legal powers to tax, collect tribute, or demand labour services, leaving the commoner-led CDRs as the sole official structures.[7]

Above the villages were new departments, numbering 300, or an average of ten per province. Each department was managed by a council selected by village and town CDRs, but headed by a government-appointed prefect. The communes were for the thirty towns selected as provincial capitals, run by "special delegations" also named by the central government. Their mayors, however, were picked by CDRs, except in Ouagadougou, where the mayor and provincial high commissioner were the same individual, a CNR appointee. Ouagadougou itself was sub-divided into thirty sectors, and Bobo-Dioulasso into twenty-five, each governed directly by CDRs.[8]

On paper, the new structures appeared far more representative. Yet the CNR's local officials were not always welcomed. They faced sceptical populations because of general distrust of the central government, the continued influence of chiefs and religious leaders, and fear of zealous defence committee activists who occasionally tried to enforce new policies with little prior consultation. In Oudalan, an exceptionally arid province in the far north-east inhabited largely by semi-nomadic livestock herders, the provincial high commissioner found it hard to mobilize people to build houses for the victims of a severe flood in Gorom-Gorom, the provincial capital, because many thought the houses would in fact go to civil servants or military personnel. Only after homeless flood victims began moving into the houses did the distrust fade.[9] In Passoré, where Aïcha Traoré was high commissioner, merchants strenuously resisted her efforts to rebuild the central marketplace in Yako, while former dignitaries tried to use the presence of a woman in such a high office to rally men against the government.[10]

Since the central government did not have the money to recruit more civil servants to staff the new provincial structures, it reassigned about 10 percent of the employees of the central ministries to the provinces.[11] Given the dominance of state-appointed personnel and the absence of local resources managed by the departments or provinces themselves, some scholars questioned the government's designation of its policy as one of "decentralization," arguing that it would be more accurate to consider the new entities as a form of "deconcentration," that is, a delegation of authority by the central government to its designated representatives at the local level.[12]

From the perspective of chiefs, religious leaders, wealthy merchants, and other local elites who had once enjoyed great autonomy from Ouagadougou, the CNR's efforts to strengthen local government (however it was labelled) appeared to be an aggressive intrusion of the central authorities into rural life. Yet at the same time, many of those in the villages who had chafed at the old order (youths, migrants, ethnic minorities, women, the very poor) appeared to welcome this central state presence. Through the semi-state CDRs, they saw a means to enhance their social position, and therefore an opportunity for making more autonomous decisions of their own.

## TRANSFORMING THE CIVIL SERVICE

At the state's centre, chiefly Ouagadougou and a few other large towns, the CNR's main goal was to overhaul the existing structures enough to ensure greater effectiveness, provide basic services, and, if possible, open them to more public scrutiny. That meant trimming the bureaucracy's established privileges and prerogatives, instilling an ethic of public service, and more clearly separating the duties and obligations of office from the private concerns of the officeholders themselves. As one Burkinabè legal scholar put it, the civil service had to become less an obstacle to the country's economic and social development and more a vehicle for its advancement.[13] Increased efficiency, it was reasoned, would yield a stronger, more robust state, one that could enact essential domestic reforms as well as assert some degree of independence internationally.

The CNR initially took power with notable popular support. Young people in particular seemed to expect much of the new leaders. But coming after a succession of incompetent, arrogant, and venal politicians and officers, the CNR also encountered cynicism about those in authority. So to foster some confidence in the new government's commitment, the authorities took a series of dramatic—and sometimes consciously theatrical—steps to demonstrate a sharp break with the past. Almost immediately, government ministers and other senior officials lost their expense accounts and some of their benefits. Delegations travelling abroad were reduced in size and officials had to fly economy class.[14] When Sankara visited New York in 1984 to address the UN General Assembly, his entire delegation stayed at the Burkinabè mission to avoid the cost of hotel rooms. Two-thirds of the government's auto fleet was sold off, and only small cars were kept. Sankara himself used a small, inexpensive Peugeot 205. Officials who were assigned individual cars were strictly prohibited from using them for private purposes.[15]

Public perceptions of the civil service were based not only on the extravagant lifestyles of those at the top. In such a poor country, even a lowly office secretary or clerk was seen by ordinary villagers as relatively well-off. In 1987, even after public salaries and benefits had been seriously squeezed for several years, the average civil service salary was still 15.4 times the country's per capita income. It was the widest gap among eighteen countries (mostly former French colonies) in West and Central Africa. Under such circumstances, commented one researcher, a civil servant "lives in a different world than the peasant."[16]

Justifying its actions on the basis of this gulf, the CNR soon froze civil service salaries and reduced housing allowances by 25–50 percent. Promotions were halted, or made without a corresponding salary increase. Deductions for child support were eliminated from the tax schedule, and the retirement age was reduced from 55 to 53 years. In addition, public employees were expected to contribute to a variety of special funds and levies to aid drought victims or finance development projects.

There were other exactions. To expand the market for domestically manufactured textiles and clothing, the government obliged civil servants to purchase one or more "Faso dan Fani" outfits, made by local seamstresses from cotton fabric produced by the Faso Fani textile plant. As part of a health campaign, the CNR also required office workers to take part in weekly group calisthenics and other activities, a policy that caused almost as much resentment as the financial constraints.[17]

To reduce the scope for corruption, new disciplinary councils were given broad powers to dismiss civil servants, withdraw pensions, and impose other sanctions for a variety of infractions. By 1986 the grounds for disciplinary action could include not only "diversion of public goods," but also "overt hostility to the revolution," a vague notion that opened the way for abuses.[18]

In August 1985 the CNR unexpectedly relieved all cabinet ministers of their titles and reassigned them to oversee collective farming projects. Sankara called it a "revolutionary pedagogic formula" to destroy the "myth" that ministerial appointment was an irrevocable sinecure: "Everyone must know that a minister is only a servant."[19] When a new cabinet was reconstituted at the end of the month, almost all the old ministers were returned to office, although not all at the same ministries.[20] The same thing happened the next two Augusts.

The ministries and their staffs came under more regular scrutiny. The work of each ministry was overseen by an administrative committee and "people's commissions" that included CDR delegates, as well as by bodies comprised of provincial high commissioners, defence committees, and students' and women's associations.[21] The commission meetings subjected ministers and directors to gruelling questioning and obliged them to explain what they had done, or not done.[22] The first national conference of people's commissions, held in September 1986 in Ouahigouya, drew 1,000 delegates from all ministries and provinces. It was not quite the free and open "popular debate" that Sankara judged it to be.[23] But the scope of the discussions and the breadth of participation were nevertheless greater than anything the administration had previously experienced.

## NEW COURTS TO "FRY BIG FISH"

By themselves, new mechanisms of monitoring and control would take some time to make the state bureaucracy more diligent and honest. To demonstrate its seriousness, the CNR had to show some teeth quickly and dramatically. Accordingly, its sweep began at the top. Scores of former presidents, generals, cabinet ministers, and state enterprise directors were charged and tried. As one scholar of corruption in Africa put it, by "frying ... big fish in public," a new government could signal a clean break with the previous era, end the old culture of impunity, and show some determination to carry through wider state reforms.[24]

To conduct such a major judicial undertaking, the CNR could not rely on the old court system. In the public eye, those courts were largely equated with prisons for the poor but impunity for the rich, and were thoroughly compromised by corruption and lethargy.[25] Since independence, they had only brought a few cases of corruption to trial, some thirty between 1960 and 1980.[26]

The government thus created new courts for their anti-corruption drive, the People's Revolutionary Tribunals (TPRs). These were thoroughly modern institutions, but also partially reflected elements of the country's judicial legacy that had been preserved in a very distorted way in the customary courts of the colonial and post-independence eras.[27] Unlike regular state courts, in which a single magistrate ruled over a case, the TPRs were constituted as panels of judges to hear and decide cases collectively, generally made up of seven members: one professional magistrate (who also served as the TPR chair), five CDR members, and initially one military or police officer (a slot later replaced by another CDR member). Only the TPR chairperson, drawn from the country's pool of regular judges, was appointed; the rest were named by the CDRs.[28]

Virtually all TPR cases were economic in nature, involving civilians or military officers who had held political or administrative office. In a dataset compiled by the author of cases against 743 defendants tried during thirty-two tribunal sessions, all but a tiny proportion of the 1,264 identified charges dealt with white-collar crimes: diversion, corruption, bribery, misuse of funds, collection of irregular bonuses, fraud, use of forged documents, illicit enrichment, and the like. The charge of "diversion" ("détournement" in French) was by far the most common, filed against three-quarters of all defendants. It was a catchall charge, covering embezzlement, misappropriation, theft of public goods, or any other misuse of public office by either public employees or private citizens. It had been on the statute books since the last year of French colonial rule, but before the CNR it had been used only rarely.[29] "Illicit enrichment" was the next most common charge, laid against somewhat more than half of all defendants, usually public employees who could not account for their extensive properties or excessive lifestyles.

With illicit enrichment and a number of other charges, the standard "burden of proof" was reversed, requiring a defendant to prove his or her innocence. This prompted some criticism by legal experts and human rights organizations, but proponents of the tribunals countered that corruption cases were notoriously difficult to prove by ordinary court standards since documentation was often doctored or missing. In practice, the tribunal panels were guided by common sense and usually did not convict solely on illicit enrichment charges, but in conjunction with other illegal acts.[30]

According to the government, the TPRs gave citizens an opportunity "to achieve justice yourselves, directly, without detour."[31] That idealized view did not match the reality, but the tribunals did provide some opening through which popular conceptions of justice were expressed. In contrast to the excessive formalism of the old courts, the new procedures were designed to make the judicial process more accessible: direct, simplified, speedy, and transparent. Like traditional notions of justice, the tribunals emphasized collective concerns in place of individual interests and rights. The TPRs also relied largely on direct oral testimony, questioning, and debate, a bias that was "in harmony with African oral traditions."[32] The tribunals' system of collective judgment likewise drew on the spirit of consultation that usually prevailed in customary courts. Finally, as in customary courts, tribunal judges were expected to look beyond the specifics of the case and consider the infractions in a broader social context, for purposes of highlighting relevant lessons or morals. As then interior minister Ernest Nongma Ouédraogo later recalled, the tribunals sought "to contribute to the moralization of public life. The goal was to awaken people, to put them on guard against corruption, and to prevent those who might be tempted by corruption to pull back."[33]

One measure of the TPRs' popular character was the massive audiences they attracted. The tribunal sessions in Ouagadougou were held at the Maison du peuple, which seats about 3,000 people, and for the more spectacular trials the hall was often filled to capacity. Despite formal prohibitions against loud outbursts, audiences often responded with applause or hoots of derision during testimony.[34] The main TPR sessions were broadcast live over the radio, with summaries and commentaries in Mooré, Dioula, and Fulfuldé for the African-language programmes. During important trials, it was common to see people walking on the street or even riding their bicycles with transistor radios held to an ear. Cassette tapes recorded from the trial broadcasts made their way to marketplaces, selling briskly, not only in other parts of Burkina Faso but in Côte d'Ivoire as well.

### *"Political gangsters" in the dock*

During the first wave of TPR trials in 1984, dozens of former government officials were called to account for funds improperly diverted during their tenures in office, mainly during the 1978–80 Third Republic of General Lamizana and the 1980–82 CMRPN military junta of Colonel Zerbo. All charges were essentially economic: diversion, tax fraud, illicit enrichment, the misuse or mismanagement of funds, and bribery. Yet because the defendants had been high government officials, the trials bore a pervasive political stamp.

The first trial was of Lamizana. It began on 3 January 1984, the historically charged date marking the eighteenth anniversary of the 1966 insurrection against Maurice Yaméogo, which originally brought Lamizana to power. To emphasize the political implications, Sankara addressed the opening session, stating that it was intended to "put political gangsters on trial" and "allow the wounds of the neo-colonial regime to be revealed for the world to see." They were "political trials, which call into question the political system of neo-colonial society."[35]

Halidou Ouédraogo, who previously chaired the Ouagadougou Appeals Court and now served as head of this first TPR panel, castigated waste and mismanagement under Lamizana's government. "You now find yourself alone before the people, who demand an accounting," he told Lamizana. Most questioning concerned Lamizana's use of a special fund. Some money, Lamizana testified, went to the intelligence services, some to government ministries, and some to support various domestic social associations, the women's federation, filmmakers, and publications. He acknowledged handing out favours to those who came to him. When asked for documentation, Lamizana replied, amidst applause from the audience, "When I helped a student's parents or a farmer, there was no receipt." Over the next two days, a long line of witnesses took the floor to back up Lamizana's assertions. Confronted by such testimony and the audience's evident sympathy for the former president, the judges decided by majority vote to acquit him of all charges.[36] Based on the evidence, the TPR probably could have argued that Lamizana's use of state resources was irregular, designed to curry partisan favour with various individuals and organized groups. Other tribunals made such arguments in their cases. But in this instance there was no evidence that Lamizana had taken advantage of his position to enhance his own individual or familial wealth. The judges thus made an apparent distinction: that operating as a beneficent patron was not, by itself, sufficient to convict, even on charges of mismanagement.

If anyone took the judgment as a sign that the CNR would be lenient, they were soon set straight. During a dozen trials from January to July 1984 included in the author's dataset, a total of forty-four government officials of cabinet rank or above were tried. About half were officials of Lamizana's Third Republic and half from Zerbo's CMRPN. Overall, a dozen were acquitted, but the rest were found guilty of economic infractions and sentenced to fines, reimbursement orders, and prison terms. A number were leaders of political parties and officials of Lamizana's Third Republic who engaged heavily in political patronage activities. But unlike Lamizana, they appear to have diverted some funds into their own pockets. Issa Welté Palé, a former minister of rural development, was forthcoming in admitting his motivations: "You have to sort things out so that you don't leave [office] empty-handed."[37]

The head of the CMRPN, Zerbo, and his second-in-command, Colonel Barthélémy Kombasséré, received the stiffest sentences of all the high-level defendants. This reflected some measure of political reckoning. As a pro-CNR commentator acknowledged, "The trial of the CMRPN was always on a political level, a trial of the French neo-colonial army, with all its faults: dictatorship by a handful of officers, scorn for the people."[38] In the legal-rational tradition of jurisprudence, such an explicit political agenda would be considered highly improper. In the TPRs, it took centre-stage. Past political practice did not necessarily determine guilt—quite a few CMRPN members and cabinet ministers were acquitted or ordered to pay only modest fines and reimbursements. Yet it did seem to weigh in sentencing.

### *Local justice*

The trials of "big fish" received most public attention, yet the TPRs also dug down to less well-known targets: sundry underlings and accomplices and officials of a variety of state institutions, including the grain marketing board, national airline, livestock agency, sugar enterprise, and public health service. Sometimes judges went beyond the defendants' actual misdeeds to highlight the consequences of their actions: public roads that could not be maintained or wells that could not be dug because investment funds had been pilfered, medicines that cost more because health personnel diverted them to private merchants, farmers who were cheated when they sold their grain to the official marketing agency. Some tribunals focused on private merchants, other businesspeople, and professionals who abetted and/or benefited from public sector corruption or favours. And to ensure that such exposures were presented not just to residents of Ouagadougou and Bobo-Dioulasso, the TPRs began more systematically to hold sessions in provincial capitals and smaller towns, to try officials of cooperatives, village associations, local governments, and various rural development agencies.

Despite the tribunals' image of severity, their outcomes reflected a degree of leniency. Nearly one-fifth of all defendants in the dataset were acquitted. Of those convicted, most received prison terms plus monetary penalties (fines and restitution). Prison-only sentences generally remained low, averaging 7.3 percent of the total judgments throughout 1984–87. Some prisoners were released or had their sentences shortened. In 1986 Gérard Kango Ouédraogo, a former prime minister, was granted clemency and Zerbo was shifted from prison to house arrest.[39]

While the national TPRs reflected the social and political imperatives of revolutionary justice (as defined by the CNR), lower tribunals provided scope for more localized concerns. Among them were the Tribunaux populaires de conciliation (TPCs) to hear cases in villages and urban neighbourhoods.[40] Beginning in 1986, they were constituted as panels of eight lay judges popularly elected for renewable one-year terms. Their trial procedures were even more simplified and flexible than those of the TPRs. The sessions were usually held once or twice a week (at least in urban neighbourhoods). Anyone could attend or give testimony. Their jurisdiction was limited to cases of litigation involving less than CFA50,000, the setting of brushfires and destruction of crops, violations of price restrictions and speculation in basic necessities, disputes and disturbances that made "community life intolerable," and in general any "anti-social behaviour considered to be so by the population." Their fines could not exceed CFA1,000, they could order only up to ten days of community labour, and they had no authority to jail anyone.[41] The basic goal of the TPCs was not necessarily to render judgment on who was at fault, but to bring the parties together in some mutually agreed settlement.

In those respects, the TPCs resembled the old customary courts, which were formally dissolved by the same ordinance establishing the new tribunals. But unlike the customary courts, they did not uphold traditional norms of hierarchy or social behaviour. One of their key tasks was to eliminate "cultural defects," including "backward customs" relating to women.[42] Bruno Jaffré described a September 1987 session of a Ouagadougou neighbourhood TPC that included a domestic fight, in which the wife, contrary to custom, was not required to return to her husband.[43] A delegation from the Ministry of Justice estimated that in thirteen provinces it visited up to October 1986, more than half the TPC cases dealt with "conjugal abandonment," mainly wives leaving their husbands. The delegation chairman attributed this to the advancement of new notions of freedom among women.[44]

### *Judicial reform*

Meanwhile, many old courts functioned in parallel with the new institutions. Although they continued to hear ordinary criminal and civil cases, they were targeted for reforms designed to overcome their inefficiency. Brief and intense commando-type campaigns in October 1985 and June 1986 sought to clear out part of the enormous backlog of cases and appeals that had accumulated over the years. Most professional magistrates, plus court assessors, TPC judges, and CDR delegates, were mobilized to examine evidence and issue rulings in several thousand cases. During the first operation, 794 defendants received prison terms, of whom 210 were released for time served. Another 541 were found guilty, but given fines and other monetary sentences, while 185 were simply acquitted.[45]

The reforms extended to the prison system as well. Old facilities were refurbished and new ones added, including workshops, vegetable gardens, and literacy classes. During a 1987 visit to the capital's central prison, this author found a new medical clinic, three buildings for religious worship, a school with two classrooms, a soccer field, and workshops for teaching welding, sewing, and other crafts. By moving some prisoners to less crowded facilities and releasing others, the total number had been brought down to 450, from some 1,400 before. According to Sambo Antoine Komy, secretary of state for justice and a TPR judge, it was not right to consider "prisoners as lost people."[46]

Komy was one of a number of professional magistrates who played an active role in the TPRs and efforts to reform the justice system as a whole. A few magistrates were dismissed, but many others were promoted, reassigned to other jurisdictions, or newly appointed.[47] A new judicial school was set up in 1984 within the old college for high-level administrators. Besides courses in new conceptions of popular justice, the school required trainees to follow their classroom instruction with a ten-month stage of practical training in the provinces. It also placed a high priority on advancing women judges. Out of its first class of fifteen magistrates, seven were women.[48]

Some established magistrates appeared uncomfortable with the changes, especially the revisions of established legal procedures and a tendency to belittle their professional qualifications in favour of a concept that saw any citizen as a potential judge. But others actively supported the tribunals and the reforms. Some of those "revolutionary judges" had launched their own association in March 1983, prior to the CNR's seizure of power in August of that year.[49] Later renamed the Syndicat autonome des magistrats burkinabè (SAMAB), its secretary-general, Halidou Ouédraogo, chaired the first TPR and other members sat on later tribunal panels.

While facilitating the launch of the TPRs, the politicized nature of this judicial sector also brought some problems. As in other aspects of the CNR's functioning, factionalism and dogmatism bedevilled the tribunals' work. A large portrait of Joseph Stalin that hung at the back of the main hall in Ouagadougou's Palais de justice exemplified the limited concern for defendants' rights or for civil liberties more generally. That disdain was reinforced by the minister of justice, Captain Compaoré, who declared at the opening of a TPR session in Pô: "In Upper Volta, there has not existed nor will there ever exist human rights, full stop."[50] By 1984–85, as several of the small political groups that had members among the judiciary came into direct conflict with the CNR, relations between the government and SAMAB grew tense. Halidou Ouédraogo was accused of consorting with government opponents (specifically the underground PCRV). At its September 1984 congress, SAMAB reaffirmed its support for the tribunal system, but also raised critical points: defence of both collective and individual rights, opposition to the retroactive nature of some laws, and assertions of judicial independence from government pressures.[51] A few months later, after SAMAB signed a labour declaration critical of the government's economic policies, Halidou Ouédraogo was ousted from the judicial service. About two dozen other SAMAB members were similarly dismissed over the next two years.[52] The conflict with the magistrates' union, although driven overwhelmingly by partisan differences, served to harden the government's general stance against any notion of judicial independence.

As distinct institutions, both the TPRs and the regular courts thus found themselves under pressure from two different directions. On the one hand, the judicial system was opened up to greater input "from below," especially with the involvement of ever greater numbers of lay judges and newly trained components of the legal profession. On the other hand, they were clearly subordinated to the imperatives of those who controlled the central state. As long as the CNR was in power, that state connection gave the TPRs in particular considerable power and authority. But the October 1987 coup highlighted the vulnerable side of that link. The tribunals were to limp along for a few more years, but in the early 1990s were scrapped entirely, in favour of a full return to the regular court system.

## AN ARMY OF THE PEOPLE?

Despite the evident fractures at the command level, the military was still one of the country's most solid and formidable institutions, continuing to exercise an inordinate influence over the state system as a whole. It had played a key political role ever since Lamizana's 1966 assumption of power. Judging by the number of officers in the CNR and other state bodies, it clearly continued to do so. Yet like other state institutions, the military also came under review. The political rhetoric that accompanied that process was often overheated. Leaders of the CNR stressed the need to "decolonize" the army, to transform it from an instrument of the bourgeoisie into a servant of the oppressed, and to raise the revolutionary consciousness of the ranks. As Sankara put it, "a soldier without [political] training is a criminal in power."[53]

The process of reforming the armed forces was far more orderly and measured than the verbiage suggested. It was also somewhat limited. The military chain of command continued to operate normally—except that its very pinnacle was essentially lopped off, first by the compulsory retirement of the army's generals and then by the death or imprisonment of those senior officers who had opposed the radical military wing before and during the August 1983 takeover. Since no other officers were subsequently promoted to the highest rank, the Burkinabè army remained devoid of generals for years after.

From the CNR's perspective, the problems of the armed forces were similar to those of the state administration more generally. The goal was to put an end to the "army of parades," a military cut off from people's daily sufferings and mired in corrupt and profiteering practices. Different components of the armed forces (especially its equipment and supply service, the officers' mess, the air base, the medical corps, and the military engineers) had suffered from thefts, embezzlement, and other malpractices, often involving senior officers, a number of whom were tried by the TPRs. Unlike with other sectors of the state administration, however, there was no move to trim the armed forces' size and budget. Total regular troop strength remained at 9,000 throughout the CNR period, while military expenditures, as a share of total spending, rose from 18.7 percent in 1985 to 22.2 percent the following year, before falling slightly to 17.3 percent in 1987.[54]

Things did not remain static, however. The disciplinary councils set up throughout the civil service were also established within the military to hear cases of embezzlement, theft, unauthorized absence from duty, and other infractions.[55] New garrison committees were established similar to the civilian CDRs, with representatives elected by general assemblies of officers and ranks. Little information emerged about their activities or modes of functioning, but their influence appeared to have been limited and they did not seem to have compromised or competed with regular command structures.

Previously, most officers had been sent abroad for advanced training, usually to military academies in France or bases in some of its former colonies, such as Morocco or Madagascar. In October 1984, however, the first Burkinabè officers' academy was opened at the paracommando base in Pô, and a year later its first cohort graduated. It was expected that officers who needed specialized training would continue to study abroad and that France would still provide some equipment and technical expertise, but the opening of the academy was nevertheless seen as a step towards asserting a degree of sovereignty in military affairs and changing the military's basic orientation. "On the one hand," declared the academy's commander, Lieutenant Daniel Traoré, "these cadres trained in the hard realities of Burkina, on Burkinabè soil, will be better fit to serve their country. On the other, it is we who determine the training programme, what we teach them." In addition to regular military skills, he pointed out, this included production methods and political ideology, derived from Sankara's political orientation speech.[56]

Although the size of the regular armed forces did not change, the CNR initiated far more extensive military training of other organized sectors of its support base. Foremost were the CDRs themselves, many of which had their own armed units. In most major military facilities, large numbers of selected defence committee activists underwent training in basic military skills: the handling and maintenance of arms, the mastery of rudimentary logistics, and the ability to operate in tightly organized and well-led groups.[57] Besides creating a reserve that could be mobilized in the event of war, it was expected that these activists would apply some of their new organizational and operational skills to their civilian work, such as building roads or directing social mobilization campaigns. For similar reasons, thousands of youths in the national service programme received several weeks of training at the Pô academy and other bases.[58]

Special attention was paid to the military training of women, a particularly radical notion in a country where women's social and political status was so marginal. In some cases, as at the Pô base, that began with courses for the wives of soldiers, to enable them to play stronger leadership roles in the defence committees and other organizations. But more formal training was also established for other women around the country, most of them members of the defence committees. For example, in the country's second military region, comprising several provinces in the north-west, about 310 women received two weeks of training in drill, armaments, and other skills. In Passoré, the outspoken provincial high commissioner, Aïcha Traoré, encouraged them to translate their new leadership skills into stronger mobilizations of women more generally. She also cautioned them not to use their knowledge of combat within their households, suggesting that it would be better to instead organize "mini-TPRs" to deal with wife-beaters.[59]

By engaging in such widespread military training, Sankara maintained: "We have demystified the military art. You don't have to attend a military academy to learn military science ... The defence system is not composed only of the army. It is composed of all the people."[60]

While broader citizen participation was still far from the reality, the "demystification" aspects of this approach nevertheless served some public relations purposes, by slightly altering the image of the armed forces as solely concerned with military affairs. Wherever they were based, soldiers grew food and raised livestock, planted trees, dug wells, and built schools, health clinics, roads, and other facilities. There were four specialized units in the more fertile south and south-west that concentrated almost entirely on farming, using advanced technologies to produce rice, maize, sorghum, groundnuts, and other crops.[61] Besides showing civilians a different side of the military, such productive activities were also intended to dissuade those in uniform from seeing themselves as superior to other Burkinabè. "Soldiers must learn to suffer with the people," said Sankara. "Now they are farming, so they will understand what that involves ... This is the way we are going to produce a new mentality in the army."[62]

Yet the Burkinabè army still was an army. Soldiers, through their organization and access to firearms, knew they had greater power than other sectors of society. Despite efforts to maintain discipline, abuses of civilians sometimes occurred.

While a powerful domestic force, the Burkinabè army was a more modest presence on the regional stage, as became evident during Burkina Faso's brief border war with Mali in 1985. The Malian president, General Moussa Traoré, made no secret of his dislike of the CNR's revolutionary politics, its alliance with Libya and other radical regimes, and the encouragement it might provide to domestic opponents of the Malian junta. As tensions mounted, the Malian military received new arms shipments from France, despite protests by Sankara to French President Mitterrand.[63] Then, in early December 1985, Burkinabè census-takers, apparently accompanied by armed CDR members, entered several villages in the Agacher region, a ninety-mile strip of territory along Burkina Faso's northern border, which Mali claimed as its own. The Traoré regime seized on the census operation as a justification to attack on 25 December. Having only a small air force and very few tanks or armoured cars, the Burkinabè army was no match for the larger and better-equipped Malian forces, and suffered serious setbacks. At least four provincial capitals were bombed by Malian warplanes and dozens of civilians and troops were killed. Finally, after five days, a ceasefire was signed under pressure from neighbouring countries. Both sides agreed to take the border dispute to the World Court, which a year later delineated a definitive boundary between the two countries.[64]

For the Burkinabè authorities, the war demonstrated several things. One was the utility of the CDRs and their newly trained vigilance brigades, which provided some logistical and support services for the regular army. Pierre Ouédraogo, the national CDR secretary-general, emphasized that they had helped free up soldiers from other duties, staffed roadblocks and checkpoints, and enforced the curfew.[65] Still, the sobering reality was that such mobilizations could not compensate for the military's fundamental weaknesses. Sankara acknowledged that the CNR had neglected equipping the army, believing that it would have been "criminal to spend money on arms." But in the future, he added, "we will be obliged to devote part of our resources to equipment for our army."[66] Military spending did increase in 1986. On the political front, the war gave the CNR an incentive to try to improve relations with its immediate neighbours, including not only Mali but also Benin and Niger.

Whatever the reforms of Burkina Faso's military structures and practices, the leaders of the CNR never contemplated reducing the army's substantial role in political life and state affairs, let alone subordinating it to civilian control. Neither the officers in the political leadership nor their closest civilian allies saw any real problem with this, although a few civilian members of the CNR sometimes grumbled quietly about the heavy-handed way the "activists in uniform" engaged in political debate. Yet from the CNR's own perspective of making the state more accountable to society, the failure to even question the military's place within the state was seriously short-sighted. It would ultimately prove fatal.

# 6
# ON FRAGILE GROUND

The attempts by the National Council of the Revolution to restructure the state were closely related to its sweeping vision of economic and social development. The CNR proclaimed that its ultimate goal was nothing less than the construction of an "independent, self-sufficient, and planned national economy at the service of a democratic and popular society."[1] Yet the CNR had little in its coffers to finance that vision. That was one factor behind its drive to eliminate superfluous and expensive administrative functions, combat corruption, and crack down on tax evasion and fraud. The weakness of existing state structures also spurred it to promote local community mobilizations.

Although the CNR, like its predecessors, remained highly dependent on foreign aid, it attempted, with some modest success, to reduce the level of that dependence and diversify the sources of funding. Throughout its tenure, the government rejected the policy proposals of the International Monetary Fund (IMF) and World Bank, fully aware of the politically disruptive consequences that such "structural adjustment" prescriptions had brought to many other African countries. Justin Damo Barro, briefly finance minister during the first year of the CNR, later revealed that he had tried on four occasions to persuade Sankara to ask for IMF assistance, but the president declined on the grounds that the policy conditions the IMF would demand in exchange could well cripple the revolution.[2]

## BUDGET CUTTING IN PUBLIC VIEW

Since some measure of austerity was necessary, the CNR decided to take its arguments before the Burkinabè public. Previously, each ministry prepared a budget for its own sphere and these were then discussed and aggregated by the Council of Ministers. To open up that opaque process, the government organized public sessions in December 1983 to discuss the following year's budget. Not only ministers and directors, but also many other state employees—including some secretaries and typists—took part and asked questions. The proceedings were broadcast live over national radio. Then in December 1984 came an even more ambitious effort for the 1985 budget: a two-day national budget conference, including CDR activists from all but one province and several labour representatives. Participants identified new revenue sources and some cuts in operating costs. A few asked embarrassing questions about military expenditures.[3]

No such public conferences preceded the 1986 budget, according to some officials because of the December 1985 border war with Mali. Then came another budget conference in December 1986. As before, the basic question posed to the 400 delegates was how to reduce the budget deficit, which was brought down from CFA17 billion to CFA12 billion, mainly through new taxes and better collection of existing revenue sources. Sankara closed the event by inviting citizens to find further ways to economize and criticized civil servants and state enterprise personnel who still engaged in absenteeism, self-enrichment, laziness, and disorganized working methods.[4] That highlighted another element behind the CNR's national budget debates: to leverage public pressure behind its efforts to squeeze and discipline the bureaucracy.

## STATE ENTERPRISES UNDER A MICROSCOPE

Negligence, poor performance, embezzlement, and waste existed across the civil service, but the approximately thirty state-owned companies exhibited some of the worst instances. These firms often had different structures, styles of management, and methods of control, making it hard to draw a clear picture of their financial position, let alone supervise their functioning or contain their chronic deficits. As one columnist noted, the enterprises were a "poisoned legacy" of the previous state system. Ministers and other members of the old political elites had often used the state firms for their own benefit or to give jobs to relatives, friends, and political clients. "To a remarkable extent laxity, waste, and profiteering have replaced ethical rules," commented the state-run daily newspaper.[5]

The most grievous cases of outright theft and embezzlement were handed over to the revolutionary courts. Some senior enterprise personnel were dismissed for incompetence and negligence and replaced by others considered better qualified or more trustworthy. In August 1984 the CNR issued new, more uniform rules for state enterprises, with each run on a day-to-day basis by a director appointed by the Council of Ministers. Each also had an administrative council composed equally of government appointees and representatives of the trade unions and CDRs to supervise performance, budgets, investment plans, personnel policies, salary scales, and other matters.[6]

Along the model of the budget debates, scrutiny of state companies also had a public side. In July 1986 and March 1987 open hearings were held in Ouagadougou's Maison du peuple to examine the performance, financial records, and management policies of almost all enterprises. Their directors, administrative councils, and financial experts had to give accounts for the previous three years before some twenty cabinet ministers, sometimes headed by Sankara himself. The questioning was often tough. In many cases excessive management pay was reduced. Housing, transport, and other allowances were either trimmed or eliminated entirely. In some enterprises the central authorities acknowledged the need to raise base salaries to improve incentives for better performance by ordinary employees. At the close of the final session in 1987, Sankara ordered all directors, senior accountants, and financial and administrative officers to make full disclosures of their assets within a few days. "All [enterprise] personnel must be sensitized to the risks of corruption," he said. "Those who are corrupt and those who corrupt them must be denounced."[7]

## REINFORCING TAX COLLECTION

Because of the administration's limited capacity, tax collection had never been very effective. The easiest taxes to secure were those deducted directly from the salaries of public and private employees. Most other taxes, except on substantial fixed properties, were relatively hard to assess or collect. According to tax authority estimates, about 80 percent of those in the liberal professions evaded taxes to some extent, as did 64 percent of craftsmen, 41 percent in service occupations, and 34 percent of retail merchants. The resulting shortfalls in state revenue were estimated at some CFA2.6 billion annually during the three years before the CNR came to power. The government reorganized the tax authority in October 1984 and gave it more tax verification brigades to monitor whether businesses and professionals were paying their taxes. Defence committee members also supplied information on suspected evasions. As a further check, anyone seeking to secure a loan, purchase goods wholesale, or win a state contract had to produce a certificate verifying they had met their obligations.[8]

In the spirit of the CNR's other "commando" mobilizations, the government mounted an extensive tax recovery operation in May–June 1987, mobilizing hundreds of customs agents, CDR activists, policemen, and troops and gendarmes. At the end of the first week, the Ministry of Finance estimated that CFA2.8 billion had been collected in Ouagadougou, CFA429 million in Bobo-Dioulasso, and CFA120 million in Banfora.[9] Several new taxes were introduced, taxes on salaries, certain imports, and other goods were increased, and fees were raised on government registration and other services.[10] In 1985, owners of urban rental property were hit especially hard when the CNR decreed a "rent-free" year; in fact, tenants continued to pay their normal rents, but directly to the state treasury, not to the owners.[11]

Through such efforts, the government moderately increased its collection rate. As a percentage of gross domestic product (GDP) tax revenue rose very modestly from 9.2 percent in 1983 to 10.6 percent in 1987. Overall government revenue, which included non-tax sources, saw a clearer improvement, from 13.5 percent of GDP in 1983 to 16.3 percent in 1987.[12] That reflected changes in the customs service, where corrupt personnel were weeded out and greater supervision of importers ensured that they paid their duties and tariffs. Meanwhile, the increase in domestic tax receipts slightly reduced the economy's external dependence. In 1987 taxes on international trade were 29.4 percent of total tax revenues, down from 41 percent in 1983.[13]

## "HOME-COOKED" RIGOUR

In the CNR's broad development strategy, the state was assigned the central role. Most members of the CNR were certainly aware of the state's inadequate reach and capacities, but saw little alternative. The economy was so underdeveloped and fragmented and the private sector so limited that only the state could mobilize the capital needed to build essential infrastructure or stimulate productive activities.

Since the government's own treasury was small and little additional funding could be expected from abroad, raising significant investment financing required seriously economizing on existing operations. Thus almost as soon as the CNR took power, civil service salaries were frozen. The first full annual budget unveiled in February 1984 was a "budget of rigour," as Finance Minister Barro put it, with a contraction in spending.[14] Subsequent budgets featured higher expenditures on health, education, and other social programmes and significantly greater investments in infrastructure and productive projects, but within a context of strict spending controls.

The heavy emphasis on stringency, painful cutbacks (at least for urban residents), and frugal management led some Burkinabè analysts to later equate the CNR's policies with those of the structural adjustment programmes adopted elsewhere in Africa under the tutelage of the Washington-based financial institutions. However, since the CNR's approach was fashioned on its own initiative and not dictated from outside, it was usually qualified as "self-adjustment," "self-imposed adjustment," or even "home-cooked adjustment."[15] Researchers at the industrialized countries' Organisation for Economic Co-operation and Development saw the CNR's policy as "a strange hybrid of Thatcherism and Maoism."[16] Such characterizations began only in the late 1980s, after the CNR had been overthrown. From the perspective of the IMF and World Bank, which were arguing energetically that African countries really had no alternative to structural adjustment, Burkina Faso's relatively good macro-economic performance in the 1980s was an unwelcome indicator that there might indeed be another route. Labelling the country's experience as an idiosyncratic variant of adjustment was one way to gloss over the differences.

Yet major differences there were. First, the CNR's concept of self-reliance extended further than simply refusing to request policy advice and financing from the IMF and World Bank. It also sought to reduce its dependence on aid overall and to mobilize greater domestic revenues. "Foreign aid, technical aid, will only be as a support, no longer the determining factor in the construction of the national economy," Planning Minister Youssouf Ouédraogo told this author.[17] Expressed as a share of Burkina Faso's growing economy, total aid levels did in fact fall from 16.7 percent to 13.4 percent of gross domestic product between 1984 and 1987.[18] France, traditionally the country's main source of foreign finance, maintained some project funding, but halted all general budgetary support after 1983, while the World Bank ended its project financing in 1985.[19]

Second, contrary to most structural adjustment programmes, the government did not seek a wholesale shift from the public sector to the private. Nor did it carry out any sweeping liberalization of either domestic or foreign trade. Its general approach was to create a more robust state entity, freed of corruption and bureaucratic inefficiencies and better able to stand up to pressures from the social elites and external powers.

Third, while the CNR's budgets and its five-year development plan, initiated in 1986, included much that was austere, basic social services—those generally of greatest benefit to the poor—received greater funding. Public health spending rose from CFA388 per person in 1983 to CFA491 in 1987, and education from CFA1,128 to CFA1,605.[20] That was quite different from most African countries undergoing structural adjustment in the 1980s, in which health, education, and social services were often the first to be cut.

Although proponents of structural adjustment would have predicted otherwise, the macro-economic results of the CNR's "unorthodox" policies were largely positive. Real growth of Burkina Faso's GDP tended to fluctuate with rainfall (which strongly affects agricultural performance), but it nevertheless averaged 4.6 percent annually during 1983–87, higher than the 3.8 percent average in 1970–82 and quite respectable compared with the rest of sub-Saharan Africa in the 1980s.

## SEEKING NEW SOCIAL ALLIANCES

CNR leaders often framed their social agenda in class terms. They soon discovered, however, that social realities on the ground did not easily fit the labels they were accustomed to. As in large parts of Africa, the uneven penetration of market forces meant that many social strata were fluid, ill-defined, and fragmentary. Sankara himself acknowledged as much, noting that Burkina Faso had not only a "numerically weak" working class but also "no strong national bourgeoisie."[21]

As in the political realm, the government's economic policies tried to shift the social landscape and consolidate a new range of alliances. Dramatic changes in public spending clearly favoured certain sectors and hurt others. The emphasis on building a national economy opened opportunities for indigenous producers and entrepreneurs, as against those linked more directly to external markets. Above all, the focus on improving the conditions and capacities of poorer Burkinabè turned more attention and resources towards rural folk. That change was accompanied by a severe squeeze on the salaries and benefits of (mainly urban) public employees, in turn sharpening tensions with the trade unions.

Urban importers resented higher customs duties designed to better protect domestic goods from stiff foreign competition. Rural grain merchants faced tighter government controls and new marketing institutions designed to boost the prices paid to farmers. Yet many wholesale and retail traders were often able to successfully evade official restrictions, including by smuggling goods across the country's porous borders.

Meanwhile, manufacturers engaged directly in production—identified as "national capital"—were courted by the CNR, provided they were not linked to networks of corruption. "Private property is a normal thing at this stage of our society," Sankara noted. "It is normal that it should be protected. But what Voltaics cannot accept is private property dishonestly acquired."[22] Linking up with national business interests was not simple, however. Much locally owned manufacturing faced serious difficulties, stemming in part from some of the highest energy and transport costs in the region and the absence of suitable physical and commercial infrastructure. Moreover, the CNR's revolutionary rhetoric frightened a number of entrepreneurs into shifting their operations to neighbouring countries. As of 1985, out of seventy small and medium-sized industrial enterprises registered, fifteen were no longer operating.[23] Government officials tried to assure Burkinabè businessmen that the private sector would "play the role that it has long held, to invest in the productive sectors of the economy and promote jobs and training for Burkinabè."[24] That message was symbolically reinforced by the very visible role of Oumarou Kanazoé, probably the country's richest businessman, in various road, dam, and other public infrastructure projects.[25]

The investment code, amended in 1984, included tax and customs breaks for businesses in priority sectors, along with pledges against arbitrary expropriation. The benefits were weighted much more heavily than before towards smaller-scale enterprises, owned by Burkinabè entrepreneurs, using local materials, producing basic consumer goods, and located in less-developed parts of the country. Entrepreneurs were encouraged to develop new industries to supply agriculture or use agricultural raw materials: fertilizer, farm tools, and food and livestock processing.[26] Meanwhile, enterprises exclusively owned by foreign capital received fewer incentives and faced tougher restrictions.[27]

The foremost element of the CNR's development vision was its effort to promote agriculture and improve the conditions of rural villagers. Between 1973 and 1980, only around 25 percent of all public investment went to agriculture, a proportion that had slipped to 21 percent in the 1977–81 development plan, the last to be completed before the CNR. The level of commercial bank credit to agricultural ventures was always among the lowest in Africa.[28] Except for cotton, which absorbed much of the available financing, farming remained an extremely rudimentary activity, with crops dependent overwhelmingly on rainfall and the big majority of farmers using nothing more advanced than the *daba*, a short-handled hand hoe.

Proclaiming the need to radically transform this "backward" agricultural sector, the CNR initiated a range of measures to provide poor farmers and livestock herders with more extensive public services, productive inputs, price incentives, marketing assistance, irrigation, environmental protection, and other assistance. A greater share of the budget went directly to agriculture, permitting a modest rise in fertilizer use and irrigation. Between 1986 and 1987 the number of tractors more than doubled. Basic social services also increased in the countryside. By January 1986 more than 7,460 primary health posts had been established, or one for each village, staffed by a health agent and a midwife trained in basic health care and supplied with medicines and first-aid kits. Some 2 million children were vaccinated against the major childhood diseases, and about 36,000 villagers were taught basic literacy.[29] In the five-year plan started in 1986, 71 percent of investment in productive sectors was allocated to agriculture, livestock, fishing, and wildlife and forests. Another CFA150 billion was planned for irrigation, sanitation, and other water-related projects, with major portions of health, education, and transport investment destined for rural areas.[30] The government also abolished the colonial-era head tax, by which each rural family member had to pay from CFA500 to CFA1,000 a year. The move did more than lift a monetary burden from villagers; it eliminated a mark of their subject status, both to the central government and to the traditional chiefs who had collected the tax.[31]

With higher rural investment, the government aimed to stimulate output, especially of cereals, in order to enhance national food security, raise the incomes and well-being of farming and stock-raising families, and boost local rural economies. During the relatively few years when the CNR was in power, agricultural indicators, although still very low by African standards, demonstrated a notable improvement, despite weather-related fluctuations (see Table 6.1).

***Table 6.1 Burkina Faso: agriculture indicators***

| Indicator | 1983 | 1984 | 1985 | 1986 | 1987 |
|---|---|---|---|---|---|
| Cereal production, '000 metric tons | 1,100 | 1,113 | 1,587 | 1,927 | 1,638 |
| Cereal yields, kg/ha | 507 | 565 | 716 | 717 | 645 |
| Cotton producer price, CFA/kg | 70 | 90 | 100 | 100 | 95 |
| Sesame producer price, CFA/kg | 96 | 96 | 113 | 175 | 175 |
| Fertilizer use, '000 metric tons | 13.3 | 11.5 | 12.2 | 16.3 | 17.9 |
| Irrigated land as percentage of total cropland | 0.41 | 0.40 | 0.40 | 0.45 | 0.51 |

Sources: Savadogo and Wetta (1992), p. 64; World Bank (2000).

Through its control over the state cotton enterprise, which had an effective monopoly on cotton purchases, the government had little trouble ensuring that higher producer prices could be delivered to cotton farmers. But boosting prices to poorer cereal farmers was more difficult. There was hardly any effective state regulation of the domestic grain market, while the state marketing agency, the Office national des céréales (Ofnacer), was generally able to purchase only between 10 and 20 percent of marketed output. This gave traders wide scope to engage in profiteering. With transport and capital, they could set the prices paid to poor farmers, who lacked the means to find alternative buyers or storage capacity to hang on to their crops until prices improved.[32]

In response, the CNR authorized the defence committees to crack down on *véreux* (shady) merchants. Hundreds of village cereal banks were built through collective labour mobilizations organized by the CDRs, village associations, and other rural organizations. In the village of Doundouni, for example, without an organized storage system, villagers often sold their grain to merchants for CFA500 per sack, only to repurchase it later, when they needed it, at CFA1,000. But with the new cereal bank, managed by the village association, they could buy it back for just CFA550.[33] The CDRs also directly supported the state's own marketing bodies. In 1985–86 they mobilized to collect thousands of tonnes of grain for Ofnacer and helped staff agency stores in Ouagadougou and elsewhere.[34]

In addition, any merchant trading cereals across provincial boundaries was required to obtain a licence from a local defence committee. A portion of the cereals collected was to be sold to the local Ofnacer centre. Violators were subject to revocation of the licence or confiscation of property by the CDRs. Meanwhile, official cereal prices were set at provincial level, during public assemblies at which CDRs, merchants, consumers, and cereal producers were represented.[35]

Noting the continued weakness of Ofnacer's capacity, Labazée commented that "while awaiting a general reform [of the marketing system], the CNR is counting on the effectiveness of 'popular control' to reduce the impact of speculative practices."[36] From most indications, however, such control had only a modest impact.

To further alter relations in the countryside, the government adopted an agrarian reform law in 1984. It proclaimed that henceforth all land would be state property, including lands held under customary communal tenure. It sought to abrogate the chiefs' previous powers of land allocation by specifying that tenure rights would henceforth be allocated by new commissions that included members of the village CDR bureau.[37] By nationalizing the land, the new law aimed to hinder land appropriation through the acquisition of private titles (by a few wealthy farmers or, more commonly, urban functionaries), and through the practice among some chiefs of demanding payment from villagers in exchange for use rights. As of 1984, there were only 3,456 titles, but proponents of the agrarian law maintained that by closing off avenues towards future land alienation, those who were already working land or wanted some for cultivation would have greater security of tenure. An essay in the national CDR journal argued that the law involved "a confirmation of the rights of the poor peasants, the most numerous, with the aim of helping to free them from the power of property owners and feudalists," the prevalent term for traditional chiefs.[38]

The CDRs soon found that the power of the chiefs was not that simple to overcome, especially since the chiefs did not draw their authority only from land allocation powers but also from complex "hierarchies, ranks, and values" to which many villagers still adhered.[39] As a result, implementation of the agrarian reform got bogged down in confusion: chiefs could no longer legally allocate land, but new alternative structures were not yet in place. Few land-use maps were available. The common practice of lending land made sorting out tenure rights even more complicated. So when plans for the land management commissions were redrafted in 1987, they made provision for involving local land chiefs, in part because of their detailed knowledge of tenure patterns and rights.

Taken together, the government's numerous economic and social initiatives pointed towards a demonstrative effort to realign the state's social linkages and support base. As Otayek noted, ever since independence successive governments rested on support from the public administration, traditional chiefs, and Catholic and Muslim religious leaders. The CNR, however, aimed at "the dismantling of this pact and the establishment of a new alliance, this time with the peasantry, to the detriment of the social strata normally associated with the running of public affairs."[40] Yet it was easier to dismantle one set of alliances than to successfully build a new one. Many rural Burkinabè appeared to welcome the government's new orientation and participated in the numerous community development mobilizations and other activities that the government and CDRs initiated. But there were few indications that this acceptance translated into a solid and active political base for the new state-in-formation. Country folk were dispersed across more than 7,000 villages. They had little access to organization other than the CDRs—which some distrusted because they tended to embrace mainly the young, not a representative cross-section of rural society. There was thus a disjuncture between the government's social aims and the hard reality of trying to bring real change to the countryside.

## NATION-BUILDING

The CNR was able to project a broad social orientation: against the established elites, in favour of the poor. Yet it had difficulty mobilizing people on the basis of more precise class identities. Besides the ambiguity of social stratifications overall, one factor that tended to hinder ordinary Burkinabè from viewing the world through the prism of class was the prevalence of ethnic identities. As with other social attitudes, ethnic outlooks were not rigid. Nor were they particularly antagonistic. But they were tangible enough to provide the CNR with some firm footholds for advancing a broader nation-building project.

The decision to rename the country "Burkina Faso" exemplified that goal. First, the change affirmed the African identity of the new state the CNR was trying to fashion, a state that did not derive its legitimacy from a colonial geographical designation, but from the indigenous peoples who lived there. Second, it was simultaneously a pan-territorial, polyglot identity embracing the country's multiple cultures. The name itself was a multilingual composite: *burkina* from Mooré, the language of the Mossi, meaning "worthy people" or "men of dignity," and *faso* from Dioula, signifying, among other definitions, "house" or "republic." The "bè" suffix in Burkinabè came from Fulfuldé, the language of the Peulh.[41]

From the perspective of the young modernizers who came to power with the CNR, the limited extent to which the peoples of the country identified themselves as citizens of a common nation was a serious shortcoming. Whether they drew their ideas from Marxism or revolutionary nationalist traditions, they viewed the construction of a unified "nation" as an essential corollary to building a modern state and society. Like many other African countries, the territory they governed was to a great extent an arbitrary creation of the colonial era. Given the extensive reach of the old Mossi empire, the country's geographical boundaries were perhaps less artificial than those of some of its neighbours. But the relative lateness of the colonial creation, the colony's sub-division among Côte d'Ivoire, Mali, and Niger between 1932 and 1947, and the absence of a strong nationalist movement for independent statehood had slowed the development of a robust national identity. Then after independence the state's minimal contact with people in the countryside did not provide much of a framework within which a sense of common citizenship could arise. On the positive side, the relations among the different ethnic groups were relatively easy-going, unlike in many other African countries (although that did not mean that ethnic relations in Burkina Faso were problem-free, given the tendency of the Mossi to dominate).

As part of its efforts to extend the state's social penetration and territorial reach, the CNR pursued a consciously inclusive approach, to open up social and political life to more of the country's different ethnic groups. The CNR had numerous Mossi in it, but also Bobo, Gourounsi, Peulh, and others. Sankara himself was from a marginal and low-status sub-group known as the Silmi-Mossi (of mixed Mossi and Peulh ancestry).

The country's different indigenous cultures and languages were actively promoted through the state-owned media. Television news was no longer delivered only in French, but also in Mooré and occasionally other languages. Because very few Burkinabè had access to television, radio remained the main means of communication, and it employed eleven indigenous languages (Mooré, Dioula, Fulfuldé, San, Nuni, Liélé, Gulimacema, Lobiré, Dagara, Bissa, and Bwa). Few radio announcers and translators who spoke those languages could actually read or write them, so a national media committee organized training courses to teach elementary composition and journalism.[42] At public anti-corruption trials it was common for a translator to sit in a corner with a microphone to record a summary of the proceedings in Dioula or one of the other languages for later broadcast.

A literacy campaign in 1986 known as Alpha Commando was conducted entirely in nine indigenous languages. That was partly in reaction to the previous official educational policy, dating back to the colonial era, of promoting French as the sole language of instruction. As a result, research into Upper Volta's national languages had lagged. By the 1980s, only thirty-six of the approximately sixty identified languages had been studied in any depth, and only fourteen of those were given a written form. This posed many practical problems for the literacy campaign. With the partial exception of Mooré, Dioula, and Fulfuldé, which had previously been used on an experimental basis in some primary schools, written materials in the other languages were scanty. In the aftermath of the campaign, which reached some 30,000 villagers (mostly members of farmers' associations), plans were made not only for follow-up courses but also the production of more written materials in those languages. That included educational texts, newspapers, journals, and bulletins. A weekly Mooré paper, *Manegda*, started to appear.[43] According to Léonard Compaoré, whose Ministry of Peasant Affairs was responsible for following up on the literacy efforts, "The state is trying to develop each of these languages. A language dies when it is not used."[44]

The government also promoted or directly organized cultural festivals, at which members of different groups could share their varied forms of musical and artistic expression. At a week-long national cultural festival in Gaoua in December 1984, dance troupes, musicians, weavers, sculptors, writers, and painters from different ethnic groups displayed their talents and competed for prizes. A jury declaration emphasized that while individual works could be considered in competition, that was not true for the cultures themselves, since "each culture has its own value ... This festival is an occasion for our different nationalities to discover themselves, to make themselves known, and to mutually enrich themselves, for the birth of a genuinely national culture."[45] Major political rallies, professional conferences, and other events were frequently preceded or followed by dance and musical performances by troupes from Burkina Faso's various ethnic groups.

However, in a period of political turbulence, tensions were sometimes expressed through the lens of ethnicity. In the western regions, disputes over land tenure occasionally pitted Bobo chiefs, who decided land rights, against Mossi settlers, who sought freer and more secure land access. Since CNR support groups in some of those areas tended to represent Mossi migrants, the conflicts took on an ethnic colouration.[46] Similarly, because many merchants were either Dioula or Yarse (a Muslim, Mooré-speaking group), the government's sharp criticism of traders sometimes led to sweeping ethnic characterizations by overzealous defence committee activists. But for the most part such expressions were relatively restrained.

In retrospect, the period of the CNR was one in which African cultural and ethnic representations blossomed as they never had since the start of the colonial era. Many Burkinabè acquired a strong sense of pride in their specifically African identity and in the cultural richness of the country to which they belonged. Years after that government's demise, significant sectors of the population, including leading critics of the CNR, seemed to readily accept their identification as citizens of Burkina Faso, as Burkinabè.

# 7
# MOBILIZATION FROM ABOVE AND BELOW

The CNR's initial takeover stirred wide popular expectations. Mobilized support, however, was limited mainly to small organized sectors in the cities, principally students, unionists, intellectuals, and soldiers. For the vast majority in the countryside, who had little or no routine contact with state institutions, politics remained a game of townspeople. To them, the new figures in Ouagadougou had yet to prove themselves.

The incoming government therefore quickly reached out to unorganized youths and other potential supporters. The main vehicles were the Committees for the Defence of the Revolution (CDRs). The committees had multiple tasks: defend the new government against domestic and external opposition, spur economic and social initiatives that could bring some rapid and visible progress, and serve as building blocks for restructured local state institutions. In his first radio broadcast as president, Sankara appealed to everyone, "men and women, young and old," to begin forming such committees.[1] Without any detailed guidance, people in Ouagadougou's poor neighbourhoods began setting up the first ad hoc CDRs within a few days. Committee leaders were chosen by direct, open election, and competition was fierce. "Usually, there are many, many candidates for the CDR bureaus," commented one committee leader in the capital.[2] The earliest committees were organized strictly on a residential basis. By October 1983 "service CDRs" also began to emerge in workplaces, schools, and markets, and along trade and professional lines.[3]

The committees involved many people from among the poorer strata of society who had never previously taken part in political or associational activity. Initially the committees were politically weak and haphazardly organized. This was despite the government's creation within a few weeks of a national CDR coordinating body, the Secrétariat général national (SGN), headed by two officers, including Captain Pierre Ouédraogo as secretary-general. With few experienced cadres, the CDRs' organization and public participation were very uneven. In some areas leading positions were initially won by supporters of outlawed political parties or traditional chiefs. In some villages and urban neighbourhoods "natives" monopolized the CDR leaderships, excluding more recent residents or members of minority ethnic groups.

Given wide authority, some CDR leaders and members inevitably abused their powers, used the committees to settle personal scores, or carried out exactions against community members.[4] Sankara sounded an early alarm in his October 1983 political orientation speech:

> The activities of some militants who harbor the counterrevolutionary dream of amassing property and profits through the CDRs must be denounced and combated … One does not make a revolution simply to take the place of the despots who have been deposed. One does not participate in the revolution for vindictive reasons, driven by the desire for a privileged position.[5]

Nine months after the committees' first appearance, official CDR statutes sought to systematically define their functions and structures and bring them under better central direction. The committees were to be simultaneously "an emanation" of the CNR and "the people's authentic organizations in the exercise of revolutionary power." The fundamental decision-making body of all CDRs, whether organized geographically (village or urban neighbourhood) or by occupation (trade, workplace, school, military unit), was the general assembly, a periodic meeting of all members to discuss and vote on whatever questions arose. Each local CDR elected a nine-member bureau to direct activities and liaise with higher-level CDRs. At least two members of each bureau had to be women, the deputy chairperson and the delegate responsible for women's mobilization. The local CDRs were seen as the base of a pyramid extending to the departmental, provincial, and national levels, the latter comprising the SGN and a biannual national congress. While local general assemblies could recall or replace CDR bureau members, the SGN also could dissolve a "faltering" bureau. There were no formal restrictions on simple CDR membership. Election to a bureau, however, was barred to anyone convicted of theft, embezzlement, or smuggling, former leaders of "reactionary" parties, known "political opportunists," or members of the "state bourgeoisie, comprador bourgeoisie, and backward forces," the latter term generally referring to chiefs and royal families.[6]

The CDR statutes reflected an evident tension between the central authorities' hopes for local community mobilization and legitimacy and their desire to maintain control over their activities. The latter motivation was especially pressing amidst continuing political insecurity and early signs that some militants, if left unchecked, could alienate potential supporters. CDR Secretary-General Pierre Ouédraogo explained to this author that the committees' subordination to the CNR did not preclude the ranks from proposing development projects or nominating managers and other officials. But giving authority to the CDRs could "only be a gradual process, because it would not be right to say that all power belongs to the people right away." It would even be "extremely dangerous to give all the power to the masses when some do not even understand what the revolution is."[7]

Two instances in September 1983, a little more than a month after the takeover, reinforced that concern. Both involved activists of the PAI, a party then represented in both the CNR and the cabinet. It had a strong base in some of the most militant unions and soon came to dominate many of the CDRs in the capital. First a PAI-led union mobilized workers at the state electricity company to oust its managing director. Then a group of CDRs controlled by the party planned a march to demand the removal of Ouagadougou's mayor, a holdover from the previous government. Both initiatives were interpreted as a partisan bid to exert PAI hegemony. The government officially repudiated these actions, but also deposed the mayor, thus acknowledging the validity of the grievances while simultaneously asserting the CNR's exclusive authority to dismiss public officials.[8]

Despite such rare challenges, the CNR had little option but to assign a range of local responsibilities to the committees, given the "insufficiency of official services" otherwise available to the state.[9] These initially included extensive security duties. Thousands of activists received basic military training and formed armed People's Vigilance Brigades to patrol neighbourhoods, staff checkpoints, and assist the army and police.[10] The move brought considerable controversy. With limited screening of brigade members, some used their arms to extort money or wield arbitrary power. Years later many urban residents still recalled the fear induced by the brigades, even though their activities were just a fraction of the CDRs' total efforts.

There were many other ways in which CDRs supported the state. Some organized assemblies to expose corrupt officials. Others took on the main responsibility for allocating land parcels to residents of Ouagadougou's peripheral areas, bypassing both traditional chiefs and land speculators. Within two years, they officially allocated 57,333 residential land parcels, nearly twice the 30,000 allotted in the previous quarter-century.[11]

Urban and rural youths flocked to the CDRs. One attraction was the committees' links to a modernist government that included many individuals still in their early-to-mid thirties. Moreover, in a society that accorded most formal authority to elders and family patriarchs, CDR participation enabled youths to assert their own views and social worth. The abrupt ascension of so many youths into local leadership positions may have alarmed some older Burkinabè, but it also imparted vitality to the CDRs' activities.

Other Burkinabè who had few previous outlets for public activity also joined. Local CDRs were filled with people of humble social origins, although those educated in French were disproportionately represented in the urban bureaus, partly because they had the social connections and organizational skills to get things done. Women were most active in community self-help mobilizations, but rarely in other activities, although the quota system for elections to the CDR bureaus ensured that at least a few women rose to leadership positions.

The CDRs' community roots were a clear advantage in mobilizing people for local projects. But in a country of rudimentary communications, low literacy, and some sixty spoken languages, coordination was not easy. There were few newspapers, books, or printed CDR documents of any kind. Of these, almost all were in French, which could be read by only about 10 percent of the population. That enhanced the importance of oral communications, radio broadcasts, and general assemblies. In Pô, CDR leaders often conducted meetings in French and the two main local languages, Kasséna and Nankana. The CDRs' political organizer, Jean Baptiste Natama, who came to Pô from Ouagadougou and spoke just French and Mooré, had difficulty communicating with those who spoke only local languages.[12]

The CDRs were hybrid entities, straddling the state and civil spheres. Analysts who viewed state and society as separate and dichotomous minimized that dual nature. By emphasizing the CDRs' links with the CNR, some saw them strictly as state emanations, inherently antithetical to the development of civil society.[13] The reality was more nuanced. With their combined roles, the CDRs acted both to strengthen the state *and* to reflect the interests and concerns of ordinary citizens. At times the outcomes were one-sided or contradictory. At others they were mutually reinforcing, advancing the development of the state as well as society's capacities to organize. In any event, the CDRs did not seek to monopolize civil space or crowd out other associations (with the partial exception of the politicized trade unions). Between 1983 and 1987, the period of the CNR, 166 new civil associations were officially registered nationally, comparable to the number created during the previous five years.[14]

## CONFRONTING RURAL COMPLEXITIES

For the CNR, the defence committees were nowhere more important than in the countryside. There the state had little presence and public life, if it existed, was structured by traditional chiefs and other influential patrons. The young urban modernizers who came to power in Ouagadougou thought, rather naively, that if they could just displace the old rural hierarchy they would easily be able to gain villagers' support.

Identifying traditional chiefs among the "enemies of the people," the CNR mounted a two-pronged challenge: by the state and by village youths acting through the CDRs. Formally at least, many of the chiefs' powers and responsibilities were handed over to the defence committees, in essence an attempt to shift authority to commoners, an especially radical undertaking in the Mossi heartland. It also marked the first serious effort since independence to forge direct links between rural people and the state, in place of the previous reliance on indirect rule through chiefs.

Proclaiming the supremacy of the defence committees was one thing, achieving it quite another. In late 1983 and early 1984 chiefs or their appointees sometimes managed to secure election to CDR bureaus, particularly in Yatenga, Passoré, Kourittenga, and other predominantly Mossi provinces. After some hesitation, the national CDR leadership ordered local committees to hold new elections, with "backward forces" specifically excluded. Yet keeping out the chiefs' supporters still depended on villagers' capacity to act autonomously, a process that acquired some traction only here and there.

In many places, the defence committees remained weak. In Ouarégou, a Bissa village in the centre-east, the CDR attained its peak influence in 1983–85. Then in 1986, amidst factional rivalries, a new bureau chose as its chair someone who spoke only Bissa and thus could not draft reports, fill out forms, or meet with French-speaking officials. Meanwhile, Ouarégou's traditional chief had the skills and connections to arrange donor aid to build a local school, secure UN sponsorship for a pilot food project, and attract Saudi financing for a new mosque. Combined with local anxieties over the impending agrarian reform, those initiatives helped swing the balance of power in Ouarégou back towards the traditional authorities.[15]

Initially, the most ardent CNR supporters made little distinction between higher-ranking political chiefs and land chiefs, who customarily allocated cultivation rights to communally owned land. The 1984 agrarian reform law sought to shift that land allocation authority to new commissions that included the village CDR representatives.[16] That proved unworkable. Sometimes the only person with comprehensive knowledge of which families had rights to which land was the land chief. By 1987, CDR militants and rural development personnel concluded that they could not simply bypass the land chiefs and incorporated them into the land management commissions. More generally, village activists found that literacy programmes, collective labour mobilization, and other development activities won broader support if chiefs and other elders chose to participate.

Defence committee activists also learned that rural society did not match the neat class categories favoured by official revolutionary discourse. Stratifications and conflicts not only followed but also cut across social hierarchies, ethnic identifications, caste and occupational status, and other distinctions.

Sometimes CDRs were drawn directly into inter-community land conflicts, as in the neighbouring villages of Béguédo and Niaogho, about 100 kilometres south-east of the capital, a dispute that was only settled after intervention from Ouagadougou.[17] In other cases CDRs brought latent tensions to the surface by introducing a new element of political and social power. While some villagers, often of subordinate status, looked to the committees for support, others reacted against what they saw as a challenge to their established power. The Silmi-Mossi, of mixed Mossi and Peulh ancestry, were able to step into positions of responsibility within the CDRs that were denied them in both traditional Mossi and Peulh societies, a process that received a psychological boost from the rise of a president (Sankara) who happened to be Silmi-Mossi. Similarly, among the semi-nomadic Peulh of the Liptako region, the lower-ranking Rimaybe (descendants of non-Peulh war captives, slaves, and vassals) were "very satisfied with the revolution of Sankara," in part because they saw a chance to advance their standing against the aristocratic Rimbe.[18] Among the Mossi and Peulh hierarchies, the CDRs were resented for attracting both commoners and previously subordinate ethnic and caste groups. In the different context of the west and south, recent Mossi settlers migrating in from the drought-prone central plateau chafed at the dominance of Bobo, Samo, and other non-Mossi traditional authorities, who generally favoured indigenous land claimants over newcomers. In those areas, Mossi joined CDRs in large numbers, partly in the hope of gaining land rights.

Across the country, ongoing farmer–herder conflicts over land intensified as severe drought pushed more herders southwards in search of pasturage. The CDRs, conceived primarily as geographic bodies, were thus more accessible to settled farmers than to nomadic herders. Tensions erupted when the government mounted a campaign to protect farmland from uncontrolled grazing by decreeing that cattle caught destroying crops could be shot and those wandering unattended seized, returnable to their owners upon payment of a fine.[19] In some areas, CDR members took things to extremes, shooting cattle accompanied by their owners and even a few herders who tried to protect their animals. According to a local press report, "To save their animals and their own lives, many herders crossed the borders into neighbouring countries." Half the herders in Sissili province were believed to have fled.[20] A national CDR conference in 1986 acknowledged that the anti-grazing campaign was a failure, with a CDR commission noting with understated irony that "the systematic slaughter of animals did not have the support of the rural world."[21]

## SOCIAL MOBILIZATION

For the most part, the defence committees tried to promote social unity, not division. In seeking to mobilize communities CDR activists repeatedly appealed to notions of egalitarianism and mutual support. Although customary community ties had weakened somewhat, ideals of social solidarity, communal work, reciprocity, and the general welfare still had some weight in the countryside. They were also attractive to urban youths, who saw collective mobilization as an opportunity to "level down" the more powerful by requiring them to take part in labour activities with everyone else.

Although the initial calls for mass development mobilization came from the central authorities, they easily won support from ordinary citizens. Most projects directly benefited local communities, which often made their own proposals during general assemblies. The first mobilizations involved cleaning school and hospital courtyards, gravelling roads, building mini-dams, and, when building materials could be secured, even starting construction on schools, community centres, theatres, and other facilities. Bigger projects required more organization. In Kaya, neighbourhood and workplace CDRs located and transported large stones and sand, civil servants gathered gravel, and different neighbourhoods organized daily shifts to produce bricks. The pace initially seemed quite hectic. Over the weekend of 12–13 November 1983, for example, thirty-three separate CDR labour mobilizations were reported in major towns.[22]

By October 1984, the community mobilizations were systematized in the Programme populaire de développement (PPD), which lasted fifteen months. It coordinated local initiatives nationally and extended them to new areas. Across the thirty provinces, people's contributions of money and labour averaged 27 percent of total costs, with the remainder funded by the provincial and national governments and by external donor agencies. The level of public participation varied, from an exceptionally low 4 percent of the population of Oudalan in the north (inhabited mostly by nomadic Peulh) to a high of 89 percent in Passoré.[23] In some areas, villagers abandoned projects included in the PPD in favour of others not originally planned. They sometimes built more schools than anticipated, obliging the government to find additional teachers, desks, and other supplies if it could. Overall, the PPD saw the construction of 351 schools, 314 dispensaries and maternity clinics, 2,294 wells and boreholes, and 274 water reservoirs, among other facilities.[24]

Especially dramatic were the short, intense campaigns known as "commando" operations. The most celebrated was the Vaccination Commando. In September 1984 the government decided to launch, within two months, a drive to vaccinate most children against the key childhood killers (measles, meningitis, and yellow fever), and to do it in only two weeks. In opting for such a concentrated campaign, the authorities disregarded external donor advice to move more cautiously. Previous vaccination efforts involved mainly official medical personnel. This one was different. As an external observer noted:

> There were radio programmes and posters in local languages; there were travelling theatre groups ... The CDRs and their affiliated women's groups spread the message about the value of vaccination and organized popular fund-raising events. They carried out the census of children, gave out

> vaccination cards, and made sure that people turned up at the right place and the right time for vaccination. The response was overwhelming. Mothers almost took the vaccination points by assault. They walked long distances, and formed queues often more than a kilometre long, waiting whole days and nights for their turn.[25]

By the end of the two weeks, some 2 million children had received a vaccination, raising the rate of immunization against the three diseases from 11–19 percent of all children in the target age group to 60–75 percent. Sensitization of the population as a whole to health issues was "the most spectacular aspect of the operation," stated a joint evaluation by the Ministry of Health and UN Children's Fund, one of the few donor agencies to back the effort.[26] Its success meant that the usual epidemics of measles and meningitis were much less severe in 1985, preventing anywhere from 18,000 to 50,000 child deaths.[27]

The commando model was applied to several others, including the Alpha Commando literacy campaign in 1986. It mobilized mainly volunteer instructors (students, CDR activists, civil servants, and some teachers) to bring basic literacy and numeracy skills to some 30,000 rural people, most of them members of farmers' associations. With follow-up, about half eventually acquired functional literacy.[28] Since literacy allowed these farmers to read the weights of their marketed grains, noted the minister of peasant affairs, Léonard Compaoré, they were less easily cheated by merchants or corrupt state grain-buying agents.[29] Several national "big battles" were also carried out, with mobilizations in phases or shifts over periods more prolonged than in commando operations: digging irrigation canals in the Sourou River valley, planting millions of trees to combat deforestation, and manually laying nearly 100 kilometres of track to extend the railway from Ouagadougou to Kaya.

## VILLAGE AND FARMERS' ASSOCIATIONS

In the countryside as in the cities, the defence committees operated alongside various civil organizations. There were village assemblies, farmers' groups, cooperatives, youth associations, and other non-governmental organizations, some with an important local presence or established links with national institutions and external donor agencies. A few pursued methods of mobilization similar to those of the CDRs, but without their political agenda or direct government links. Several appear to have influenced the way the CDRs worked.

Autonomous farmers' groups, usually limited to several villages or a particular region, had been a feature of rural life for some time. Most common were the *naam* labour societies among the Mossi, in which young men and women formed collective work groups.[30] A similar form emerged among the Dagara in the 1980s. Reflecting the egalitarianism of traditional Dagara society, it grouped councils from eleven villages, made decisions through open village assemblies, and carried out projects through collective labour mobilizations. Eighty percent of the members were women.[31]

The largest and best-known association was the Union de fédérations des groupements naam (UFGN). Launched in the 1970s with a particularly strong base in Yatenga, it drew heavily on the tradition of Mossi *naam* collective work groups and focused on preserving the environment (soil conservation, water harvesting, tree planting) and promoting better agricultural techniques.[32] While adopting Mossi chieftaincy titles for their leaders, the UFGN groups nevertheless shunned rigid hierarchies and often included in their leaderships young people and members of ethnic minorities, descendants of former slaves, and lower-ranking castes such as the *forgerons* ("blacksmiths").[33] Commented an article in the state-owned newsweekly, "It is the only so-called Mossi association where no social inequalities exist. Everyone is on an equal footing: neither birth, wealth, nor sex matter in the elections. The only thing that counts is the individual's character, temperament, altruism, social consciousness, and technical competence."[34]

The CDRs sometimes competed with these other associations and occasional tensions were evident among individual leaders, especially in Ouahigouya, where the UFGN was headquartered.[35] Yet generally they were able to collaborate. The projects favoured by the *naam* groups were generally similar to those of the defence committees. While taking care to guard its independence from the state, the UFGN participated in joint consultative bodies with government officials and CDR activists. It also sat on provincial committees that helped prepare the first five-year plan (1986–90) and a committee that coordinated collective labour mobilizations.[36] Referring to the CNR, Bernard Lédéa Ouédraogo, the central leader of the UFGN, told an interviewer:

> This government is the most supportive one we've had. Our concept of development fits in well with the government's concept … With previous governments, party politics came first. If you supported the party in power, you would get your rewards. If not, nothing. This government is different;

> it truly has the welfare of the villagers at heart. In that way we are luckier than many of our brothers and sisters elsewhere in Africa.[37]

Thanks to the supportive climate, the UFGN expanded significantly beyond its original base to fifteen provinces by 1987.[38] Between 1983 and 1987, the number of its individual *naam* groups more than doubled, from 1,024 to 2,453, with total membership rising spectacularly, from 5,120 to 151,910, of which 56 percent were women.[39]

## WOMEN'S ORGANIZATION

Like male youths, Burkinabè women previously had few opportunities to mobilize to advance their interests, organize politically, or engage directly with state institutions. The weight of traditional, patriarchal relations effectively relegated most women to the status of minors, whatever their age. Most basic life decisions remained in the hands of fathers, husbands, uncles, and other male relatives. Yet autonomous women's organizations were not completely absent. There were a few national women's associations composed primarily of professionals or the wives of high-ranking officials. Local village women's cooperatives or women's sections of farmers' groups also provided some means for rural women to act together.[40]

The CNR's takeover opened new doors. From the beginning, the new leaders emphasized women's emancipation as a central goal. Speeches by Sankara and other leaders repeatedly chastised "corrupt" and "feudal" husbands for treating their wives and daughters as "beasts of burden" and pledged to act against the many customary practices considered oppressive to women. Government programmes with specific measures for women included literacy classes, primary health units in each village, and support for women's cooperatives and market associations. A new family code set a minimum age for marriage, established divorce by mutual consent, recognized a widow's right to inheritance, and suppressed the bride-price. There were vigorous public campaigns against female genital mutilation, forced marriage, and polygamy.

Such practices were deeply rooted in Burkinabè society, however, and could not be eliminated by decree. Most efforts confronted stiff resistance, including from some women themselves. Addressing a women's conference, Family Minister Joséphine Ouédraogo denounced oppressive practices such as polygamy. A woman in the audience spoke up:

> Everything you have said about women's suffering is true and your conviction touches us. However, you, our sisters from the city, can never understand what we live with in the countryside. The problem you raise [polygamy] is the smoke you see from a distance; you can't see the fire that creates the smoke ... We women peasants will never fight against our husbands or co-wives. They're too useful to us![41]

In the political sphere the government had some power to take unilateral steps. It appointed women to cabinet posts, including as ministers of family affairs, culture, health, and the budget—at a time when hardly any women reached high office anywhere in Africa. Although largely a symbolic gesture, many women were nevertheless encouraged. Still, the CDRs had difficulty involving women beyond community mobilizations. During the first defence committee elections for local CDR bureaus, few women stepped forward as candidates.[42] That was one reason why the CDR statutes later mandated that at least two positions in each bureau had to be filled by women. Bringing women into CDR leadership bodies went only so far. Béatrice Damiba, a leading female activist, commented that women

> were silent in the general assemblies, absent from the evening debates, and one hardly heard them in the CDR bureaus ... The idea of integrating people of both sexes within the CDRs proved unrealizable in the short term. Girls and women who became active were [socially] ostracized. Revolutionary husbands kept their wives at home. The creation of women's cells became imperative.[43]

After some hesitation, the CDR national secretariat announced on 8 March 1984 (International Women's Day) that women's cells could be formed within the defence committees. A special body within the national secretariat was to coordinate their work nationally. The cells tried to increase women's participation in general assemblies, community development projects, literacy classes, and militia training, although with uneven success. By the second national conference of CDRs in 1987, one-third of the elected delegates were women.[44] However, during the regional preparatory conferences preceding the national meeting, women rarely took the floor. Fatoumata Barry, a CDR leader in the remote northern province of Oudalan, explained that "we Sahelian women are not accustomed to speaking very much in public in front of people we do not know."[45]

A national women's seminar in 1985 recommended a separate national women's organization.[46] It was launched later that year as the Union des femmes du Burkina (UFB). Local UFB bureaus were elected by general assemblies of women, but the chairperson, initially, was the CDR bureau member responsible for women's mobilization.[47] The UFB gradually acquired a distinct profile. During the 1986 Alpha Commando literacy drive, a UFB representative sat on each five-member regional management committee. The UFB vocally complained that only limited places had been allotted to women in the literary classes, prompting Sankara to promise that future drives would increase women's participation, proportionate to their numbers in society.[48]

## LABOUR

Given the Marxist outlook of many CNR members, official pronouncements often assigned labour a leading role in the revolutionary process and presented the CNR's seizure of power as a logical culmination of labour conflicts under previous regimes. That assessment was shared by some unions, including the union of secondary and university teachers. "The National Council of the Revolution, which is leading the revolutionary process, has struck blows against the reactionary bourgeoisie by taking just measures in the interests of the workers and the people," Secretary-General Etienne Traoré declared at the union's December 1984 congress.[49]

While the CNR had support from some sectors of the salaried workforce, it essentially failed to establish a secure base in labour. There were several reasons. Unlike most other social sectors, labour was extensively organized before the CNR's takeover, with highly politicized union leaderships that resented the authorities' efforts to establish CDRs in the workplaces. Some unions were linked to banned political parties, so did not identify politically with the new government. Whatever their political orientation, most unionized workers were affected by the government's measures to squeeze public sector salaries and benefits. Finally, the authorities' reaction to displays of union displeasure was heavy-handed, further alienating organized labour.

By late 1983 "service" CDRs had been set up in most public and private enterprises, eventually reaching 340 in number.[50] Their activists grappled with how to approach the unions. They initially sought to work mainly with "revolutionary unions," that is, those politically aligned with the government.[51] Since in some larger enterprises there were multiple unions, affiliated with different federations, that sometimes drew the defence committees into conflicts among rival unions. The CDRs mostly avoided traditional "bread and butter" labour issues, concentrating instead on political education and exhortation. When they did address economic matters, it was to support government campaigns to increase productivity or justify cuts in bonuses. During official ceremonies, workplace CDR leaders sometimes appeared alongside government and military personnel, further emphasizing their association with the state.

It was thus unsurprising that the service CDRs had difficulty winning support among workers. One Burkinabè researcher found that the ideas of the August 1983 revolution had "stopped at the factory gates." Industrial workers worried mainly about preserving their individual and collective interests, including through patron–client ties with their employers.[52] Workers' distrust spread demoralization within the service CDRs and by 1985 official press commentaries complained that their activities had slowed down and their bureaus met infrequently.[53]

Nationally, relations with trade unions were often strained, fuelled less by shop-floor competition between the unions and CDRs than by political divergences at the top. By coincidence, the CNR's 4 August 1983 takeover came just as the main primary school teachers union was holding a congress. The SNEAHV, which was politically aligned with the parties of Joseph Ki-Zerbo, promptly accused the CNR of "fascism," condemned the CDRs, and appealed for external pressure against the government. In March 1984 security forces arrested several SNEAHV leaders on charges of plotting against the state. The union reacted by calling a three-day strike, leading the authorities to escalate the confrontation by firing 1,300 teachers and replacing them with hastily trained instructors, many of them CDR youths.[54] The crackdown's severity shocked many Burkinabè. Although some teachers were later rehired, the firings sent a clear signal to all unions that the CNR would not tolerate overt opposition.

At the time, the government enjoyed the open support of one of the larger and more active union federations, the Confédération *syndical* burkinabè (CSB, as the CSV had renamed itself). The federation was led by Soumane Touré and other members of Lipad, which in turn was affiliated with the PAI. Leaders of both groups belonged to the CNR, held key cabinet positions, or were prominent in the defence committees. Within a few months, however, the relations between the Lipad/PAI and other currents in the CNR deteriorated (see Chapter 8). That rift led to a more critical stance by Touré and the CSB. At the union's 1984 May Day rally, Touré warned, "If the CNR does not want to make a revolution, we will assume our responsibilities and the workers will take the place of the CNR." In August, a cabinet reshuffle ousted most Lipad/PAI ministers; several were briefly detained, as was Touré himself early the following year. The CSB subsequently became one of the government's bitterest critics.[55]

Another current, the PCRV, also had a base in several autonomous unions in the health, mining, tax collection, judicial, education, and construction sectors. The PCRV was politically hostile to all the currents in the CNR and the PCRV-led unions formed a Front syndical (Union Front) that was critical of many government policies. In January 1985 they were joined by the CSB and a couple of other unions in signing a declaration accusing the government of violating basic democratic and trade union rights. "Increasingly," the unions declared, "the government only wants to see unions that sing its praises and blindly support its measures." They called on workers and students to mobilize for the survival of their organizations "independent of the government in power." A wave of repression followed. Most signatories were fired from their jobs or detained. In the provinces, local authorities banned some union meetings, while CDR members physically broke up others.[56] Under heavy government pressure, a number of the unions installed new leaderships less inclined to openly resist official policies.

Paradoxically, the government's relations were less contentious with the politically conservative labour federations. The Confédération nationale des travailleurs burkinabè (CNTB), Union des syndicats des travailleurs burkinabè (USTB), and Organisation nationale des syndicats libres (ONSL), which together represented a majority of unionized workers, rarely organized strikes or protest marches, preferring instead low-key, orderly negotiations that achieved modest, incremental gains. Although opposed to some CNR policies and wary of its ideological views, they sometimes expressed more alarm over the strident rhetoric of the unions led by the PCRV and Lipad. Accordingly, they declined to sign the January 1985 protest declaration and the leaders of the CNTB and ONSL openly met with President Sankara while the crackdown on the other unions was under way.[57]

## DESPOTS, GANGSTERS, AND IMPOSTERS

Factionalism and infighting among the groups supporting the CNR were persistent problems within the defence committees, especially in Ouagadougou. Leading figures rarely discussed these difficulties openly, instead stressing the CDRs' dynamism and spirit of collective action. While shortcomings were occasionally noted, they were generally presented as resulting from material shortages, the strength of conservative social forces, and/or the inexperience and immaturity of young cadres suddenly thrust into leadership positions. Meanwhile, political critics of the CNR often portrayed the defence committees as repressive, totalitarian organs composed of young toughs. Each perspective was one-sided, yet each captured an aspect of a complex phenomenon. For some Burkinabè, the CDRs were a positive force for change. For others, especially in the cities and among the better-off, the CDRs' conduct was intrusive, even frightening.

In rural areas, the defence committees remained hobbled by weak organization, poor communications, and social conservatism. When serious problems arose, local CDR activists often sought support from officials higher up. Since few rural people had the necessary skills to carry out key organizational tasks, young activists were often brought in from the towns and cities. Many took their assignments seriously, but lacked concrete knowledge of local conditions. Their abilities, combined with a certain domineering approach, meant that they frequently "monopolized" leadership of rural CDRs, as Sankara admitted.[58] There was a tendency among some to operate in a top-down fashion. The practice of issuing directives, in a military style, led a commentator in a state-run publication to assert, "In the countryside, certain CDRs are sometimes worse than the feudalists during colonial times."[59]

In the cities, the defence committees were afflicted by additional problems. Political debate was often more intense, yet sometimes reflected simple struggles for power rather than genuine differences. Political education within the CDRs, noted a report of the 1986 national conference, frequently involved little more than rote learning of terminology, definitions, and slogans, the mastery of which enabled some to secure positions of political responsibility and fend off potential rivals through the use of "intellectual terrorism" in political debates.[60] The armed patrols by undisciplined youths in vigilance brigades led to some abuses against ordinary citizens. Although assigned to unmask corrupt state functionaries, some activists were themselves guilty of embezzling funds, stealing, breaking into homes during curfew hours, and collecting "taxes" and "contributions" for their personal use. During the urban land allocation campaigns, some CDR leaders illegally sold or diverted land plots.[61]

As early as 1985 Sankara sharply criticized "subjectivism and abuses" within the defence committees, perpetrated by "adventurers, imposters, and opportunistic hypocrites," as well as those who "exercise authority as a dynastic right." Serious steps were needed to correct "these aberrations, for which we have had a thousand excuses."[62]

That critique set the cue for the first national CDR conference in March–April 1986. It was a frank affair. There were positive assessments of the defence committees' accomplishments, but also critical tallies of their failings. The conference complained that "inexcusable and revolting" actions by some CDRs had given a poor image to the revolution and contributed to "the demobilization of the masses."[63] Sankara, in his closing address, used even stronger language. Some CDR leaders "set themselves up as veritable despots in the local districts, in the villages, and in the provinces ... Reigning and holding sway like warlords, they are fascists." Referring to "unspeakable things" done by some defence committees, Sankara continued:

> We have seen CDRs arrest someone, lock them up, and then say, "That's it. Those are the rules, that's justice. We will deal with you." No! Every Burkinabè has the right to the CDRs' protection. The CDR office must not be a locale of torturers but the complete opposite: an office where you find people in charge who lead, who organize, who mobilize, who educate, and who struggle as revolutionaries … [A]buse of power must be considered alien to our struggle.[64]

At the year's end Operation Spearhead was launched by the CDRs' national secretariat. It convened local general assemblies to assess the committees' functioning and elect new bureaus, affecting some 200,000 positions across the country. The aim, according to CDR Secretary-General Ouédraogo, was to flush out those who had "a poor understanding of power" or who had "abused the masses."[65]

There were subsequently fewer reports of CDR malpractices. The second national CDR conference, held in Dédougou from 30 March to 3 April 1987, shifted greater emphasis towards economic production and marketing issues, with a lower profile for security functions. The way the national conference was organized reflected an increased concern with extending CDR activism and leadership beyond the educated few. Not only were women more than a third of all delegates, but the conference was staged in Dédougou, a modest provincial town. An elaborate system of simultaneous translation enabled sessions to be held in French, Mooré, Dioula, and Fulfuldé. Expanding use of the national languages, noted one Burkinabè commentator, would help ensure that the committees did not represent only those who had attended a "white school."[66]

Given time, such steps could possibly have widened involvement in the defence committees and helped allay public anxieties and apprehensions. But such prospects were undercut by deepening divisions within the top echelons of the CNR, in part over how to balance persuasion and coercion in the political leadership's interactions with the population. Time was already running out.

# 8
# COUP AND "RECTIFICATION"

In its final two years, the National Council of the Revolution experienced a variety of troubling cross-currents, in the wider political, social, and international environment as well as among its own contentious factions. Directly and indirectly, that turbulence contributed to the October 1987 coup. It is difficult, however, to pinpoint which factors were most determinant, given the secrecy of the CNR's internal functioning. It is also not clear precisely how foreign interventions intersected with the domestic cleavages, although the circumstances strongly point to such a link.

The brief war with Mali at the end of 1985 highlighted the regional strains confronting the CNR, at a time when the conservative, pro-French governments of neighbouring Côte d'Ivoire and Togo also exhibited open hostility to the Burkinabè government, including by hosting exiled opponents. Meanwhile domestic social tensions became more evident, involving not only traditional chiefs, merchants, land speculators, and other layers directly affected by CNR policies, but also portions of the government's own support base. Most visibly, relations with the trade union leaderships had become conflictual. And although the popular mobilizations spearheaded by the CDRs registered significant social and economic accomplishments during the first few years, sustaining a high level of activity proved difficult. An official evaluation of the 1984–85 People's Development Programme noted that implementing so many different projects overtaxed participants and spread committed activists too thinly: "In certain cases the population was drained by the intense pace, leading to chronic demobilization towards the end of the work."[1]

The CDRs had difficulty keeping their own members mobilized week after week. A 1986 conference of provincial activists in Bazega observed that participation in CDR undertakings had fallen sharply and that some headquarters had simply been abandoned. Among the causes cited were resistance from chiefs, the government's inability to provide enough support services, and a "poor understanding" by CDR leaders of their responsibilities.[2]

## BETWEEN CONCILIATION AND COERCION

While there had always been tactical differences among leaders of the CNR, other state structures, and the CDRs, the emergence of broader public scepticism and signs of fatigue tended to heighten divergences over the optimal balance of persuasion and coercion. These were not always expressed clearly, but two broadly contrasting approaches could be discerned. Sankara and those aligned with him tended to follow a more conciliatory approach when confronted with complex new challenges, although they also approved force against identified "enemies of the revolution." Others, however, reacted in a more consistently authoritarian, top-down manner overall, not only against overt political opponents but also against supporters who were less than zealous, questioned certain aspects of official policy, or fell on the wrong side of the internal fights that bedevilled the CNR's deliberations. As the differences within the CNR deepened, these hardliners coalesced around Blaise Compaoré, the second highest ranking figure.

The efforts from within the CNR to pursue conciliation began at least two months before the Mali war, when Sankara appealed to Burkinabè political exiles to return home.[3] The government then transferred from prison to house arrest several detained politicians, with Sankara insisting that the revolution was for everyone: "It's better to count the number of its adherents than to count the number of its victims."[4] He later stressed that repression should be reserved strictly for "exploiters" and "enemies." The revolution "must mean only persuasion for the masses—persuasion to take on a conscious and determined commitment."[5]

Such pronouncements were accompanied by concrete gestures. In early 1986 the government reinstated more than 250 of the teachers who had been fired for striking.[6] Other public employees who had been suspended or dismissed for political infractions were also re-employed. In January 1987 compulsory deductions for a "people's investment effort" ended, bringing immediate increases in net pay.[7] Although not always consistently, over the course of 1986 and 1987 the government shifted away from intensive, ad hoc commando mobilizations towards more institutionalized, sustainable methods. Sankara emphasized that it was time to pause to assess past errors and more patiently explain the government's goals.[8]

Others within the CNR, however, exhibited little patience and reacted to signs of reluctance in a heavy-handed manner. They viewed the CDRs not as mechanisms for explaining and promoting official policies but as institutions to keep the population in line. When difficulties emerged, their approach often slid back into the bureaucratic and repressive modes of the past. Although their authoritarian leanings became more pronounced during the CNR's final year, some signs were evident early on. Captain Compaoré, while interpreting the Leninist concept of "democratic centralism" during a June 1984 radio interview, insisted that "it is the top, the leadership, which decides and the grassroots have to submit."[9]

Military officers were on both ends of the persuasion/coercion spectrum. Nevertheless, some analysts and even a few civilian members of the government attributed the strength of the repressive current to the predominance of army figures in the leadership, who had a habit of lacing their arguments with threats of force. Less than two months before the coup, Basile Guissou, who held several ministerial positions under the CNR, told this author that "we are facing a very strong wing of militarist orientation" within the CNR.[10] He later made the same point in his public writings.[11]

## SOCIAL TENSIONS AND INFIGHTING

The divergent attitudes towards persuasion and coercion were partially reflected in the factional divides among the political groups supporting the CNR. On the surface, their fights focused on ideological or tactical differences. But the vehemence of their polemics also reflected underlying social tensions.

Without overtly challenging the CNR's anti-imperialist foreign policy, some appeared to favour softening criticisms of France and Côte d'Ivoire. Others expressed displeasure with Sankara's ad hoc methods and frequent efforts to bypass the bureaucracy to directly engage ordinary Burkinabè. The prospect of opening up the state to public involvement challenged their narrowly state-centred perspective, especially since their own positions gave them considerable power. Nor did the CNR's efforts to weaken the influence of chiefs and incorporate more marginalized ethnic communities enjoy universal agreement. In the months before the coup anonymous leaflets called on Mossi to unite against the government of the "stranger," an implicit rallying cry against Sankara, a Silmi-Mossi, and for Compaoré, from a Mossi royal lineage.[12]

Some appeared uncomfortable with Sankara's austere vision of public service and drive against corruption. Just a few days before his death, Sankara noted to journalists: "Today there are people in power who live better than the population, who engage in small-scale trade with Syrian and Lebanese merchants, who find positions for their families, their younger cousins, yet all the while speaking in very revolutionary language."[13] He did not mention any name, but some in the president's immediate entourage were aware that Compaoré was among those who harboured strong personal ambitions. Ernest Nongma Ouédraogo, the minister of interior (and Sankara's cousin), later maintained that when the anti-corruption commission was launched in early 1987, Compaoré was unhappy with having to publicly declare his assets. "Subsequently," said Ouédraogo, "he was reproached for having hidden certain properties of his wife, such as a massive gold clock given to her by President Houphouët-Boigny."[14] Compaoré's wife, the former Chantal Terrasson de Fougères, was an adopted daughter of Côte d'Ivoire's president and made little secret that she preferred the finer things in life.

Some contemporary analyses of Burkina Faso's revolutionary process devoted considerable effort to trying to delineate the evolution and shifting positions of the organized political groups that gravitated around the CNR.[15] With one or two exceptions, however, most had small memberships. They exerted influence mainly by virtue of their presence in strategic leadership positions in key state institutions, the CDRs, or the military.

The first signs of serious conflict surfaced in 1984, chiefly involving the PAI, then better known by its front group, the Lipad. The PAI was the oldest and most substantial left-wing group to ally with the radical officers who spearheaded the August 1983 takeover. It initially played an influential role within the council, the government, CDRs, and the labour movement. Soumane Touré, a Lipad leader and head of the CSB union federation, had long been one of Sankara's personal friends. Rather than working collaboratively with the smaller formations backing the CNR, however, the PAI pushed hard for partisan advantage. In reaction, most PAI leaders were ousted from the government and CNR.[16]

With the exception of a miniscule PAI splinter group and several unaffiliated intellectuals, that left the ULCR as the main civilian component in the CNR. Of Maoist background, it had been at fierce ideological loggerheads with the Soviet-inclined PAI. Some of its leaders, along with Sankara, nevertheless tried unsuccessfully to reconcile with the PAI in April 1985. During those negotiations, Sankara and his military colleagues created a formal political group of their own, of strictly military composition, the Organisation militaire révolutionnaire (OMR). According to Andriamirado, that was to "counterbalance the influence of the ULCR."[17]

Around the same time, a few other groups emerged. One, the Groupe communiste burkinabè (GCB), was inconsequential in membership, but several figures had influential connections, including Jean-Marc Palm, whose brother Captain Jean-Pierre Palm was in the security apparatus and was close to Compaoré. More significant was the Union communiste burkinabè (UCB), founded in July 1984. Like the GCB, it formally entered the CNR in May 1985. The UCB was composed of two strands. One included radical civilian intellectuals at the university and in the state media, numbering perhaps two dozen, according to Somé. The other, weightier wing was military. Over time the group came under the control of a hard-line coterie of civilian intellectuals and military personnel, aligned closely with Compaoré.[18] Another small group arose slightly later, in February 1987, following a split in the ULCR. It took the latter's original name, the ULC.[19] It gained no representation within the CNR, perhaps because two of its top figures were suspected of corruption.[20]

The UCB and GCB, and to some extent the other groups, exhibited a highly dogmatic, intolerant approach. Beginning in early 1986, this "Stalinist current," as the academic Pascal Labazée termed them, argued that it was time for a "radicalization" of the revolution. Their proponents disagreed with Sankara's emphasis on easing up the pace and granting clemency to political opponents. They opposed any attempt to reconcile with the PAI and systematically sought to undermine the influence of the ULCR, which backed Sankara's approach.[21] Publicly, however, they maintained a posture of unity and even vowed to build a "single vanguard organization."[22]

Sankara also mentioned unity, but generally projected the need for a wider front. He tried to keep the doors open to the PAI, still the largest group, with a real base in the labour movement. He also repeatedly spoke about drawing in the many unaffiliated young activists belonging to the CDRs and other organizations. Less than two weeks before his death, he sharply rejected any party that was monolithic and politically stultifying, saying that he preferred instead an organization that would be "pluralist, diverse, and enriched by many different thoughts and actions, thoughts and actions rich with a thousand nuances."[23]

While not yet daring to publicly challenge Sankara, his rivals acted to undermine such moves towards openness. In May 1987 members of the CDR in Ouagadougou's Sector 29 arrested several prominent unionists, including Soumane Touré, charging them with printing leaflets for anti-government demonstrations. That CDR and several others called for the unionists' execution. According to ULCR leader Somé, when a CNR meeting took up the execution calls, numerous UCB leaders and several captains, including the GCB's Jean-Pierre Palm, urged that Touré be put to death. Only the ULCR and Sankara opposed it. Sankara's intervention "was decisive in saving Soumane Touré's life," Somé wrote. Sankara reportedly felt he could not publicly repudiate the arrest itself, since it was initiated by a CDR and he had previously been criticized for ordering the release of his friend after other detentions.[24] Presidential aide Frédéric Kiemdé, who was to be killed with Sankara during the coup, explained to this author that Sankara was nevertheless against the unionists' detentions because they had "done damage to the revolution."[25] Several of the less prominent unionists (but not Touré) were released.

In June 1987, Compaoré, as minister of justice, dismissed nineteen judges who had voiced criticisms of aspects of the government's judicial policies. Two months later, when Sankara asked all cabinet ministers to consider re-employing more dismissed teachers and other civil servants, Compaoré opposed him.[26] Sankara stood firm, stating that too many state personnel had been dismissed unjustly. "We can no longer condemn a citizen on the basis of individual or subjective considerations or statements," he told a press conference.[27] At a CNR meeting in early October 1987, he announced that another eighty-eight detainees would be freed, stirring more grumbling from the hardliners.[28] "There's now a campaign against me," he told a group of foreign journalists. "I'm accused of being a sentimentalist."[29]

The UCB and other critics eventually became more overt. On 2 October, at a political rally in Tenkodogo, the university CDR chairman Jonas Somé openly contradicted Sankara's calls for tolerance. His speech—which had been approved in advance by a cabinet minister and the deputy secretary-general of the CDRs, both UCB leaders—denounced "opportunists and counterrevolutionaries who have infiltrated the CNR." In response, Sankara, who spoke last, insisted even more strongly on the need for tolerance. That evening, amidst rumours of an assassination plot, Sankara's security guards whisked him out of Tenkodogo. The next day, the provincial government in Bobo-Dioulasso, also dominated by the UCB, declared its support for Jonas Somé, further escalating the group's now open challenge to Sankara.[30]

## THE OCTOBER 1987 COUP

Meanwhile, Compaoré and his supporters prepared to force a resolution. Some of their manoeuvres involved lining up external support. Compaoré travelled extensively the year before the coup, including repeated and prolonged visits to Paris. Following France's apparent role in Sankara's removal as prime minister in 1983, relations had remained quite frosty. Although no definitive evidence has emerged indicating a direct French role in the 1987 coup, Jacques Foccart, a key French intelligence figure with extensive networks throughout Africa, may well have been aware, if not actively engaged in, the coup plans. Those seeking to uncover documentation about France's possible involvement have been stymied ever since by secrecy laws, although researchers, French parliamentary deputies, and even a Burkinabè investigating judge have filed petitions to lift the veil.[31]

Compaoré also pursued other contacts, including with Libya's strongman Muammar al-Qaddafi, whose relations with Sankara had become strained over the latter's efforts to mediate among different warring factions in Chad (a war in which Libya had intervened).[32] Several Liberian exiles, among them the future warlord Charles Taylor, had solicited Sankara's support for an insurgency in Liberia, but the Burkinabè president turned them down. Compaoré—who openly sided with Taylor in the subsequent Liberian civil war—reportedly offered the Liberians such support if they took part in his plan against Sankara.[33] Years later, two of the warlords (Prince Johnson and John Tarnue) publicly claimed to have taken part in the coup, although their precise roles were not clear.[34]

Probably the most decisive external actor in the coup plot was Côte d'Ivoire's Houphouët-Boigny, a very close ally of France and known for his hostility to Sankara's radicalism. Frédéric Korsaga, Burkina Faso's ambassador to Côte d'Ivoire, reportedly functioned as an intermediary for Compaoré—who in any case was now an in-law of the Ivorian president, having married his adopted daughter. According to Somé, after repeated solicitations from both the Burkinabè plotters and conservative Ivorian politicians, Houphouët-Boigny finally "ended by giving the green light."[35]

Whatever their foreign links, the conspirators had resources of their own. Compaoré commanded the fifth military region (which included the capital) and maintained active operational ties throughout the military command. He still headed the paracommando training base in Pô, which his closest aide, Lieutenant Gilbert Diendéré, managed on a day-to-day basis. Some of those paracommandos were seconded to the Conseil de l'Entente complex in the capital, the headquarters of the CNR, and thus formed part of the security force responsible for protecting CNR members. It was later revealed that the paracommandos in Pô were paid extra bonuses in the weeks before the coup. Covertly, officers in secondary command positions at other military bases were won over to the plot.[36] According to Somé, "many millions of CFA francs were distributed in the barracks."[37]

The morning of 15 October, Sankara met with Somé. They discussed the tensions among the various currents within the CNR and Sankara drafted a speech for a meeting of the OMR later that evening, in which he would propose a "purification" of the council and implementation of a new leadership code of conduct.[38] Before the OMR meeting, however, Sankara had a scheduled gathering with several aides at the Conseil de l'Entente. According to Alouna Traoré, the only surviving eyewitness among Sankara's staff, the meeting started around 4:15 pm. After a brief while, perhaps around 4:30 pm, shooting erupted in the small courtyard outside, in which the president's driver and two bodyguards were killed. Upon hearing the gunfire, everyone inside took cover. Sankara got up and told his aides to stay there for their own safety. "It's me they want." He left the room, hands raised, to face the assailants. He was shot numerous times, and died without saying anything more. The gunmen, all in military uniform, then entered the meeting room and sprayed it with automatic weapons fire, killing everyone but Traoré, who survived and soon fled the country.[39]

While the precise identity of the gunmen was subject to conflicting accounts, the evidence indicates they were under the overall command of Compaoré and Diendéré. Diendéré himself admitted that his men did the shooting, although he maintained that their intention was simply to arrest Sankara, who fired first: "At that moment all the men let loose, everyone fired, and the situation totally escaped control."[40] Compaoré denied that he had issued orders for Sankara's assassination and claimed he was at home in bed with an illness at the time. Many found it hard to believe that his men would have acted on their own. Andriamirado, after a year's investigation of various accounts, concluded that while Compaoré may not have given an explicit assassination order, he "nevertheless knew what was going to happen."[41] (In 2015–16, after Compaoré's overthrow, military prosecutors filed formal assassination charges against Compaoré, Diendéré, and a dozen others.)

Parallel to the assault at the Conseil de l'Entente, the plotters quickly eliminated potential resistance within the military. At the Kamboinsé base

10 kilometres outside Ouagadougou, the commander, Lieutenant Michel Kouama, a known Sankara loyalist, was struck down by a small assassination team. His second-in-command planned to march against the coup forces in Ouagadougou, but Kouama's killing left his troops in disarray and no counterattack materialized. At other bases loyalist troops and officers hesitated, unsure what to do now that Sankara was dead. For nearly two weeks, however, a special 400-man airport security battalion based in Koudougou, under the command of Captain Boukary Kaboré (nicknamed the "Lion"), defied the new authorities in Ouagadougou. Although Kaboré managed to slip away to neighbouring Ghana, nearly a dozen of his followers were summarily executed when pro-Compaoré forces finally took the Koudougou base.[42] The takeover was the deadliest the country had yet experienced.

Back in Ouagadougou, many known supporters of Sankara within the CNR, military command, CDRs, and civilian political groups (especially the ULCR) were detained, went into hiding, or fled the country. Within less than two hours of the killings at the Conseil de l'Entente, the national radio started carrying announcements that the CNR, the cabinet, and the OMR had been dissolved. A new "Popular Front" headed by Compaoré was running the country. Initially there was no official confirmation of Sankara's fate. Yet the news of his death spread quickly. Many people in the capital exhibited evident shock and anger. By the day after the coup, large crowds began gathering at the weed-infested Dagnoën cemetery on the outskirts of Ouagadougou where the slain president and his aides were buried in shallow graves.[43]

Despite its name, the new front exhibited little popularity. It tried to organize support marches, but none materialized. Front officials seen in public were sometimes greeted with stones and catcalls. At a CDR meeting in Ouagadougou's Sector 9, a majority of participants expressed open anger. Students at the Zinda secondary school, the largest in the capital, walked out of their classes chanting, "Sankara or no one."[44]

Although Compaoré's ascension was not easy and entailed notable bloodshed, the rapid demise of the CNR and its associated institutions warrants some comment. In part, the success of the coup benefited from the shock and disarray of those who looked to Sankara's CNR for leadership, especially since the blow came from within. Many simply did not know what was going on. The differences within the CNR had not been aired publicly and were understood only by insiders or astute activists who could decipher the coded language of the conflicting tendencies. The Popular Front, moreover, proclaimed that its goal was not the overthrow of the revolution, simply its "rectification." Confusion reigned for some time. With no effective organized resistance to the coup, many of Sankara's supporters in the administration and military remained at their posts, some rationalizing that they were trying to preserve what they could of the revolution.

As an institution, however, the CNR's roots proved shallower than was apparent during its four years in power. It had done much to re-found the state and extend it beyond the large towns. It succeeded in stimulating citizen engagement. But the momentum of that process appears to have depended to a great extent on the acumen, energies, and vision of an individual. His supporters saw that as a demonstration of Sankara's unique leadership skills. But beyond Sankara himself, the wider leadership structures were rather thin. Only a few of his closest allies and personal friends openly stood with him as the conflict escalated, and they were insufficiently organized to avert the showdown. The CNR, despite its pretensions to collective revolutionary leadership, thus exhibited some of the institutional weakness and personalized features of political systems across much of Africa.

For many Burkinabè, the revolution was closely identified with its charismatic leader. Now that he was gone, so was the revolution. Among the many handwritten messages left at Sankara's gravesite, one captured that essential point. Alluding to the four top military figures of the CNR, Sankara, Compaoré, Zongo, and Lingani, it proclaimed: "Four minus one equals zero."[45]

## FLEXIBLE HELMSMAN FOR A CONTRADICTORY COURSE

In their early statements, Popular Front officials explicitly recognized Sankara's "charisma." For them, that was not a compliment, but a criticism. They instead adopted a deliberately lacklustre, technocratic discourse designed to appeal to administrators and office managers. Behind the bureaucratic language, however, the Popular Front and its successor governments were also marked by personalized power, even more than was Sankara's CNR. Whatever the ideological colouring of the moment, Compaoré remained at the centre of official life for the next quarter of a century.

Compaoré's personality was strikingly different from that of his predecessor. During the CNR he rarely spoke publicly. His first addresses as president were halting and visibly pained. His skills at oration did improve over the years, but few considered him charismatic. He studiously avoided conveying clear messages and intentions. "Sphinx," "chameleon," "enigma," "shady," and similar terms were often used to describe him.[46] When Compaoré shifted positions, he did not say that he had been wrong, but that the circumstances had changed. His supporters regarded that elusiveness as a conciliatory trait that enabled him to build and rebuild heterogeneous political coalitions. His critics called it opportunism.[47] Compaoré attributed his affinity for strategic, bureaucratic methods to his military training: identify the mission, define the strategy, survey the terrain, and then choose steps to achieve the goal. As one local scholar put it: "This military approach to Burkinabè political problems explains the realism or pragmatism of a political strategist little inclined towards revolutionary romanticism."[48]

Compaoré's ability to straddle expectations served the Popular Front well. During its first couple of years, the authorities sought to retain a revolutionary image, both to placate the small hard-line groupings that aided Compaoré's takeover and to assure the wider public that the CNR's more popular programmes would not simply be abandoned. They simultaneously promised to be less stringent, giving some hope to the heterogeneous conservative currents gravitating towards the new government.

A January 1988 conference of CDRs, trade unions, and officially sanctioned "mass organizations" included many vitriolic criticisms of the CNR's four years in power. But speakers from the floor also cited gains in health care and education, the campaign against corruption, the emphasis on food production, and other popular programmes.[49] An official Programme of Action subsequently cited a checklist of similar goals, from the reduction of illiteracy to the organization of peasants' cooperatives.[50]

In implementing such programmes, however, the new authorities shunned the intense campaigns of popular mobilization that had been a CNR hallmark. While presented as a rejection of Sankara's ad hoc "voluntarism," such restraint also reflected a stark reality: this was a period of popular *demobilization*. Across the country, few people turned out for construction projects and many CDR headquarters were simply abandoned. The CDRs themselves were drastically restructured and renamed Revolutionary Committees (CRs). Unlike the old CDRs, which represented the central state in local communities *and* provided some channels for transmitting concerns upward, the new

CRs were strictly top-down, serving primarily as training grounds for future state functionaries.[51]

The first elections to the new CR base committees in April 1988 drew very limited participation.[52] This author's brief tour through a number of Ouagadougou neighbourhoods in October 1988 found most committee offices empty and shuttered. On the first anniversary of the coup, the authorities tried to give an appearance of mobilization by bringing in several thousand cadres from throughout the capital area. Yet when Compaoré and other speakers tried to lead the crowd in chanting, the response was embarrassingly feeble.[53] The general secretary of the national coordinating body for CRs, Captain Arsène Bongnessan Yé, was surprisingly frank. In both the countryside and towns, he said, the committees suffered from "a feeling of emptiness." When asked how he would assess the activities of his national coordinating body, Yé replied that "one cannot expect non-existent structures to act."[54]

With persuasion not proving very effective, that left coercion. Nearly two years after the coup, the UN-recognized International League for the Rights and Liberation of Peoples put the number of political prisoners at thirty.[55] Many had been leading supporters of Sankara, including top figures of the ULCR. Valère Somé later gave graphic descriptions of his torture.[56] The authorities were intolerant of any public expressions of support for the former regime. When in May 1988 thousands of students rallied at four secondary schools in Ouagadougou, carrying placards that read "Vive Sankara," heavily armed troops and gendarmes rushed in to disperse them.[57]

## IN SEARCH OF NEW ALLIES

While repression would remain a hallmark of Compaoré's decades in power, lasting stability required finding new pillars of support, both abroad and at home. Despite continued assertions of a vague "anti-imperialist" worldview, the Popular Front sought to re-establish close ties with the same powers that had been hostile to Sankara. Within three days of his takeover, Compaoré met the French chargé d'affaires in Ouagadougou to convey his readiness to "maintain and even reinforce cooperation with Paris."[58] In 1988, Jean-Marc Palm, the foreign minister, said that relations with the US administration had been "normalized" after his brother, Captain Jean-Pierre Palm, quietly visited Washington for official talks.[59] Regionally, the government drew closer to its conservative neighbours, especially President Houphouët-Boigny, Compaoré's father-in-law. Togo's President Gnassingbé Eyadéma was an honoured guest at the August 1988 anniversary ceremonies, as was the vice-president of the dictatorial regime in Zaire (as the Democratic Republic of the Congo was then known). Meanwhile, the Ghanaian government of Jerry Rawlings, who was personally close to Sankara, severed all but the most minimal ties with Ouagadougou.

With numerous contradictions and inconsistencies, the Popular Front also gradually shifted its basic domestic orientation to favour the social elites. René Otayek, an academic who had been sharply critical of the Sankara government, saw "a recomposition of class alliances displacing the country's political centre of gravity from the countryside to the cities."[60] Rural people still held a place in the authorities' developmentalist discourse, but they no longer enjoyed the attention they had under the CNR. With the local revolutionary committees little more than empty shells, traditional chiefs were able to reassert their dominance, a shift that received official sanction as chiefs were accorded places of honour at major national ceremonies organized by the Popular Front.

In the cities, Compaoré promised greater freedom to merchants and businessmen. "Without shame, we must appeal to private investors," he said a few months after the coup.[61] A year later he declared, "We need to develop capitalism ... We have never considered socialism."[62] By then, Compaoré had already invited the IMF and World Bank to exploratory talks on a structural adjustment programme.

For senior civil servants who chafed under the CNR's vigorous anti-corruption drive, the coup offered immediate relief. The People's Revolutionary Tribunals were still there for a while, but operated in low gear. Sankara's anti-corruption commission was scrapped, as was the requirement that top officials publicly declare their assets. Mercedes Benz cars, which had virtually disappeared under the CNR, were back on the streets. Construction resumed on luxury houses. Compaoré himself set an example of opulence by starting construction on a new presidential palace and buying a luxury jet (previously used by the US pop star Michael Jackson).[63] Inevitably, the relaxation of controls encouraged functionaries to revert to their old ways. Even the official press felt obliged to acknowledge:

> Laxity, hustling, bureaucratic stupidities, absenteeism, contempt for public property, use of state funds and equipment for personal ends, bureaucratism, corruption, so many ills are again popping up in our administration and institutions—like mushrooms after the first rains![64]

Urban workers also received some benefits, as the new authorities sought to buy a measure of public acceptance. Salaries, frozen since 1982, were allowed to rise. Many teachers and other civil servants who had been suspended for political reasons got their jobs back (accelerating a policy that had begun under Sankara). The trade unions enjoyed a significant easing of repression. As a result of such concessions, most unions formally endorsed the "rectification." During the January 1988 conference assessing the period of the CNR, they generally welcomed the reduction in rights violations. Yet the fact that some of those in the Popular Front leadership had previously clamoured most loudly against the unions lent an element of caution to the labour response. The CSB, which had suffered the greatest repression, vowed to maintain its independence from the government and "reject any vassalization of the union."[65]

## POLITICAL ADAPTATION

The government's efforts to find new bases of social support had a political corollary. In an August 1988 address, Compaoré explained (mainly to the leftist groups allied with his regime) that the country's backward economy and social structure required an alliance with the "progressive bourgeoisie." He then added: "Such an alliance at the economic level entails alliances at the political level."[66]

Although the Popular Front was initially dominated by military officers and leaders of the tiny groups that supported Compaoré's coup (UCB, GCB, ULC), other formations soon emerged and sought admission. One of the first and most visible was a party led by Hermann Yaméogo, son of the country's first president, Maurice Yaméogo. It welcomed a number of the government's initial measures, including its promise to create the conditions for all currents to participate "without exclusion."[67] Other parties were also admitted to the Front, among them several that traced their roots back to the old parties that had dominated in the 1960s and 1970s.[68]

One party, however, refused to join the Popular Front: the PAI. Its Central Committee noted that many of the Front's members previously "had acted like torturers towards the people and especially towards militants of our party." Moreover, "violations of democratic liberties are unfortunately still in vogue under the Popular Front." Despite those misgivings, the PAI affirmed that it would not, for the moment, adopt a hostile stance towards the authorities.[69]

The conservative complexion of a number of the Popular Front's new members stirred disquiet among those who still harboured illusions about the government's revolutionary course. A draft programmatic platform of the UCB, ULC, and GCB that circulated in mid-1988 quoted liberally from the works of Stalin, cited the need for "revolutionary violence" against perceived reactionaries, and warned "anarcho-syndicalist" trade unions that the Popular Front "will certainly be the most authoritarian."[70]

To better manage such tensions, a new political party was launched in April 1989 by the president's leadership core. As was evident from its name, the Organisation pour la démocratie populaire/Mouvement du travail (ODP/MT) continued to utilize pseudo-revolutionary language. Most of its leaders previously belonged to the UCB.[71] The ODP/MT was henceforth the dominant political force, with its leaders controlling the Popular Front's executive committee and occupying most key ministerial posts.[72]

Although apparently cobbled together in an ad hoc fashion to enable the Popular Front to navigate its contradictory tendencies and direction, the utility of such an overlapping network of political alliances was to prove itself over the long term. At its centre was a core of Compaoré loyalists skilled in factional infighting and manoeuvring, as ideologically adaptable as they were politically ruthless. At varying distances around that core were circles of political hangers-on, momentarily satisfied with small fragments of power but always hopeful of gaining admittance to the top echelons. One strength of the model was its ability to entice potential challengers to position themselves around the periphery of the ruling party and government, undermining the emergence of a strong, institutionally distinct opposition.

For those not entirely convinced of the virtues of Compaoré's brand of political inclusion, the alternative was very costly. After a pro-Compaoré officer was killed in a grenade attack in Bobo-Dioulasso in 1988, seven rank-and-file soldiers from Boukary Kaboré's Koudougou battalion were executed. Among the Sankara supporters who remained in detention, university lecturer Guillaume Sessouma died in 1989.[73] When former leaders of the CSB union federation demanded in September 1989 that the Popular Front stop interfering in its internal affairs, Soumane Touré was again arrested.[74]

That year also saw the abrupt elimination of two of the most senior military figures, Commander Jean-Baptiste Lingani and Captain Henri Zongo, who were summarily executed on 19 September. Both had been key leaders of the August 1983 revolutionary takeover. Although they tacitly sided with Compaoré during the rift within the CNR, they were not known to have played any role in

Sankara's assassination. Following the coup, the two became deputy chairmen of the Popular Front, with Lingani also defence minister and commander of the armed forces and Zongo minister for economic promotion. There were occasional rumours of tensions between them and Compaoré. Lingani openly expressed opposition to the Front's "rightist deviationism," including its admission of conservative political groupings. According to the official version of their supposed plot, Lingani and Zongo planned to assassinate Compaoré. But after they sought to enlist into their plot Captain Diendéré, he exposed their plan. A day after the executions, Lingani's taped confession was broadcast over the radio. In key respects it contradicted the official account. Lingani said it was Diendéré who originally proposed ousting Compaoré. Lingani admitted that in hindsight he was a bit naive in trusting Diendéré and characterized the coup proposal as "a frame-up in which I was put forward so that I could be gotten at easily."[75]

Soon, a reshuffle of both the Popular Front executive and the cabinet further consolidated the domination of Compaoré loyalists. The top executive positions went to ODP/MT leaders or military officers, with Diendéré reconfirmed as secretary for defence and security. In the cabinet, Compaoré himself took the defence portfolio. He gave foreign affairs to Prosper Vokouma, a cousin, an early sign of the weighty political role of members of the president's family.[76]

With no more rivals in the military leadership and most political currents incorporated into the Popular Front or simply silenced, Compaoré entered the 1990s on a more solid footing than when he first seized power. That would enable him to successfully steer through the next few turbulent years of transition to a new constitutional order.

# 9
# "DEMOCRACY" WITH A HEAVY HAND

The opening of the last decade of the twentieth century was an especially turbulent time in Africa. Beginning in a handful of states in 1989 and then spreading rapidly across the region, powerful movements for democratic and social reform buffeted dozens of countries. Long-ruling military juntas and autocratic single-party states, then the norm on the continent, confronted widespread opposition rallies, street demonstrations, labour strikes, rioting, and other forms of defiance. The agitation was ignited in part by popular grievances over persistent economic austerity and stagnation. Social demands soon escalated into overt political claims, as citizens started pressing for greater freedoms as well.

While driven mainly by domestic concerns, these movements took inspiration from outside developments. The dramatic release of Nelson Mandela and other anti-apartheid leaders in South Africa in 1990, followed a few years later by democratic elections, demonstrated to many that even the most exclusionary and intractable political systems could be forced to cede. The fall of the Berlin Wall and eruption of protest movements across Eastern Europe conveyed a similar message. For Africa, the end of the Cold War not only weakened those rulers who had directly benefited from Soviet bloc aid, but also contributed to a decline in Western backing for authoritarian African regimes more generally. From Benin to Zambia, leaders were urged by Western officials to open their political systems and permit multi-party elections.

Under such internal and external pressures, many an autocrat was either pushed from power or obliged to allow some political liberalization. New parties proliferated, legal rights expanded greatly, and relatively open elections were organized in country after country. Between 1990 and 1995 the number of African states with competitive elections rose from less than ten to thirty-eight.[1] A continent marked overwhelmingly by military or one-party regimes was transformed into a region characterized largely by formally democratic electoral systems.

Burkina Faso was one of the states swayed by those winds of change. It felt the pressures early on, as many of its French-speaking neighbours were caught up in the turmoil. Benin was the first, starting with student protests in early 1989, then escalating into massive nationwide strikes and demonstrations. The unrest obliged the long-time president to permit a representative national conference in February 1990 that stripped him of effective power and led to multi-party elections a year later. Following Benin's example, nascent opposition forces across Francophone Africa called for similar sovereign national conferences, with the authority to fundamentally change their political systems. There was also direct pressure from France. President Mitterrand, at a June 1990 meeting with African heads of state in La Baule, France, explicitly urged them to reform: "a representative system, free elections, multi-partyism, freedom of the press, independence of the judiciary, no censorship."[2]

Local and external admirers of Compaoré later portrayed the Burkinabè president as an eager champion of democratic reform, even before the fall of the Berlin Wall and Mitterrand's La Baule speech.[3] The actual record, however, reveals a halting, reluctant, and tightly managed transition from the Popular Front to a formally multi-party electoral system, one that could meet donors' new political preferences and offer a domestic safety valve for previously excluded elites. Compaoré would prove adept at navigating those tumultuous waters, making concessions only when necessary to preserve his hold.

## CONTROLLED CONSTITUTIONALIZATION

At the first congress of the Popular Front in March 1990, Compaoré repeatedly referred to democratic reforms. Yet he did not once mention competitive, representative elections. Instead, he talked of "popular democracy" through the political structures of the Popular Front and its subordinate Revolutionary Committees. He did point to the need to adopt a constitution, as distinct from the non-constitutional "states of exception" that prevailed during the years of military and revolutionary rule. But such a new, written constitution would conform to the Popular Front's Programme of Action and seek to enshrine the principles of a "revolutionary and democratic state of law." In case there was any doubt about his intentions, Compaoré added that such a state of law would be completely different from "the hypocrisy of bourgeois democracy."[4] Captain

Bongnessan Arsène Yé, head of the Revolutionary Committees and soon to become the government's constitutional spokesman, interpreted Compaoré's comment to mean that there would be no "separation of powers."[5]

For the pseudo-Marxist groups in the Popular Front, the congress offered some assurance that the government would not simply cave in to demands for political pluralism, open elections, and human rights. For others, the congress was a disappointment in its continued attachment to revolutionary rhetoric, centralized political control, and Popular Front dominance. Yet the references to a constitution and wider political participation also gave some hope that things might evolve.

After the congress, the Popular Front's executive drafted a preliminary outline of a constitution. It stipulated that the presidency would have pre-eminence over a future legislature, that most (but not all) parliamentary deputies would be directly elected, and that political parties could be permitted to operate outside the Popular Front.[6]

A Constitutional Commission was set up to elaborate on those points. Unlike some of the sovereign national conferences or constituent assemblies that arose elsewhere in Africa, Burkina Faso's commission lacked effective autonomy. It was launched by the Popular Front. Of the 104 commissioners, sixty-four represented the Popular Front directly, including its dominant party (the ODP/MT), the Revolutionary Committees, or other member "mass organizations." There were, in addition, nine staff from the Ministry of Justice, seven sitting judges, and several other government officials, giving the authorities a predominant voice. The chair of the commission, Captain Yé, was named by government decree.[7]

When the commission began its deliberations in May 1990, there were immediate objections to both the preliminary outline and the commission's composition, coming mostly from non-Popular Front organizations, but also from some of its own members. A subcommittee then produced a revised draft with only a few minor changes. But under further pressure, the authorities' representatives on the commission agreed to more significant concessions by the final sessions in July: no official leadership role for the Popular Front, direct election of all parliamentary deputies, and a limit of two seven-year presidential terms. The draft continued to be peppered with the Popular Front's old jargon and only "anti-imperialist" parties would be legally authorized.[8]

In December, some 2,200 delegates assembled for a national conference to fine-tune the draft. Although many more parties, civil society associations, and other non-governmental groups were able to take part in that conference than in the work of the Constitutional Commission, the balance of power in favour of the authorities did not shift appreciably, since official representation also increased. According to one tally, some 1,800 delegates (81 percent of the total) were pro-government.[9] Nevertheless, domestic and donor pressures increased further, prompting the government to concede yet more. All remaining "revolutionary" and "anti-imperialist" references were stripped from the text, opening the way for parties across the political spectrum to function. However, provisions for an advisory second house of parliament, known as the Chamber of Representatives, were inserted over the objections of opposition parties, which saw it as a ploy to perpetuate representation for the Revolutionary Committees and other generally pro-government forces, including traditional chiefs.[10]

The final step towards the new constitution was a public referendum. On 2 June 1991, with all recognized political parties calling for a "yes" vote, the constitution was approved by a resounding 93 percent of those who went to the polls.[11]

Despite reservations about some aspects, the opposition parties, like Burkinabè citizens more generally, saw the constitution's adoption as an important step towards establishment of somewhat regular and regulated institutions. Whatever its limitations, the constitution marked an end to the "state of exception" era, in which arbitrary and unpredictable decision-making was the norm and conflicts were settled mainly by the balance of informal political power and access to armed might. The courts were still not independent, but at least in theory blatant violations of the constitution could be legally challenged and all laws had to be in conformity with its basic precepts. The constitution, moreover, guaranteed a wide range of political and human rights, including those of assembly and expression. Already, the first private FM radio station had been authorized, and soon three independent newspapers emerged.[12] The constitution gave such freedom of the press additional legal protection.

Pro-democracy advocates nevertheless worried that the authorities themselves were not committed to constitutional rule, and had agreed to it under duress simply to hang onto power. Government officials and leaders of the Popular Front, ODP/MT, and other ruling bodies themselves made clear their intention to remain in control. There were also the lessons of history. The country already had three previous constitutions, each adopted overwhelmingly by public referenda (1960, 1970, 1977), only to be subsequently scrapped or subverted.

## BITTER ELECTIONS

Political tensions had already been mounting by the time of the constitutional referendum, and then quickly escalated further. The conflict was fuelled partly by the authorities' patent fear that they might still be swept out of office, as had happened in several other African countries. The opposition in turn believed that Compaoré and his colleagues would do everything they could to win the upcoming presidential and legislative elections, including using outright fraud and intimidation.

The opposition was a diverse lot. Several somewhat conservative parties first arose as members or supporters of the Popular Front, but once it became clear that the front would lose its official dominance under the new constitution, they increasingly distanced themselves from it. The Rassemblement démocratique africain (RDA), which initially functioned in the Popular Front under a different name, came out in 1991 under its own banner, led by Gérard Kango Ouédraogo, who had been a prime minister in the 1970s.[13] Another, the Convention nationale des patriotes progressistes/Parti social-démocrate (CNPP/PSD), was expelled from the Popular Front in March 1991 after adopting a more critical stance. Hermann Yaméogo, an especially prominent figure in the early days of the Popular Front, formed a new party, the Alliance pour la démocratie et la fédération (ADF), at the end of 1990; somewhat inconsistently, he subsequently moved into more direct opposition. Several other currents emerged from a different part of the ideological spectrum. The PAI, the country's oldest Marxist formation, secured legal recognition under Philippe Ouédraogo and Adama Touré. Ernest Nongma Ouédraogo, interior minister in the Sankara government, launched the Bloc socialiste burkinabè in December 1990, the first "Sankarist" party to form openly. In addition, several figures in the governing ODP/MT broke with the party as it increasingly dropped its revolutionary pretentions. These included Etienne Traoré and most prominently Oumarou Clément Ouédraogo, the ODP/MT's first general secretary.[14]

Deeply distrustful of Compaoré and his comrades, many parties called more forcefully than before for a sovereign national conference to establish a new transitional administration to oversee free and impartial elections, a demand that Compaoré rejected outright. The president then tried to entice party leaders into taking ministerial posts in ostensibly coalition cabinets. In July 1991 nine leaders of purported opposition parties joined the government, including Hermann

Yaméogo of the ADF. But after a few weeks he and two ADF colleagues pulled out and were replaced by six other opposition representatives.[15]

The manoeuvres failed to stem a growing polarization. In September, six opposition parties formed a new alliance, the Coordination des forces démocratiques (CFD), soon joined by seven other parties. Its main demands were for a sovereign national conference and holding legislative elections before the presidential poll. As the remaining CFD government ministers resigned, the coalition called its first mass public demonstration on 30 September, drawing an estimated 3,000 protesters in Ouagadougou. They were attacked by several hundred ODP/MT militants, causing numerous injuries, and the ADF's headquarters was burned. Two more mass demonstrations followed in October, each involving about 10,000 protesters, with further attacks by riot police and government supporters. The ODP/MT and twenty-six other pro-government parties formed an alliance of their own and in mid-October held a large demonstration in Ouagadougou, comparable in size to those of the CFD.[16]

While the two sides challenged each other in the streets, the electoral contest for the presidency became a starkly one-sided affair. Five opposition parties had initially named candidates to run against Compaoré, but the CFD, to express its lack of confidence in the authorities' impartiality, withdrew all five from the contest. The opposition parties would have had only the dimmest of chances anyway, since they were divided and unable to agree on a common candidate, were poorly organized outside just a few urban centres, and confronted an incumbent who not only had the advantages of state power but also control over the electoral machinery. Yet by depriving Compaoré of any challengers, they at least succeeded in diminishing his election's domestic and international legitimacy. Besides the absence of contenders, Compaoré's capture of 86 percent of the vote was further tarnished by an exceptionally low turnout rate of just 25 percent.[17]

The start of Compaoré's first elected mandate was punctuated by further violence. On election day itself, Bobo-Dioulasso experienced looting and opposition supporters sacked ballot boxes and burned voting booths. Then on 9 December Ouagadougou was rocked by a series of attacks on opposition figures. Moctar Tall, a university lecturer and leader of a small opposition party, was shot and seriously wounded. About a kilometre away someone threw a hand grenade into Oumarou Clément Ouédraogo's car, killing him on the spot. Opposition activists blamed the government, speculating that Ouédraogo was silenced to prevent the former ODP/MT general secretary from revealing potentially embarrassing secrets. (An army sergeant later boasted of involvement in the assassination, but charges against him were dropped in 2005 when he retracted that claim and no other evidence was available.)[18]

That Christmas Eve, Compaoré was officially sworn into office as the president of Burkina Faso's Fourth Republic. In his oath before the Supreme Court he pledged to "honour, preserve, respect, and defend the constitution."[19]

In another bid to reduce polarization, Compaoré opened a national reconciliation conference in early 1992, but it soon collapsed. He was more successful with a coalition cabinet in February. Although several key opposition parties were excluded, others belonging to the CFD did agree to participate, most notably the RDA and ADF, with the latter's Hermann Yaméogo given the high-ranking position of minister of state.[20]

That brief détente smoothed the way for the legislative elections. Although the constitution accorded much greater power to the executive, the legislature was nevertheless seen as an important arena for the opposition parties. Encouraged by the very high abstention rate in the December presidential election and by the electoral successes of oppositions elsewhere in Africa, they abandoned their previous boycott stance and joined the fray. Out of some sixty parties that had been legally registered by that point, twenty-seven fielded slates of candidates for the 107-member legislature. Only four, however, had a sufficient base to run candidates in all thirty provinces: the ruling ODP/MT and the opposition ADF, CNPP/PSD, and RDA. Contrary to opposition expectations, the results of the 24 May parliamentary election were very lopsided. The ODP/MT secured a decisive majority of seventy-eight seats, and five small allied parties took six more, leaving the opposition only twenty-three.

Various factors contributed. Most obviously, the ODP/MT, as the governing party, was able to use state resources, influence, and the promise of patronage jobs to attract local powerbrokers and the blocs of voters under their sway. Its links to the powerful executive also facilitated an electoral alliance with the many small parties that had supported Compaoré's presidential campaign. The opposition, by contrast, was fragmented, had little presence in rural areas, and failed to forge any electoral coalitions. Their divisions ensured that the ODP/MT could win numerous constituencies without even a majority of the electorate. Thus with just 48.5 percent of the national vote it obtained 73 percent of all parliamentary seats.[21]

Compaoré was then able to leverage that skewed result into an even more dominant position after the election. He formed yet another coalition cabinet, attracting leaders of the three strongest opposition parties to accept ministerial posts, further diminishing their independent profile. The demoralized opposition also experienced deeper internal divisions. Many members and local leaders of the ADF and RDA defected outright to the ruling party, while the CNPP/PSD suffered a major split. One leader of the CNPP/PSD openly accused the government of directly instigating factional quarrels within the opposition.[22] A Burkinabè academic commented: "The situation very much resembled the evolution towards a single party during the first years after independence ... the opposition, trounced in the elections, rallied to the victor through discouragement, promises, or pressures."[23]

So by the early 1990s, many elements were already in place to give the Compaoré government its durability and flexibility over the next two decades: a strong ruling party that controlled most state institutions and could dominate electoral contests, a weak and divided opposition incapable of mounting a real challenge, occasional coalition cabinets to give an appearance of inclusion, and when inducements and token concessions were insufficient, selective repression.

## AN ENCOMPASSING "PARTY-STATE"

Because of the disjuncture between Burkina Faso's new democratic trappings and the more dismal practice of daily political life, a number of academics and political actors observed that the Fourth Republic tended to function at two levels. One was official, that of constitutionalism, pluralist elections, accountability, and the rule of law—a "shadow play" put on to please donor agencies. The other was unofficial, the world of real politics in which crude power, monopoly, and arbitrary rule prevailed.[24]

That did not mean that the first level was a fiction designed solely to fool outsiders. Citizens could cite the constitution in defence of their rights, officials were obliged to periodically subject themselves to electoral scrutiny, and various new institutions opened some space for critical engagement, including an ombudsman's office to take up citizen complaints and a formally non-partisan communications council to regulate the media. The problem was that those institutions could be ignored, subverted, manipulated, or altered by the politically powerful. Once Compaoré's ruling party had consolidated its hold and pushed the opposition to the margins, it took only a simple parliamentary vote to remove the two-term limit on the presidency (in 1997) or to repeatedly reshape the electoral code to the majority's advantage. The legislature's second house, the advisory Chamber of Representatives, was finally established in 1995, at a time when the authorities considered it beneficial. But then they readily dropped it seven years later as part of a package of concessions to the opposition.

The centrepiece of the authorities' power (both official and unofficial) was the ruling party. Initially known as the ODP/MT, it had already emerged in a clearly dominant position in the 1992 legislative election. The party subsequently induced half a dozen opposition deputies to cross the aisles. Then in February 1996 the ODP/MT absorbed thirteen other parties, including the remnants of the CNPP/PSD, christening the new formation the Congrès pour la démocratie et le progrès (CDP). The mergers automatically brought the party's parliamentary representation up to eighty-eight. Then in the next election in 1997 the CDP took an even bigger share, winning 101 seats (in a slightly enlarged legislature of 111). The CDP became an "ultra" majority party, to such an extent that even its deputy secretary-general, Salif Diallo, regarded the outcome as "rather embarrassing for a democracy."[25]

CDP leaders often argued that it was the party's solid record in government that won over the electorate. But the party also controlled formidable financial resources and personnel that no formation outside of government could hope to match. Although the CDP's overwhelming hegemony did indeed find expression at the ballot box, the party did not owe its quasi-monopoly solely or even mainly to its electoral performance. In essence, that power rested on control of the state and the state's institutions and resources. Again in the words of Salif Diallo, one of the party's most candid figures: "We have an advantage, it must be honestly recognized. And that's that we have the state apparatus. In African countries, when you have the state apparatus, you are far ahead of the opposition."[26]

Despite the adoption of a constitution that spelled out a formal separation of institutions, the fused "party-state" concept of Compaoré's Popular Front carried over into the Fourth Republic in various unofficial ways. In rural areas and smaller towns, local governments and institutions drew many of their cadres directly from the former Revolutionary Committees of the Popular Front era. Those personnel now operated simultaneously as state functionaries and CDP activists.[27] Nationally, observed the scholar Augustin Loada, state and party were informally connected "through the establishment of partisan cells within the state administration, creating in practice a partisan administration. Almost all the administrative and economic elites were obliged to join the ruling party (or believed they had to) in order to get by or survive."[28]

During election campaigns in particular, civil servants understood that their positions depended greatly on participation in CDP activities. It was a form of exchange: partisan commitment in return for career advancement. In this, the CDP functioned like many other ruling parties in Africa. In Burkina Faso as elsewhere, "The elites played the game of 'big men'," noted Hilgers and Mazzocchetti, "by engaging in redistribution practices, putting their networks of dependents at the government's service with the aim of acquiring resources to perpetuate themselves."[29]

That was the description of a typical patronage system. While patron–client relations operate in a variety of contexts, some strictly in the economic and social realms, those related to public office are common across Africa, often with state property and jobs allocated to ethnic or political supporters in networks connecting powerful patrons with dependent clients. Such networks can be small and local, or may be linked together in pyramid-type structures that reach the summits of social and political power.[30] Some scholars have described African states built on patronage systems as "patrimonial" or "neo-patrimonial,"[31] building on Weber's concepts of patrimonialism.[32]

At their heart, patron–client relations involve a two-way trade in material, social, political, and other resources between patrons and clients in which both benefit, albeit to unequal degrees.[33] Usually, clients provide patrons with services (labour, votes, other forms of political support), while patrons offer protection, information, contacts, or more tangible goods such as scarce commodities, jobs, or business contracts. These are especially important where laws, courts, police systems, and other official mechanisms are weak, ineffective, or under the control of a particular group. That allows patrons to help their supporters on a selective, discriminatory basis.

For those holding central state office, relations with local patrons can extend their authority, at least indirectly, into areas they could not otherwise penetrate.[34] The structural characteristics of patron–client ties make them especially flexible building blocks for this purpose: a village patron, for example, may himself be a client to some district patron, who may in turn support a regional or national figure, thereby aggregating clienteles all the way to the top. The state does not need to provide services directly to everyone, nor does it need their direct support. Everything flows through intermediaries.

Because such mechanisms are informal and frequently illicit they are rarely talked about in official discourse. Yet in the case of Burkina Faso, practically everyone was aware of them. That knowledge was reflected in common jokes about the names of the ruling party. When it was the ODP/MT, popular wordplay suggested that the acronym stood for "Office de distribution du pain; mange et tais-toi" (Office for bread distribution—eat and shut up). When it became the CDP, that changed to "Congrès pour la distribution des postes" (Congress for distributing jobs).[35]

At times, the dim outlines of how this system operated became visible, most often during election campaigns or when particularly egregious scandals surfaced. In Koudougou, the CDP-dominated municipal council took over a 2 hectare fruit-tree orchard in 2008, ostensibly to divide it into lots for general residential use. The elderly owner later went to court to challenge the expropriation. After receiving no satisfaction, he turned to the independent press in 2011 to air his grievances. Reporters soon discovered that the mayor, without consulting the rest of the council, had designated allotments to himself and to various dignitaries. A cadastral map someone leaked to the press specified the intended recipients—the names read like a who's who of the government and ruling party. They included Prime Minister Tertius Zongo, CDP President Roch Marc Christian Kaboré, François Compaoré (the president's brother), as well as General Brice Bayala and other luminaries. Following a public uproar, the government removed the mayor, annulled the allotments because of their "flagrant ethical violations," and agreed to pay the owner compensation. The affair prompted many denunciations, with some noting that cases of corruption in urban land allotments were common.[36] After the Compaoré regime's ousting, a parliamentary commission of inquiry determined that at least 105,000 plots of land were illegally allocated in fifteen cities between 1995 and 2015, mainly to politically connected individuals.[37]

Complaints about unfair practices and abusive authority came not only from the opposition, but sometimes from within the CDP itself. In early 2000 in the north-eastern town of Kaya eighteen CDP municipal councillors issued an open letter denouncing their own mayor's financial mismanagement, arbitrary decision-making, illicit enrichment, and corrupt land dealings.[38] That same year a junior CDP legislator, Alidou Soré, styling himself the "voice of the voiceless," took the floor in the National Assembly to condemn mayors who sold confiscated land for their own profit, questioned the way Ouagadougou mayor

Simon Compaoré issued public procurement contracts, and appealed to the national leadership to end such "clientelist" practices.[39] Just before a national party congress in 2003 a group of CDP youths from the province of Passoré accused party "barons" of selecting their friends and family members as candidates, keeping unpopular and ineffective individuals in key positions, and using cabinet posts for self-serving ends.[40]

Such tensions reflected the reality that the CDP's clientelist networks were often quite fractious and in fierce competition with each other. The prospect of access to the material spoils of office gave those conflicts a virulent edge. Some factions operated from the centre, supported by particular cabinet ministers or other party strongmen. A few were holdovers of the different parties that originally merged into the CDP. In 2008 a group of six former leaders of the CNPP/PSD voiced stinging criticisms of the way the CDP functioned, including complaints that they had been "marginalized" as the core leadership remained dominated by former ODP/MT cadres.[41] (The six later split and formed their own opposition party.) But it was at the local level that factional politics often became most chaotic and contentious. Personal animosities, conflicts over access to scarce jobs and goods, ethnic and kinship rivalries, alignment with competing national factions, and chieftaincy disputes frequently imbued those contests with particular bitterness. In Bobo-Dioulasso contending CDP factions fought for control of the local municipal council, degenerating into street battles that took several lives.[42] The tensions were worsened by the fact that members of different ethnic groups (Bobo and Dioula) tended to line up on opposing sides. As long as Compaoré was able to keep the national party leadership more or less united and enough material benefits were available to adequately fuel the patronage machine, the system was flexible enough to survive such inevitable fights over power and its spoils.

The system was not confined to the CDP alone. Its tentacles extended into key economic and social sectors, enlisting other influential people to provide important support services to sustain government and party dominance. For financial resources, the CDP turned directly to the business community. In 1998, for example, the party convened a meeting of several hundred businessmen, led by Oumarou Kanazoé, president of the Chamber of Commerce and the party's national secretary of "economic operators." A CDP leader told them: "Help us so that we can help you."[43] Translated: those who contributed most generously could expect lucrative public contracts, tax breaks, or other favours.

Traditional chiefs were another major prop, especially in the countryside. From the earliest days of the Popular Front, Mossi chiefs in particular rallied behind the ODP/MT in return for the government's favourable treatment of the Mogho Naaba, the Mossi "emperor." In the estimation of Benoît Beucher, the backing of the Mossi royal court was a major factor in mobilizing votes for Compaoré: "The networks constituted by the chieftaincy played the role of a transmission belt between the capital and the provinces. And the Mogho Naaba, even though he hardly had much authority in Ouagadougou, nevertheless was a keystone of the system that pushed the Mossi population to vote for the ODP/MT."[44] One of the highest ranking Mossi chiefs, the Larlé Naba Tigré, was even elected as a CDP candidate and served for several terms as a deputy in the National Assembly (under his civil name, Victor Tiendrébéogo).[45]

Religious figures were enlisted to lend support. Kanazoé, the ruling party's wealthy financier, also headed the main Muslim federation. Although the Catholic Church would later criticize Compaoré's efforts to hang onto power indefinitely, in 2004 Ouagadougou Archbishop Jean-Marie Compaoré suggested publicly that the president was indispensable, asking about other politicians: "Who among them can really manage the country?"[46] The CDP tapped Protestant pastors as well, especially from the growing evangelical movement.[47] Tertius Zongo, who served as prime minister from 2007 to 2011, was himself involved with an evangelical church and inserted repeated religious references into his official declarations.[48]

Civil society organizations did not escape the net. While ostensibly nonpolitical, many found that they had to stay in the authorities' good graces to secure the official authorizations needed to operate. Bernard Lédéa Ouédraogo, leader of the *naam* movement, Burkina Faso's best-known rural self-help group, abandoned his earlier insistence on independence from any government by joining the CDP and winning election as mayor of Ouahigouya.[49] Karim Traoré, head of the national cotton farmers' association, was also in the party, even running (unsuccessfully) as one of its parliamentary candidates.[50]

The politics of patronage were not introduced to Burkina Faso by Compaoré and his CDP. They existed in the colonial era, and were especially robust during the periods of multi-party rule under General Lamizana. Those patronage structures of the 1970s were somewhat loose, directed less by the central authorities than by the leaderships of the RDA and other elite parties. Compared to that "polyarchy," observed Loada, the Compaoré regime "distinguished itself by its pyramid-like, quasi-'Prussian' character, with a centralization and concentration of power."[51]

Perhaps inevitably, this tight central direction became personalized. The system was anchored to the person of Blaise Compaoré, with the political influence of other party leaders determined largely by their proximity to him. He was the final arbiter of the contending factions, rewarding those perceived to be most loyal and demoting others when they disappointed him, proved ineffective, or exhibited too much independence. Compaoré found the most trustworthy associates in his own family. His wife, younger brother François, François' mother-in-law, and sundry cousins and nephews all played important roles. Although a feature of Compaoré's rule from the outset, his tendency to rely on family members became especially pronounced during his final years in power.

As long as they were sufficiently loyal and willing to acknowledge Compaoré's supremacy, other CDP leaders were also able to adopt personalized political roles. The term "baron" to characterize the most powerful party figures was not used by opposition critics or independent media commentators alone, but also frequently by CDP members themselves.

Three of those "barons" are worth highlighting in particular, largely because of their central positions in the CDP and government over many years and their later role in the breakdown of that system. The three were Roch Marc Christian Kaboré, Salif Diallo, and Simon Compaoré (sometimes known collectively as "RSS" after the initials of their first names). All had been especially intimate collaborators of Compaoré from the beginning of his rule. Diallo worked closely with Compaoré before the coup and was with him on the day of Sankara's assassination. Simon Compaoré was a member of the small ULC at the time.[52] Kaboré had belonged to the pro-Sankara ULCR, but broke with it in the immediate wake of the coup to join the ULC and others in the Popular Front.[53] All three participated in founding the ODP/MT and then its successor CDP. Kaboré served as prime minister (1994–96), president of the National Assembly, and head of the CDP for more than a decade.[54] Diallo, often called Compaoré's "right hand," for years occupied the posts of CDP vice-president and minister of agriculture and functioned as a strongman in his home region of Yatenga.[55] Simon Compaoré was the powerful mayor of Ouagadougou for seventeen years and on two separate occasions was the party's national secretary-general. As core members of the government and CDP leadership, the three were major players in the regime's vast system of political patronage, with the experience and connections that would later permit them to extend their careers beyond Compaoré's downfall. Kaboré (with Salif Diallo and Simon Compaoré at his side) would even win election as president in 2015.

## PATRONAGE UNDER ARMS

Not all barons were civilian. Given Compaoré's origins in the army and his continued reliance on military and police power to shore up his rule, it was perhaps inevitable that his network of patron–client relations would penetrate the security forces. The most prominent representative was Colonel (later General) Gilbert Diendéré, Compaoré's closest military aide since the 1987 coup. In 1996 the paracommando units previously headquartered in Pô were reconstituted as the Régiment de la sécurité presidentielle (RSP) to provide security for Compaoré in Ouagadougou and elsewhere. That force of about 1,000 men was officially part of the army, but placed exclusively at Compaoré's disposal.[56] Diendéré was in overall charge of the presidential guard for many years.

In exchange for their loyalty to Compaoré and his family, RSP members received more benefits and perks than other parts of the armed forces. They enjoyed virtual impunity for any acts they might commit, however questionable. That absence of accountability fostered abuses. The best-known was the December 1998 assassination of newspaper editor Norbert Zongo. Through his weekly tabloid, *L'Indépendant*, Zongo had already exposed a variety of high-level scandals: corruption, embezzlement, misdeeds by CDP officials, and conflicts within the security forces. His final investigation was into the death of the personal driver of François Compaoré, the president's brother. Suspected of stealing money from the household, the driver was detained by the RSP and taken to its Ouagadougou detention centre, rather than into police custody as required by law. Although his death was later attributed to "illness," Zongo cited evidence that the driver had in fact been tortured to death and also raised questions about François Compaoré's precise role in the affair. After Zongo was killed (along with three companions), an independent commission of inquiry concluded that he had been assassinated to halt that investigation. The commission named six members of the RSP as "serious suspects."[57] One was later convicted of the driver's death, but as long as Compaoré was in power none were ever tried for Zongo's killing.

The practice of providing impunity to the RSP extended, to varying degrees, to other soldiers, police, and gendarmes. Members of the various uniformed services could engage in all sorts of illegal activities, from torture and arbitrary detention to extortion and personal score-settling. The main human rights group, the Mouvement burkinabè des droits de l'homme et des peuples (MBDHP), charged in 2002 that the police had summarily executed 106 suspected criminals during a period of just three months, supported by photos of about thirty corpses, some with their arms tied behind their backs.[58]

Not only were legal distinctions blurred, so were the lines between security personnel and those in ruling party positions. Lieutenant Colonel Djibrill Bassolé, the security minister, came out of the ranks of the gendarmes, yet managed to build a party base of his own. In times of political crisis, CDP mayors, councillors, and occasionally cabinet ministers formed armed party militias to repress protesters, sometimes enlisting army officers to train them. Ouagadougou mayor Simon Compaoré was especially open about leading armed party thugs against youths protesting at Zongo's death.[59] Diendéré's wife, Fatou Diendéré, emerged as a powerful figure in the CDP and sometimes used her husband's influence to strengthen her hand in internal party faction fights.[60]

In a sense, Burkina Faso's external military relations also reflected clientelist patterns. In exchange for the regime's readiness to join Western "anti-terrorism" campaigns in the Sahel region in 2005, it began receiving greater foreign military assistance, largely from France and the US. The RSP and other parts of the army were rewarded with new equipment and training, as the country hosted both French special forces troops and US air surveillance operations on its soil.[61] From the US alone, Burkinabè military officers received advanced training valued at some $6.7 million between 2005 and 2012.[62] Diendéré in particular established close ties with US and French military commanders.

## HARVESTING VOTES

For CDP leaders, real power came from their control of the state and military apparatus, not from any electoral mandate. But elections were major events nonetheless. They conveyed a degree of legitimacy in the eyes of foreign embassies, donor agencies, and many Burkinabè. Periodic elections held out some hope that a particularly unpopular parliamentary deputy, mayor, or even cabinet minister might be displaced. Party barons found that elections offered an opportunity to reshuffle competing factions, renew patronage structures, and gauge local leaders' capacities.

Securing high tallies was a major goal for the president and his political supporters. *How* the votes were obtained was secondary. If registered voters backed pro-regime candidates out of conviction, then all the better. But promises of special favours, vote buying, threats, and outright ballot rigging all featured to some extent in the presidential, legislative, and local government elections under Compaoré's Fourth Republic.

The 1990s featured many reports of fraud. Irregularities included faulty voter lists, issuing voting identification cards to underage youths, transporting voters from one polling station to another, withholding cards from entire villages suspected of opposition sympathies, using chiefs' homes as voting places, and "indelible" ink that could be easily washed off, allowing multiple voting. During voters' registration before the 1998 presidential poll, two journalists for the weekly *L'Indépendant* visited various registration offices in Ouagadougou, obtaining twenty duly stamped and authorized voting cards between them. "They are signing up everyone who shows up," the reporters commented, terming it an "administrative corvée" to produce a high tally for the incumbent.[63]

Over time such blatant fraud declined in importance. By the 2000s the electoral commission had gained greater independence from the state administration, became more non-partisan by incorporating a larger share of opposition and civil society representatives, and increased its authority and capacity to register voters, supervise balloting, and proclaim the results. Foreign and national observers generally certified successive elections as free and transparent, with only minor irregularities that would not have changed the basic results. Quipped Salif Diallo after the CDP swept the 2006 municipal elections: "We don't need to cheat in order to win."[64]

That may have been technically true for the voting process. But the CDP and its allies were still guaranteed the upper hand thanks to the manipulation of election rules and the ability to use state resources during campaigns. In principle, the presidential term limit in the original 1991 constitution aimed to prevent the incumbent from using his position to remain in office indefinitely. But since it was not an entrenched clause and Compaoré's CDP had more than the required percentage of seats to amend the constitution by parliamentary vote, he was easily able to eliminate it. But then in 2000, in the midst of the grave political crisis that followed the Norbert Zongo assassination, the authorities felt compelled to make a few compromises. These included not only reinstituting the two-term limit, but also shortening the term from seven years to five. Some believed that would oblige Compaoré to leave in 2005, at the end of his second term. The amendment, however, did not specify *when* the new term limit would begin. That enabled the pro-regime Constitutional Court to rule that since the amendment was not explicitly retroactive, the limit would start anew with the next presidential election in 2005.[65] Compaoré thus ran again that year, and once more in 2010.

The electoral code was similarly malleable. In the 2000 political compromise, the authorities agreed that most legislators would be elected from constituencies based on the thirteen regions rather than the forty-five provinces demarcated in 1996. Together with a change in the method of calculating proportional representation, that ensured that the 2002 legislative election more accurately reflected voter preferences and made it easier for smaller parties to win seats. As a result, the ruling party was reduced from 101 seats to just fifty-seven, a bare majority. But once the regime was no longer on the defensive, it moved promptly to claw back its advantages. The CDP again modified the electoral code to change the basic parliamentary constituency from the region back to the province. Since a third of the forty-five provinces were eligible for only one deputy because of smaller populations, proportional representation could not take effect and their seats simply went to the party with the most votes, in practical terms favouring the CDP. Meanwhile, the number of deputies elected on national party lists was reduced from twenty-one to fifteen, further limiting the effect of proportional representation.[66] With the new constituencies in place, the 2007 legislative election saw the CDP bounce back up to seventy-three seats.

Rules manipulation could not fully explain the CDP's repeated victories or Compaoré's consistently high vote tallies (about 80 percent in both the 2005 and 2010 presidential elections). It was the same patronage methods through which they governed that made it possible to regularly turn out votes at election time. Control of state institutions provided the CDP with an overwhelming advantage. In rural areas, far from the sight of critical reporters or most election observers, chiefs played central roles in mobilizing the electorate. As in many other African countries, voting in the countryside was not the autonomous individual act so celebrated in liberal democratic theory. As Loada observed, the majority of Burkinabè voters cast ballots "in a communitarian environment, open to the interventions of traditional and religious authorities among whom the most fortunate candidates and parties could 'buy consciences'."[67] In a village in the province of Kénédougou, the local chief previously supported an opposition candidate mainly because of ethnic affinities, but CDP backers then gave him money, inducing him to switch his electoral allegiance to the ruling party.[68] Chiefs were not reticent about broadcasting their political preferences and frequently spoke at CDP campaign rallies. Once a chief declared his choice, that option became virtually mandatory for all subjects, with reprisals threatened against anyone discovered voting otherwise. A traditional chief in the province of Namentenga boasted that in his canton "I have nearly 20,000 inhabitants—20,000 voters. If I say 'vote for the cat,' they will vote for the cat."[69]

Nationally, the political messages that voters received were heavily filtered through the state-owned media. Although all parties and candidates were legally entitled to some coverage, in practice the national television and radio services devoted most news to the president and other CDP candidates. Official media supervisory institutions were dominated by state appointees and made only weak attempts to correct the bias. Opposition candidates had to reach potential voters mainly through private newspapers and radio stations, campaign rallies, and other face-to-face events.

Parliamentary deputies, cabinet ministers, and state functionaries who were also running for office drew little distinction between campaigning and official duties, often using the inauguration of state development projects to demonstrate the material benefits they could bring to supporters. At a CDP rally in Kaya, party speakers portrayed recent projects financed by the government and donor agencies as if they were Compaoré's personal contributions. "Blaise Compaoré, we are grateful for the dam," proclaimed one placard. Said another: "Thanks to Blaise Compaoré for the rural road—all of Kaya will vote for Blaise Compaoré."[70] Alternatively, some candidates threatened to withdraw funding from constituencies that voted heavily for opposition candidates. Many residents of Koudougou, which long had a reputation as a rebellious city, believed that the closure of a textile plant and paucity of new projects were forms of political punishment. When Compaoré held a campaign rally there during his 2005 re-election bid, the crowd's initial response was tepid, but became more animated when he cited the opening of a new university campus, the paving of roads, and the possibility of a new textile factory. On election day he carried the city with 73 percent of the vote.[71]

Many pro-government campaign events were lavish affairs, with music, T-shirts, and other festivities that projected imagery over substance: "American-style" campaigning, as the authorities called it. The evident extravagance prompted speculation that the ruling party must have budgeted more than CFA1 billion for Compaoré's 2005 campaign. Salif Diallo, the CDP's campaign manager, jokingly "denied" that allegation, reporting that the party actually spent only CFA983 million.[72] That amount was eighty times the campaign spending of the second-place finisher. In addition, the CDP's own campaign spending was supplemented by the use of state transportation and facilities and extensive in-kind support provided directly by associations of traders and other businessmen who flooded the country with T-shirts, caps, and fabrics bearing Compaoré's image and the CDP colours.

Some campaign support groups were highly personalized, with names such as the Friends of Blaise Compaoré, Association of Blaise Compaoré Youth, and so on. By 2008 those organizations were incorporated into a more centrally directed group called the Associative Federation for Peace and Progress with Blaise Compaoré (FEDAP-BC), initiated by the president's brother François and heavily funded by some of the country's richest businesspeople.

During and between elections, the regime was also surrounded by a constellation of small allied parties. Initially just half a dozen, they styled themselves the "presidential current," thus signalling their support for Compaoré if not necessarily for the CDP. They later formally constituted themselves as the Alliance des partis et formations politiques de la mouvance présidentielle (AMP), increasing in number to about two dozen. Most such parties were very small, with no parliamentary representation or at best a handful of deputies. Some were launched by defectors from the CDP or originated from splits in other parties. For Compaoré, the AMP parties served several useful functions: at election time, their backing enabled him to present his campaign as a pluralist one, with support from many more groups than just the CDP. In some localities where the CDP was less-than-popular, they could mobilize additional votes or provide junior coalition partners. In government, the appointment of one or more AMP leaders as cabinet ministers helped blunt the appearance of overwhelming CDP dominance. In the National Assembly, their deputies, who almost always sided with the government, provided extra votes for key legislation. Finally, just as the AMP sometimes operated as a refuge for losers in the CDP's internal factional battles, it could function as a landing pad for defectors from the opposition. A former opposition figure might not find it politically expedient to join the CDP outright, but could move closer to the centre of power by joining the AMP.

## A FRAGMENTED OPPOSITION

The multiplicity of parties that gravitated around Compaoré was mirrored by an even more fragmented political opposition. Even in the 1990s and 2000s there were dozens of legally recognized parties that more or less opposed the governing elites. By 2012, when the designation of "opposition" became more formalized, the number of parties identifying themselves as such stood at forty-four. A few had some presence, principally in the main cities or perhaps in the home province or region of their central leader. But most were very small, with no parliamentary deputies or just a few local government councillors. Their fortunes fluctuated greatly. At times, one or two parties seemed to do rather well at the polls, gaining enough votes to secure a voice in the National Assembly and even win control of a few municipal councils. But then their momentum quickly stalled as internal disputes tore them apart or voters deserted them at the next election. Compared with the solidity of the state-anchored CDP, the opposition parties were poorly structured, perennially short of resources, and only weakly rooted on the ground. They could not promise their followers jobs or other material perks. While several put forth lucid critiques of the existing system, as a group they offered no coherent vision for the future.

At its broadest, the Burkinabè opposition was exceptionally diverse in ideology and political strategy. The more radical parties opposed the CDP government's neo-liberal economic policies and had only limited faith in the electoral system. They therefore combined election campaigning with support for struggles by non-parliamentary groups. At times of extensive popular agitation, they were sometimes able to capitalize on their links with the movements in the streets to make advances at the ballot box.

The opposition also included a sizeable moderate wing. As proponents of liberal ideology, those parties were less critical of the government's economic policies, except to sometimes suggest that they did not go far enough in opening markets and jettisoning state intervention. Nor did they try to ally with protest movements. Their primary focus was electoral. Sometimes their electoral successes induced Compaoré to offer a few of their leaders government positions, which they often accepted. A state foothold gave them limited access to patronage resources, which in turn provided additional leverage for future election campaigns. But government participation had other consequences as well. It sometimes worsened the parties' internal faction fights, if not over the principle of participation, then over who gained access to the patronage. It also undercut the parties' claims to opposition status. They appeared less as critics of the political system than as supplicants for inclusion. That perception tarnished the public image of the opposition as a whole, especially since figures from some of the radical parties also occasionally accepted cabinet posts.

Although there were other groups that were open to cutting deals with the government, the main ones came out of the RDA tradition. In the early 1990s they operated as two separate parties, one called the RDA and led by Gérard Kango Ouédraogo and the other the ADF, led by Hermann Yaméogo. After the two merged in 1998 into the ADF-RDA, Yaméogo became its central leader, while the elderly Ouédraogo went into partial retirement. By that point, Yaméogo had already distinguished himself as an especially mercurial politician, repeatedly shifting back and forth between the government and opposition. Eventually, the authorities concluded that he was too unreliable, dropped him and his colleagues from the cabinet, and threw support behind the ADF-RDA deputy leader Gilbert Ouédraogo (son of Gérard Kango Ouédraogo) in a takeover of the party leadership. Under Gilbert Ouédraogo, the ADF-RDA adopted a more consistently accommodating stance by declaring support for Compaoré's 2005 re-election and abandoning any pretence of belonging to the opposition. Although the party was brought into the government with two ministers, including Ouédraogo, it ran separately in the subsequent legislative and local government elections, performing relatively well. The ADF-RDA campaigned for Compaoré's re-election once again in 2010 and remained in government until 2013.

Other parties maintained a clearer oppositional stance. They competed in elections as best they could, sometimes actively allied with protest movements. They essentially saw their role as opposing the government, not trying to become part of it. From the mid-1990s through much of the 2000s the largest was the Parti pour la démocratie et le progrès/Parti socialiste (PDP/PS), headed by renowned historian Joseph Ki-Zerbo. A long-time pan-Africanist and social democrat, he was an especially eloquent critic of the Compaoré regime. The authorities more than once sought to bring PDP/PS leaders into the cabinet, but Ki-Zerbo consistently refused, insisting that "in principle" opposition parties should not take government posts.[73] Following the Zongo assassination, Ki-Zerbo became a major figure in the protest collective. The stance of the PDP/PS stance attracted more voters disgusted by the regime's human rights abuses and the opportunism of the other parties, enabling it to win ten seats in the 2002 legislative election. Subsequently, however, the party suffered a string of reverses: the departure of several talented younger leaders, Ki-Zerbo's declining health and decision to hand leadership over to a less charismatic party veteran, and finally his death in 2006. The parliamentary election the following year saw the PDP/PS reduced to just two deputies, and in 2012 it won none at all.

There were other left-leaning parties as well, some more ideologically radical than the PDP/PS. The PAI actively supported labour, student, and other protest movements and was able to win a handful of legislative seats. It suffered a serious split in 1998, however. One wing, under former trade unionist Soumane Touré, reached an accommodation with the government and took up a couple of cabinet positions. But the other wing, led by Philippe Ouédraogo, remained a consistent force in the radical opposition. In the 2010 presidential election its candidate, Arba Diallo, came in (a far-distant) second.

Also consistently in opposition were most of the parties that regarded themselves as "Sankarist," that is, following the revolutionary ideals of the late Thomas Sankara. The first ones arose in the 1990s and were very active in the protest movements following Zongo's killing. In the 2002 election four Sankarist parties won a total of eight legislative seats. They were subsequently able to retain half a dozen or so deputies, most under the banner of the Union pour la renaissance/Parti sankariste (UNIR/PS), headed by Bénéwendé Sankara, a labour-rights lawyer (but no relation of the late president). In the 2005 presidential election he stood against Compaoré, coming in second. In the 2010 presidential poll he came in third (although with a higher vote total than in the previous election). From 2009 to 2012, Bénéwendé Sankara was the official head of the parliamentary opposition. The electoral impact of these Sankarist parties, which together generally polled under 10 percent of the vote, was handicapped by fragmentation and factionalism, as well as a public impression that not all their leaders were motivated by revolutionary ideals. Yet as a broad current, Sankarism was not limited to the electoral arena. Numerous Sankarist youth groups and "study circles" emerged, generally operating autonomously from the registered Sankarist parties.

On issues of common concern, such as electoral fraud or political repression, the opposition parties usually were able to come together. At times they set up structures to coordinate their activities. But such collaboration usually broke down over ideological, personal, historical, and other differences.

While the opposition's tendency towards fragmentation reflected its own weaknesses, the government and CDP did whatever they could to push things along. That included selective repression of the more radical currents, offering posts to the moderates, and openly or tacitly siding with one faction or another in internal conflicts. Sometimes the authorities handed out money to stoke opposition rivalries. In 2005, several months before the presidential election, one of the opposition candidates, Laurent Bado, revealed publicly that a small alliance he led had accepted CFA30 million from an unnamed emissary of Compaoré. That revelation reinforced the popular impression that most politicians, whether in government or in opposition, were corruptible. Salif Diallo, without specifically acknowledging involvement in the Bado scandal, later admitted that he had intervened in opposition affairs on the government's behalf: "From time to time, if we could accelerate their [the opposition parties'] internal decomposition, we did it, naturally. Personally, I can't say that I'm as white as snow in this kind of situation."[74]

## CHANGE IMPOSSIBLE?

For several years during the turbulence following Zongo's assassination, Compaoré and the CDP seemed to be on the defensive, first conceding the possibility of major reforms in the political system and then losing ground in the 2002 legislative election. For the radical opposition parties, the situation appeared somewhat more hopeful than it had since the start of the Fourth Republic. They optimistically named their electoral pact for the 2005 presidential election "Alternance 2005," using the common French term for a political alteration or shift from one regime to another. But Compaoré's confident decision to run for re-election and the resurgence of the CDP's power more generally spread disillusionment. Both among Burkinabè political activists and domestic and foreign academics, the Compaoré system appeared more unassailable than ever. A sense of fatalism set in. That pessimism was reflected in the title of a 2006 issue of the leading French African affairs journal *Politique africaine*: "Burkina Faso: l'alternance impossible." While understandable, that view stemmed from a narrow focus on the main state institutions and formal electoral process. While many of the contributors to *Politique africaine* were well aware of the contradictions in Compaoré's system and the vibrancy of those currents not caught up in its patronage net, the persistence of Compaoré's dominance nevertheless contributed a static outlook to most analyses at the time.

The next chapters of this book (obviously benefiting from hindsight) concentrate on how the seemingly solid pillars of Compaoré's system came under challenge from wider social and political trends. Economic change, especially the traumatic pursuit of market liberalization, generated new social grievances. State elites, less certain of their tenure, became increasingly predatory, focusing more on their own self-enrichment than on supplying their patronage distribution channels. As the state itself became larger and more institutionalized, its capacity *as a state*—rather than as a collection of informal networks of patronage and coercion—also grew stronger. In the process, some actors within the state moved away from personalist practices and became increasingly professional in conduct and outlook, reducing their links to the dominant patronage networks.

Finally, popular grievances adjusted their focus more directly on the state itself. Rather than operating as clients appealing for assistance from some high-level patron, more people acted as citizens, taking their claims straight to the central state authorities or to local government representatives. As Tilly noted in relation to the rise of more centralized states out of Europe's old systems of royal and aristocratic patronage, increasingly diverse sectors of the population made "demands that the state offer rewards or mete out punishments."[75] In the wider system, the main framework for bargaining shifted from *within* patron–client networks to broader arenas of social and political struggle, with collective claim-making on the rise and growing numbers of citizens becoming actively integrated into public politics.[76] Ultimately, political change ceased to be an impossibility in Burkina Faso, but became the reality.

# 10
# ENRICHMENT IN A LAND OF POVERTY

In the early 1990s the Compaoré government, following many others in Africa, joined "the bandwagon of liberalism," in the words of Zéphirin Diabré, who served for several years in various economic positions, including as minister of economy and finance. Liberalism, as he understood it, had a dual aspect, "aimed at both installing democracy and achieving economic transformation."[1] In this, Diabré was in accord with the ideological pronouncements of the main Western donor governments, which presented democracy and free markets as not only interlinked but also mutually reinforcing. From that perspective, holding multi-party elections and adopting "structural adjustment" programmes promoted by the IMF and World Bank went hand in hand. Across the African continent, as one scholar put it, there appeared to be "a broad-front liberalization, political as well as economic," an "integral liberalization."[2]

While the degree of compatibility of those processes was questionable,[3] in Burkina Faso the government's approach to economic liberalization in a certain sense did match its political practice. The authorities adopted the standard discourses of democratization and structural adjustment. Yet in reality the regime's pursuit of "liberal" economic policies was as grudging and inconsistent as its embrace of multi-party elections. Any measures that threatened ruling elite interests were ignored, subverted, or only partially implemented. The formal economic consultations held every few months in Washington, Paris, or Ouagadougou were something of a shadow play, with Burkinabè officials readily agreeing to whatever new policy prescriptions the donor institutions put forth. Backstage, meanwhile, the president, his family, key business allies, and leading politicians seized the new opportunities offered by economic liberalization and lax state regulation to amass notable fortunes—in one of Africa's poorest and least developed countries.

## ADJUSTMENT, AID, AND CONDITIONALITY

Because of the Sankara government's antipathy to the market liberalization policies of the international financial institutions, Burkina Faso had stood aside as one African government after another accepted IMF-financed structural adjustment programmes. But in the aftermath of the 1987 coup the government's financial position deteriorated and the authorities concluded that they needed a solid aid pipeline. The government first requested IMF support for an agricultural loan in 1988, but it was not until March 1991 that a comprehensive $31 million agreement was signed with the fund, followed by $80 million from the World Bank and $18 million from France.[4] That policy shift and infusion of cash came just as Burkina Faso's political system was undergoing its transition towards an elected, constitutional republic.

With its structural adjustment agreement in hand, the government gained additional bilateral financing from major Western donors. Burkina Faso soon became one of Africa's most favoured aid recipients. Over 1991–95 total aid receipts averaged about $450 million a year, with France generally accounting for about one-fifth. In 2013, Compaoré's last full year in power, total foreign grants reached $658 million.[5] Approval from the IMF and World Bank was also key to eligibility for debt relief, beginning with generous rescheduling of debt payments by official creditors in 1991. The IMF and World Bank agreed in 1997 that Burkina Faso would become the second African country (and third worldwide) to benefit from their Heavily Indebted Poor Countries initiative, as long as the government continued to implement agreed economic reforms.

Conditions were standard in virtually all agreements. Domestic critics saw in that a loss of national sovereignty. Opposition leader Joseph Ki-Zerbo sarcastically commented: "We take our instructions from the IMF and World Bank like the good pupils we are."[6] In practice, the donors were not always insistent on strict implementation of their conditions. So long as the economy registered reasonable growth rates, lapses, sometimes even major ones, were readily overlooked.

The precise policies in those programmes tended to shift over time, just as their names kept changing. But certain elements remained constant, such as reducing budget deficits and pursuing "sound" fiscal policies. Achieving those goals entailed widening the tax base (including by introducing a regressive value-added tax), containing the public sector wage bill (often leading to conflicts with the unions), and slashing "non-essential" state spending (frequently for social services).

## FROM PUBLIC TO PRIVATE

One dominant thrust of the adjustment programmes was to reduce the role and size of the public sector in favour of private market activities, based on an underlying assumption that African states were generally too large and intrusive. In Burkina Faso, that first meant avoiding significant new public investments. When the National Planning Council unveiled a five-year development plan in March 1991, the same month the first IMF adjustment deal was signed, projected investments had been scaled back to $1.8 billion, from $3.6 billion in an earlier draft.[7]

Most state-owned enterprises were flagged for sale or liquidation. During the first phase of privatization, eighteen firms were sold by the end of 1997. Six went to foreign interests at very low prices, prompting opposition parties and unions to call it a give-away of the "national heritage." The sale to Burkinabè investors of the twelve other enterprises stoked nearly as much criticism, since they were sold through restricted bidding to businesspeople close to the CDP. Surprisingly, a 1996 parliamentary commission of inquiry, chaired by the head of the CDP's legislative bloc, agreed that the handling of those privatizations "was often discriminatory," possibly involving "both active and passive corruption."[8]

Partly because of such problems, the government paused for a while. But under insistent pressure from the Washington institutions it then put up for sale several large state-owned enterprises, including a textile factory in Koudougou, a sugar complex in Banfora, and the national telephone company. As of 2001 another dozen state firms had either been sold or were in the process, while eight more were slated for liquidation because they failed to find buyers. By 2010 the privatization programme was essentially completed, leaving only thirteen state-owned firms in operation.

According to the neo-liberal ideology that informed structural adjustment programmes, reducing the public sector should have been sufficient to encourage private entrepreneurship and market expansion. Deregulating the economy was thus the focus, including through liquidation of the domestic grain marketing enterprise, abolition of all import restrictions, and elimination of price controls on most domestic and imported goods. Many Burkinabè businesses were not in a position to take advantage of the new market openings, however. Historically, indigenous private capital was very limited and the tiny business class (mostly merchants, but also a few manufacturers) had developed mainly thanks to its links with the public sector.[9] Those businesses were abruptly exposed to the full force of market competition. The drastic reduction of protective tariffs left domestic manufacturers vulnerable to a sudden influx of cheap foreign goods. Since they were small and weakly capitalized, they could not quickly adjust.[10]

Deregulation and lax customs enforcement also favoured rampant smuggling, often of very cheap, shoddy, and even counterfeit goods. The main consumers' protection association and even the National Assembly warned repeatedly that domestic markets were being inundated with dubious, unsanitary, and even toxic food, medicines, and other products.[11]

When the government consulted with businessmen, it heard many of the same grievances aired by private entrepreneurs everywhere: excessive taxation, restrictive customs regulations, the high costs of electricity and other factors of production, tardy government payments for public contracts, and seemingly endless red tape and bureaucracy. There was also anger over inequities in how the authorities dealt with private businesses. Although tax collection from the largest enterprises was notoriously lax, smaller businesses bore the brunt of occasional enforcement campaigns. Tax raids on market vendors sometimes led to physical confrontations between retailers and municipal police. Many businesspeople believed there were political biases, with those closely connected to the CDP or with the resources to bribe tax or customs officials easily able to evade their obligations, while everyone else had to pay or face punitive sanctions.

## RURAL INEQUITIES

The decline of manufacturing in urban areas was partially offset by an increase in trade and other services. But for more than 80 percent of the population, agriculture, livestock herding, and other rural production remained the mainstay. The Compaoré government, echoing the developmentalist language of the 1980s, still occasionally justified its overall austerity by claiming it needed to shift scarce resources from "privileged" urban areas to the neglected countryside. That neglect was real. Farmers frequently cited such problems as a lack of roads, potable water, health care, or affordable farming inputs.

A variety of rural development programmes were launched, often with donor funding, to address some of the shortcomings. Certain rural sectors appear to have benefited. But with marketing systems liberalized and most credits and inputs going to commercial producers, the impact was uneven. Those who already had some wealth, were near irrigation projects, or had access to official suppliers or market outlets realized the greatest gains. The rest continued to struggle. Overall, just 36 percent of households were able to use agricultural extension services and less than a third owned a plough or traction animal. Very few food farmers could afford fertilizer, so their yields were low. Without irrigation, their crops were entirely dependent on rainfall. Landholdings remained highly fragmented. The typical extended household farmed 9.6 separate plots of land, averaging 0.4 hectares each. They had difficulty growing enough food, especially when rain came late or not at all.[12]

While ignoring rural inequities, the pronounced market orientation of official policy favoured commercial crops and larger-scale farmers. The most notable example was the revitalization of the cotton sector. Cotton output had slumped during the early 1990s, leaving Burkina Faso only the thirteenth producer in Africa. But thanks to significant new investments in feeder roads and ginneries, steady increases in the official producer price, and ample credits for fertilizer, insecticides, and high-yielding seeds, production reached a peak of 740,000 tonnes in the 2006/7 season, the highest for any African country that year.[13]

The central institution in this push was the Société des fibres et textiles (Sofitex), which provided seed, fertilizer, and other inputs to farmers and marketed and ginned their crops. Originally, the government owned 65 percent of Sofitex, with the remainder held by a French company. In the privatization drive the government ceded a 30 percent stake to the cotton farmers' association in the early 2000s, thus reducing its own share to a minority. Around the same time, Sofitex lost its national monopoly on cotton marketing with the emergence of two smaller companies (one French- and one Swiss-owned) in new cotton zones in the central and eastern parts of the country. Then in 2006, with cotton output skyrocketing, both the government and the farmers' association decided to increase Sofitex's capital base eightfold. Since the French shareholder declined to increase its own investment, the government by default again ended up with a controlling interest.

The escalation of cotton output proved unsustainable. Slumping world prices led to lower payments to farmers and thus cutbacks in how much land they devoted to cotton. Total harvests in the 2007/8 and 2008/9 seasons fell to half their peak. That boom–bust cycle highlighted the fallacy of the "comparative advantage" model pushed by the international financial institutions, in which poor countries were encouraged to concentrate mainly on producing raw materials for global markets. Although Burkinabè officials and their foreign financiers often praised cotton as a means of generating national wealth, from a broader development perspective the crop actually proved to be "an engine of immizeration."[14]

Cotton contributed further to rural differentiation. That was most evident between those farmers who grew cotton, and thus earned higher incomes, and those who produced only food crops. Yet there were also inequities among cotton farmers. A few were able to cultivate large areas, owned tractors and other machinery, and hired labourers to work their fields. Meanwhile, the vast majority of the approximately 2 million rural Burkinabè whose families grew at least some cotton toiled on much smaller farms, borrowed to obtain their seeds and fertilizer, and usually hoped to complete the current season with enough to pay off their debts and perhaps earn a small profit to keep the cycle going.

Such divisions were reflected in farmers' organization. Sofitex initially promoted new "professional" cotton producer associations. Unlike earlier *groupements villageois* (village associations), they consciously did not address the broader concerns of rural communities, but only the immediate economic interests of cotton farmers. From the company's perspective, that ensured that credits and subsidized inputs to cotton farmers were not used for other activities (such as growing food) and that their income from cotton would enable them to repay their loans. In 1998 those cotton producer groups federated into a new Union nationale des producteurs de coton du Burkina (UNPCB). On its face, the UNPCB emerged as one of the country's most important civil associations, with a large membership and significant financial resources. But it had a dual nature: the official voice of cotton farmers but also a major Sofitex shareholder and thus part of its management structure.

When Sofitex began promoting the widespread use of genetically modified (GM) cotton seeds in the late 2000s, the UNPCB supported the drive, despite misgivings by environmentalists and some cotton farmers themselves. In 2006, a small agricultural workers union held a May Day march in Koumbia, in the western province of Tuy, to protest against the introduction of GM cotton. It attracted many cotton farmers unhappy with the UNPCB leadership, which they accused of favouring richer farmers, rather than small-scale producers. "We refuse to continue working to enrich the UNPCB leaders," declared Almoussa Walahou, leader of a women farmers' group.[15]

Over the years, cotton farmers (whether loyal to the UNPCB or critical of it) raised many other grievances, usually directed against Sofitex or government policies. When Sofitex officials toured the western cotton zones in 2009, they encountered widespread disillusionment and scepticism, complaints about unpredictable farm-gate prices, and high farmer debts.[16] As the official media itself acknowledged, farmers were experiencing a "crisis of confidence" in the crop.[17] That outlook would ultimately contribute to an unprecedented revolt by cotton farmers just two years later (see Chapter 12).

## NOT ALL GLITTER

It was long known that Burkina Faso had gold deposits. A state-run gold mine opened in Poura just before independence, closed in 1966, and then reopened in 1982.[18] It produced about a tonne of ore annually and was slated for privatization, but poor management, ageing equipment, weak international gold prices, and a lack of interest by potential buyers led to its ultimate shutdown in 1999.[19]

The authorities then sought to attract foreign investors. They revised general investment regulations and amended the mining code so that corporate and dividend taxes were notably lower than in a dozen other African mining countries.[20] The incentives prompted a boom in prospecting ventures, which discovered significant deposits across much of the country. Within just a few years, from 2007 to 2013, six industrial-sized mines began pouring gold ingots. They included the Canadian-owned Essakane site, with estimated gold reserves of 120 tonnes, a "world class" mine, as Minister of Mines Kader Cissé termed it.[21] By 2013 total gold output reached 39 tonnes, making Burkina Faso the fourth biggest gold producer in Africa.[22] That same year the Perkoa zinc mine, one of the world's largest, also began producing. A small manganese mine opened in 2010 and investors looked closely at the major manganese deposits near Tambao, in the far north-east. Prospecting ventures were launched to determine the extent and quality of nickel, copper, uranium, bauxite, and other deposits.

In macro-economic terms, mining's impact was staggering. By 2009 the value of gold exports for the first time surpassed that of cotton, according to Cissé transforming Burkina Faso from just a potential mining country to "a mining country, full stop."[23] As of 2013, gold accounted for 71 percent of all export earnings, and despite the relatively light taxation levels, 16 percent of government fiscal revenues. Yet because of lax regulation, fraud, corruption, unpaid dividends and royalties, and other management shortcomings, actual state income from mining was far below projected levels, a shortfall of at least $638 million between 2005 and 2015, according to a parliamentary inquiry.[24]

Nor were the benefits of mining evident from a development perspective. The IMF observed that "investment and spending capacity constraints have limited the extent to which these [gold] revenues have translated into additional development spending." The sector itself operated as an enclave, largely isolated from the rest of the economy. The biggest companies were foreign-owned, sometimes with minority private or public Burkinabè shareholders. The large formal mines together employed at most 9,000 employees directly (with most Burkinabè in unskilled and low-wage positions), and provided livelihoods to another 27,000 people indirectly, mainly in transport. By contrast, informal artisanal gold mining—largely by individual diggers and small groups of unregistered miners—employed an estimated 700,000 people directly (with much of their output sold through unofficial channels and thus beyond the reach of the state's tax authorities).[25]

Many new mining sites were in areas that previously had little economic activity except for farming or livestock herding. Their sudden appearance was traumatic. Although operating on a smaller scale than the large industrial mines, artisanal mining was no less disruptive, partly because much of the work at the approximately 600 informal sites was unmonitored by official safety and other regulators. Artisanal mining provided temporary jobs and incomes for many, but also seriously harmed the environment through the diversion of water sources and pollution from cyanide, mercury, and other hazardous processing chemicals.

Hardly a month went by without protests in communities near artisanal mines. In May 2010 a coalition of twenty civil society organizations, trade unions, and traditional chiefs marched in the south-western town of Diébougou to support a municipal council ban on artisanal mining and denounce its harmful social and environmental impacts.[26] The following month a large crowd of armed demonstrators converged on Gaoua, also in the south-west, directing much of their anger against a municipal police force perceived to be in league with artisanal miners. According to Maxime Kambou, a spokesman for the protesters, townspeople were against artisanal mining because of its "harmful consequences at all levels: education, health, environment, and even security."[27]

Many Burkinabè were aware of the vast wealth generated by mining, and often regarded the subsidiary benefits they received as far too little, expressing displeasure through the media and collective action. After construction began on the large zinc mine in Perkoa, the project stoked a severe political crisis in

August 2007 in the nearby provincial capital, Réo, partly out of dissatisfaction with the company's hiring practices and political favouritism in the mayor's handling of potential revenues for local communities.[28] Some protests turned violent. In September 2011 several hundred villagers attacked the facilities of a small Russian-owned mine in Pelegtanga, north-west of Ouagadougou, leading to serious damage. The protesters expressed fears over the use of cyanide in processing mine tailings and thought the company's local hiring and community investments were insufficient.[29] A few months later, in March 2012, youths in Dori blocked major roads to all trucks belonging to the Essakane mine 80 kilometres away, complaining about hiring practices and environmental risks. The action was broken when security forces attacked.[30]

## CRONIES, FRAUDSTERS, AND THE CORRUPT

In market systems, the better-off normally benefit disproportionately from new opportunities. The Compaoré government's policies did favour those layers. But there was a particular hallmark of his regime: those who were closest to the centres of power, whether in business or high office, got the most. As in other countries where access to state institutions is the main avenue for accumulating wealth, a form of crony capitalism developed. Much transpired in the dark, behind masks of state modernity and good governance. Ordinary citizens could only dimly perceive such dealings. As Dramane Ouattara, a farmer near the western village of Péni, put it after Compaoré's ouster: "Things happened in the shadows, and the country's money was spent in unknown ways."[31]

Although Compaoré's fall would later lift a corner of the veil, some of the leading personalities involved in dubious transactions were already well-known. They represented several key categories: members of the presidential family who used their influence to engage in nepotism and lucrative business deals; merchants and other businesspeople who depended on political connections to secure contracts and monopoly markets, either on their own or in partnership with foreign business interests, often kicking back "commissions" to individual state officials or in the form of campaign financing for the CDP; wider sectors of the business community that took advantage of lax state regulation, weak revenue collection, and corrupt customs authorities; and countless public employees, from cabinet ministers down to ordinary clerks, policemen, soldiers, and other state personnel, who embezzled funds, solicited bribes, and extorted ordinary citizens. Particular individuals or members of their families might well belong to more than one of those categories, or shift between them over time. Among such elites, any notional distinctions between "public" and "private" blurred completely.

Compaoré, his various prime ministers, and other leading officials occasionally spoke of the need for integrity, free markets, and vigorous anti-corruption measures, especially when addressing donor representatives. But the actual practices of the presidential family sent the strongest possible message to all hangers-on, at whatever level of the hierarchy: that self-enrichment was acceptable and violations of the law would be readily overlooked so long as the perpetrators remained politically loyal.

The most prominent exemplar of the presidential family's economic power was Alizéta Ouédraogo. Although she had already entered business in the late 1980s (with the acquisition of a majority stake in a French furniture marketing enterprise), her meteoric ascent began only after her daughter Salah married the president's brother François in 1994.[32] The following year, as part of the first wave of privatizations, she was among a handful of select buyers, acquiring two state-owned leather and tanning enterprises with financing from Spanish investors and local banks.[33] Thanks to a government-sanctioned monopoly on hide exports, she was able to build up sales to some $10 million a year, mainly to Italian luxury producers such as Gucci. That success eventually helped her diversify into real estate, telecommunications, and construction, with the latter move assisted by another privatization deal. In 2012 a parliamentary commission on public contracting cited Alizéta Ouédraogo's businesses for inordinate construction delays and the questionable acquisition of a contract to supply anti-malarial bed nets. At the time, her firms received some modest fines, but no other sanctions.[34] Four years later a parliamentary inquiry found that real estate companies owned by Alizéta Ouédraogo had irregularly acquired or failed to pay full taxes on more than 80,000 houses or land plots in two districts of Ouagadougou.[35] Cited by some as a symbol of women's entrepreneurial power, others regarded Alizéta Ouédraogo more as an example of "crony capitalism, corruption, environmental degradation, and disregard for workers."[36]

Few other members of Compaoré's immediate family were so directly engaged in business. At least publicly, they focused mostly on their political or administrative activities, although their power enabled them to use their official positions to advance personal and familial interests. Nepotistic appointments were common. During the Popular Front regime, Prosper Vokouma, a cousin, was briefly foreign minister. Towards the end of Compaoré's tenure, a brother-in-law, Lucien Marie Noël Bembamba, served as economy and finance minister and another cousin, Jérôme Bougouma, as minister of territorial administration and security. The president's brother François initially worked behind the scenes as a key adviser, then as head of a pro-Compaoré campaign alliance, and finally as a leading officer in the CDP itself. A sister, Antoinette, was a deputy mayor in the president's hometown, Ziniaré. His wife, Chantal, was most active publicly in a variety of philanthropic and "non-governmental" organizations, enabling her to bestow rewards to supporters in the ostensibly civil sphere.

Given the luxurious residences and lavish lifestyles of members of the "Compaoré clan," rumours abounded about their personal wealth. In addition to a new palace in Ouagadougou, Compaoré had another in Ziniaré. His brother François had his own villas in the two cities, the one in Ouagadougou right across from the main university campus—regarded by many student activists as an especially arrogant display of power. Reinforcing suspicions of hidden fortunes, Robert Bourgi, a former head of Africa policy for the French presidency, revealed in 2011 that five African heads of state had secretly helped finance Jacques Chirac's 2002 campaign. Bourgi claimed that he had visited Compaoré in Ouagadougou to collect four *djembés* (African drums) filled with about $3 million in cash, and then travelled back to Paris in the company of CDP leader Salif Diallo to deliver the drums to Dominque de Villepin, then secretary-general of the French presidency.[37] That money probably was not from Compaoré's personal accounts, however, but from political slush funds similar to those in the CDP's election campaigns.

Up until his government's overthrow, little evidence surfaced detailing the Compaoré family's wealth. In July 2015, however, the High Court of Justice provided a glimpse when it charged Compaoré's cousin Jérôme Bougouma with embezzling CFA3 billion while he was minister of territorial administration and security.[38] The following year a parliamentary commission of inquiry uncovered evidence that speculators had paid more than CFA5 billion to François Compaoré, Lucien Marie Noël Bembamba, and other ministers to secure gold prospecting licences.[39] Another parliamentary commission identified 135 land parcels illegally ceded to the Compaoré brothers in Ziniaré alone.[40]

Just beyond the presidential family were various circles of close allies and collaborators. Of those operating mainly in the business realm, none was more influential than Oumarou Kanazoé. Unlike some other businessmen, he began building his empire under previous regimes.[41] With the advent of the Compaoré government, however, Kanazoé was able to secure an especially beneficial arrangement. His position as president of the Chamber of Commerce made him an invaluable CDP fundraiser. That political clout in turn helped him advance his own business prospects. Over the years Kanazoé secured numerous government contracts to lay or repair major highways, dig irrigation canals, and build conference centres and sports stadiums. By the time of his death in 2011, the turnover of his various Burkinabè companies was estimated at more than $30 million annually, not counting businesses in neighbouring countries.[42]

Djinguinaba Barro was another prominent business crony. Like Alizèta Ouédraogo, he was an early beneficiary of the privatization programme, acquiring the country's largest flour mill and, in partnership with a Côte d'Ivoire company, a food packaging enterprise.[43] Like Kanazoé, he was a key financier and fundraiser for the CDP. That connection enabled his son, Karim Barro, to become mayor of one of Bobo-Dioulasso's administrative districts. As mayor, the son was accused of signing over several large allotments of land to his father in 2012.[44] For that and other suspected irregularities, Karim Barro was among several CDP leaders arrested in Bobo-Dioulasso in 2015.[45]

Alizèta Ouédraogo also benefited from direct government interventions. Following Kanazoé's death and her rise to the presidency of the Chamber of Commerce, the Ministry of Infrastructure rescinded a major road-building contract that had previously been given to the Kanazoé enterprises and assigned it instead to one of Alizèta Ouédraogo's firms. After Kanazoé's sons complained and the Compaoré regime was no longer there, the minister responsible was charged with that impropriety, among other irregular acts.[46]

Besides such active support for key allies, the authorities' generally lax approach to taxation and regulation helped businessmen cut corners and boost profit margins. After Compaoré's removal, a parliamentary commission reviewed his government's accounts for the years 2012–14. It found nearly $200 million in unpaid taxes in that period, the bulk owed by large enterprises. The customs service lost nearly $50 million in revenues, mainly through smuggling and fraudulent import invoicing. Government ministers, parliamentary deputies, and the heads of major public institutions owed more than $75 million on outstanding government loans.[47] The commission's vice-president, Alexandre Sankara, noted that while those who evaded their taxes and customs duties included many small-scale traders in the informal sector, the main perpetrators were large businessmen, the "big hats." They enjoyed "fiscal impunity" through "the protection and complicity of those at the highest level."[48]

Those officials providing the protection often profited handsomely themselves. The most dramatic case was that of Ousmane Guiro, director-general of the customs service. By chance, one of his nephews and several friends were picked up by police on New Year's Eve 2011 on suspicion of theft after an evening of extravagant nightclub spending. They led the police to Guiro's house, where metal coffers containing more than $3.7 million in cash were found. Guiro admitted that the money was his, and a few days later the police arrested him on charges of corruption, money laundering, and illicit enrichment. Although the authorities fired Guiro, they stopped short of bringing him to trial, and he was released for "health" reasons. Nor did the legal cloud hanging over Guiro's head keep the CDP from securing his election to the municipal council of Boulounga, his hometown.[49] Only after the Compaoré government's downfall was Guiro actually tried and found guilty.[50]

Corruption came to be rooted in the very structures of the political system. Permitting a certain amount was politically functional, providing mortar to help hold together Compaoré's patronage machine. Asked early in his tenure about the frequent reports of corruption and embezzlement in Burkina Faso, Compaoré replied, "Is there a government in the world that doesn't have such problems? Even so, Burkina appears a paradise compared to the others."[51] Set against the staggering scale of corruption in some neighbouring states such as Nigeria, the malady may have appeared fairly minimal in Burkina Faso. The country's meagre state coffers provided only limited opportunities for embezzlement, theft, and other abuses, while the country's oft-cited culture of frugality set some social constraints. Yet by the same token, cases of even minor corruption could provoke considerable public outrage. Labour and opposition declarations were filled with denunciations of corruption and the government's failure to act against those implicated. The independent press, which played an important role in exposing some of the scandals, was especially vehement:

> Officials have stolen in the full knowledge and view of everyone. They have become arrogant millionaires in our cities. Acting with impunity, they have an easy time of it ... [and are encouraged by] the policy of laisser-faire, the appeals to all-out enrichment, illicit and unpunished by the regime.[52]

Whatever its actual scale, corruption was generally perceived as serious, and getting worse. In an early survey of nearly 1,000 people in Ouagadougou in 1996, a Burkinabè polling institute asked respondents whether they thought corruption had diminished, worsened, or remained the same over the previous five years. Nearly half, 46.8 percent, felt it had increased.[53] Beginning in 2001, a coalition of civil society organizations known as the Réseau national de lutte anti-corruption (Ren-lac) issued annual reports on the "state of corruption" in Burkina Faso. Combining documentary research with systematic surveys of public perceptions, Ren-lac tracked general trends as well as specific incidents. Each year, big majorities of survey respondents judged that corruption was serious or very widespread and far more thought it had worsened than remained the same or receded. In the report for 2012, for example, 91 percent believed that corruption was frequent or very frequent and 48 percent that it had worsened over the previous year.[54] In some years, nearly half of all those polled said they had personally experienced corruption, such as shakedowns and other forms of extortion by police or having to pay bribes in exchange for urban land allotments or administrative, health, or other public services that were supposed to be free. Ren-lac's reports often ranked the most corrupt public institutions. They included a mixture of those marked by "petty corruption" (such as police, gendarmes, municipal offices, and public services that interacted directly with ordinary citizens) and those engaged in "grand corruption" through their more selective interactions with businesspeople (customs, tax authorities, courts). Among the latter, offices that issued public contracts to private businesses were often seen as the most corrupt, with officials regularly taking "commissions" worth 10 percent or more of a contract's value.[55]

## A TAINTED MILITARY

One major institution was invariably absent from the annual Ren-lac reports: the armed forces. That was not because they were above corruption, but because of the extreme secrecy that generally surrounded military affairs. Only rarely did reports of misdeeds surface. From time to time, disgruntled troops accused senior officers of embezzling funds from supply budgets, training programmes, and bonus payments. During the 1990s, when the military was in charge of regulating the transport of commercial fuelwood, agents of the forestry service reported halting vehicles with military authorization permits but suspected of trafficking wood illegally. Some troops were themselves caught transporting wood without official permission or with expired permits. Alarmed by such practices, the Environment Ministry presented a file on army involvement in the illicit wood trade to a cabinet meeting in 1994, with no government reaction. Three years later the ministry sent testimony, photographs, and other documentation to the National Assembly, again without result.[56]

Although opportunities for military graft were limited within the country, Burkina Faso's covert interventions abroad provided considerable scope for profiteering. Those activities took place under the usual cloaks of military and diplomatic secrecy, in conjunction with Compaoré's clandestine support for various insurgencies, most notably in Liberia, Sierra Leone, Angola, and Côte d'Ivoire. The Burkinabè government had multiple and complex political reasons for its engagements, but senior commanders, foreign affairs personnel, and evidently Compaoré himself were also able to use them for personal economic advantage.

The initial interventions, closely related to each other, were in Liberia and Sierra Leone. Following up on his earlier ties with the Liberian rebel leader Charles Taylor, Compaoré began sending arms and troops to aid Taylor's forces as early as August 1990. The Burkinabè government initially denied military involvement in the Liberian civil war, but as more evidence came out—and reports of Burkinabè casualties spread at home—Compaoré finally admitted sending hundreds of "volunteers" to back Taylor. In 1991 West African peacekeepers intercepted a ship flying the Burkinabè flag off the Liberian coast and discovered on board rubber looted by Taylor's troops from a large Firestone plantation, apparently intended as payment for clandestine arms purchases.[57]

Around the same time, Taylor in turn started aiding the notorious Revolutionary United Front (RUF) rebels in neighbouring Sierra Leone, in retaliation for that country's support for West African peacekeeping forces in Liberia. Sierra Leone's president, Joseph Momoh, declared on national radio that Burkinabè troops were among the units that Taylor sent to back the RUF, and that Burkinabè "operated side by side with the rebels," an accusation that was supported years later by eyewitness testimony during Sierra Leone's post-war Truth and Reconciliation Commission hearings.[58] Even more than in Liberia, the Burkinabè involvement in Sierra Leone had a clear economic motivation. In 2000, a United Nations panel of experts examining violations of an international arms embargo on Sierra Leone reported that the government of Burkina Faso had bought arms from Ukraine, then shipped them to Liberia for delivery to the RUF. In addition to citing an unnamed Burkinabè military officer who served as a key intermediary, the panel found the signature of the presidential guard's Lt Col Gilbert Diendéré on arms purchase documents.The panel reported that diamonds looted from the rebel-controlled areas of Sierra Leone were used to pay for both the arms and the Burkinabè authorities' transhipment services.[59] For many Burkinabè, the findings simply confirmed rumours that had been circulating for some time that illicit diamond wealth lay behind the very visible riches of those close to the president.

The government's assistance to rebels in Angola, a country with which Burkina Faso had few previous engagements, seemed even more closely tied to diamonds. For a time during Angola's long civil war, the anti-government forces of the National Union for the Total Independence of Angola (UNITA), led by Jonas Savimbi, controlled that country's rich north-eastern diamond fields. Barred by international sanctions from acquiring arms and other supplies through legal channels, Savimbi used looted diamonds to purchase them through black market networks. Some passed through Burkina Faso. As early as 1998, reports circulated that UNITA troops were receiving training there and that a Ouagadougou villa previously owned by Chantal Compaoré, the president's wife, was being used by Savimbi's son as a sales outlet for precious metals, in partnership with Alizéta Ouédraogo.[60] In 2000, a UN panel explicitly accused Compaoré, among a handful of African presidents, of violating international sanctions against UNITA by allowing Burkinabè airports to tranship arms bought in Eastern Europe under the cover of Burkinabè end-user certificates. Ouagadougou, the panel reported, had become a "de facto base of operations" for UNITA, with several top rebel representatives holding Burkinabè diplomatic passports and Burkinabè troops providing security for meetings between UNITA delegations and foreign diamond dealers. According to the UN panel, "Savimbi often liked to talk to his close associates about the 'envelopes' he had sent to Compaoré. It is also alleged that in addition to direct personal payments by Savimbi to Compaoré, Savimbi also made substantial contributions to Compaoré's political campaign."[61]

The decade-long civil war that erupted in Côte d'Ivoire in 2002 provided another occasion for money-making, although there the Compaoré regime's involvement was driven more by political considerations. Xenophobic attacks on Burkinabè and other foreign migrants by supporters of Ivorian President Laurent Gbagbo inclined most Burkinabè, across the political spectrum, to side with the anti-Gbagbo rebels who soon controlled the northern half of that country. Some rebel commanders received training at Burkinabè military bases, while arms and other supplies flowed freely to rebel-held zones from across the common border. Such transactions were clandestine because they violated international sanctions on both sides in the Ivorian war. Another UN panel on sanctions violations reported in 2009 that in exchange for arms, Ivorian cocoa and to a lesser extent diamonds were smuggled into Burkina Faso.[62]

## PERSISTENT POVERTY

No one expected that the diamonds brought into Burkina Faso from regional war zones would benefit more than a handful of people. However, according to the neo-classical economic models propounded by the IMF and World Bank, the country's relatively robust economic growth rates should have eventually "trickled down" to ordinary Burkinabè in the form of more jobs, higher incomes, and better access to social services.

Initially, however, fiscal austerity brought a decline in government spending on education, health, and other social sectors. Later, debt relief freed up more money, allowing a 75 percent increase in financing for education between 1999 and 2002, while expenditures for health nearly doubled.[63] In practical terms, much of the money went to hiring and training more teachers and health care professionals and building more schools and clinics. Education indicators showed some improvement, although from levels exceptionally low even in Africa. The primary school enrolment rate rose from just 37 percent in 2001 to 66 percent in 2012.[64] Adult literacy, while still low, also rose, to 34 percent in 2005.[65] With more spending on health care, certain indicators improved there as well, such as a decline in the number of children who died before the age of five from 183 to 102 per 1,000 between 2001 and 2012.[66]

The government and donor officials often pointed to their programmes to promote women's political and social advancement. A 2005 "poverty reduction strategy" report, for example, cited a significant rise in girls' access to primary education, increases in women's literacy, and a notable, though modest, presence in high political positions (as cabinet ministers, members of parliament, and regional governors).[67] While the educational changes could reasonably be attributed to policy initiatives, others reflected historical antecedents and underlying structural factors. The prominent role of women in public life began in the revolutionary era of the 1980s, when women's advancement was a high priority. Also, because of the very large historical out-migration of young males to neighbouring countries, it had long been relatively easier for literate women to secure public sector jobs in Burkina Faso than in many other African countries, with women comprising about a third of all civil servants.[68] While some urban women made notable gains, conditions remained extremely difficult for the bulk of the female population. A 2003 living conditions survey found that female headed households in rural areas had incomes 34 percent lower than those headed by men.[69] Moreover, Burkinabè women had few land rights and virtually no access to formal credit institutions. Female genital mutilation, while formally illegal, was still widely practised in the countryside and forced marriage of young girls was not uncommon. Women made up a disproportionate share of the very poor, in both rural areas and cities.

Poverty, overall, was stubbornly persistent. That was despite a gross domestic product that grew by a 5.9 percent annual average between 2000 and 2013, one of the consistently higher rates in sub-Saharan Africa.[70] It was also despite more than a decade of donor-funded programmes specifically designed to reduce poverty. Based on periodic household surveys, 44.5 percent of all Burkinabè fell below the poverty line in 1994, a proportion that climbed to 46.4 percent in 2003 and then fell slightly to 43.6 percent in 2009—although alternative IMF estimates put the latter figure at 46.7 percent. Rural poverty remained more or less consistent (at just above the 50 percent mark), but the rate of urban poverty nearly doubled, from 10.4 percent in 1994 to 19.9 percent in 2009, reflecting high consumer prices and the decline in formal sector jobs from structural adjustment and liberalization.[71]

To many Burkinabè, the stark contrast between the visible extravagance of the country's social and political elites and the prevalent poverty and suffering of most ordinary citizens suggested an increase in inequality. Among experts, however, there was some debate over the actual extent of the wealth gap, expressed in terms of the GINI index, the most standard measure of income inequality. According to the IMF, the index declined from 50.7 in 1990 to 39.8 in 2009, suggesting a better distribution of wealth. But the UN Development Programme put the country's GINI index at 50.6 in 2003, still ranking Burkina Faso as one of the more unequal in Africa.[72]

Whatever the true measure of inequality, it became a reality in popular political consciousness. Trade unions, civil society activists, and opposition leaders repeatedly highlighted the wealth gap in their public declarations. A few opposition parties warned that regional disparities, including perceptions that the government gave a low priority to infrastructure projects in the non-Mossi west, could foster ethnic resentments.[73] A rigorous public opinion survey conducted in 2012 by the non-governmental Centre pour la gouvernance démocratique (CGD) found a strong correlation between perceptions of inequality and political attitudes. Fully a third of respondents thought that narrowing the gap between rich and poor was the most important attribute of a democracy. Some 42 percent believed that the government was accomplishing that task "fairly badly" and 34 percent, "very badly."[74] The palpable public anger over the contrasting fortunes between rich and poor was captured early on in a declaration by the archbishop of Ouagadougou and nine other prominent Christian leaders: On one side was "the abundance of wealth of a privileged class," in a context of "flourishing corruption, lies, and even waste," while on the other was "the extreme poverty of the many." As a result, the clergy leaders said with alarm, the social climate was "disturbed," with a strong potential for serious conflict.[75]

# 11
# TUG OF WAR WITHIN THE STATE

The corrupt and arbitrary conduct of Burkina Faso's top officeholders made life more difficult for ordinary people, and also prevented state institutions from fulfilling their formal responsibilities. Yet those ills did not prevent the Burkinabè state from continuing to grow, multiply its links with various sectors of society, and in significant respects function as a state.

Most obviously, and despite the cutbacks and austerity of structural adjustment, over time there was simply *more* state. The country's administrative apparatus, ministerial departments, judicial system, and local government bodies grew, in both budgetary resources and numbers of personnel. In 1987, even after the expansion of state services and functions under the revolutionary government, there were still only about 30,000 public servants, equivalent to 3.5 state employees for every 1,000 people, the lowest ratio among eighteen countries in West and Central Africa.[1] By the mid-1990s the number of civil servants had increased modestly, to around 39,000, not counting about 10,000 soldiers.[2] The next two decades brought a significant increase. At the end of 2014, according to an official tally, there were 134,383 public employees.[3] The ratio of civil servants to citizens thus rose to 7.7 state employees for every 1,000 people, still a modest rate, but more than twice what it was in 1987.

State institutions also accumulated more institutional experience and some of those in state employ acquired a consciously professional ethos and outlook. Many embraced the concept of "public service." They believed that they should "unhesitatingly serve the state, not an individual or group of individuals," commented Jean Baptiste Natama, a former revolutionary cadre who later occupied several prominent positions.[4] Whether their perspective was shaped by the country's revolutionary experience or by courses at the national school of administration, they developed a notion of state service oriented towards ensuring the security and needs of the citizenry and nation. Consequently, many were uneasy with the spread of self-serving behaviour among their superiors and colleagues and grew resentful as the political elite routinely violated professional norms and procedures, promoted incompetent cronies over those with real skills and merit, and sullied the reputations of the state institutions they tried to represent. When civil society groups denounced abuses or donor agencies encouraged programmes to improve "governance," they found a ready base of support among those staffing the Burkinabè administration. Sometimes the advocates of efficiency and professionalism were able to push back against a few of the more egregious abuses or carve out small arenas of semi-autonomy.

## POCKETS OF REFORM

This chapter focuses on dissension and reform efforts by actors *within* the state and its institutions. But the political situation on the ground outside was also a major factor. As popular opposition grew in the streets (see Chapter 12) and the regime saw its firm control begin to erode, dissidents within gained more latitude and were inspired to step up their own challenges to corrupt and arbitrary rule.

Many later pointed to the crisis of 1998–99 as a key turning point. The breadth and intensity of the popular reaction to the 1998 assassination of independent journalist Norbert Zongo forced many in state service to rethink their positions. It also threw the government and its more repressive institutions into disarray. Before then, there were "practically no human rights" in Burkina Faso, noted Apollinaire J. Kyélem de Tambèla, a human rights lawyer. But because the authorities were forced to concede some ground, "there were improvements. The press appeared to be freer. Judges had greater liberties. And political organizations and associations began to multiply and operate more freely. The system could no longer control everything."[5]

An early example came in June 1999, when the government appointed a Collège des sages (council of the wise) to examine the roots of the crisis and propose reforms. Human rights activists and opposition leaders were sceptical, since the council was composed of rather conservative figures, including three former heads of state, two traditional chiefs, and six religious authorities.[6] However, the report of the *sages* was not only an "agreeable surprise," but also "audacious" in its analysis and recommendations, observed Valère Somé, one of the initial sceptics.[7] The report argued that the causes of political violence were not conjunctural, but "structural," in that "democratic debate, the exercise of fundamental freedoms, and free elections have been emptied of their content by practices aiming at victory at all costs." The result was a "lack of real democracy." Meanwhile, the *sages* added, social injustice had spread as more and more wealth was concentrated in the hands of a minority, citizens were not equal before the courts, privatization cost many jobs and squandered national resources, and corruption had increased among public officials and those businesspeople who enjoyed their favours. Among other reforms, the council recommended that the constitution's Article 37 reinstate the two-term limit on the presidency, a government of national union be formed incorporating opposition and civil society representatives, and the National Assembly be dissolved to make way for new elections. It even called for the abolition of Compaore's presidential guard, the RSP, which was directly implicated in Zongo's killing.[8] Many activists subsequently cited the council's recommendations to bolster their own demands. The *sages* report was "very advanced," said Ismael Diallo, then a UN official and later spokesman for one of the main civil society coalitions.[9]

The presidential term limit was soon reinstated. Only a passing semblance of a national union government was established, however, since the major opposition parties refused to legitimize the Compaoré regime by joining. Nor were early elections held; voters had to wait until the next scheduled legislative poll in 2002 (when they gave the opposition more seats).

Nevertheless, the momentum for change brought a reconstitution of the body governing elections, the Commission électorale nationale indépendante (CENI). Composed of fifteen members—five from parties belonging to the "presidential current," five from the opposition, and five from civil society—the new CENI had more autonomy from the government than its predecessor. The opposition parties were reassured by the commission's reliance on consensus decision-making (giving them effective veto power) and by the selection of Moussa Michel Tapsoba, a human rights activist, as the commission's president.[10] The CENI was widely credited with gradually reducing fraud, although some perceived Tapsoba as too accommodating to the authorities. In 2011 new CENI commissioners were selected and in turn chose as their president Barthélemy Kéré, a former head of the bar association.[11] Under Kéré the CENI became yet more independent, going so far as to try to bar CDP candidates from running for municipal election because of nomination irregularities.[12]

Because the government relied on donor aid, it was often obliged to launch "good governance" initiatives to project an image of openness and reform.

Such efforts were usually overwhelmed by bureaucratic lethargy and the central authorities' resistance to real reform. One initiative promised to be a little different: the African Peer Review Mechanism (APRM), promoted by the African Union to persuade member states to gradually improve the way they govern. The APRM process generally involved encouraging national dialogues among government officials, professionals, businesspeople, civil society representatives, and unions, under the guidance of respected "eminent persons" from other African countries. Several countries (Ghana, Benin) had already gone through such exercises, to general donor praise. Burkinabè held their own "self-assessment" process in 2007. A dozen civil society representatives were appointed to the national APRM governing council, and Jean Baptiste Natama became its permanent secretary. External APRM experts held meetings in all thirteen regions, involving a total of 5,000 people. A later evaluation identified some shortcomings: the civil society participants were not truly representative and the government's executive played a prominent role in administering the review.[13] Despite those limitations, the process produced a comprehensive report that highlighted many of the country's problems: very little scope for opposition or political pluralism, weakness of the judiciary, rampant corruption, and a wide gap between rich and poor. Although less pointed than the report of the Collège des sages, it still included reform proposals that activists used to back up their own arguments, among them an explicit warning not to tamper with the presidential term limit.[14]

Around that time, new institutions were also created to address corruption. Up to then, the main lead in fighting corruption was taken by the civil society anti-corruption coalition Ren-lac. Its detailed annual reports and surveys of public opinion often embarrassed the authorities, especially since they exposed the weak, half-hearted, and fragmentary nature of the government's own responses. In 2008, however, the government created the new Autorité supérieure de contrôle de l'Etat (ASCE), which absorbed the functions of three prior and separate anti-corruption entities. On paper, the authority was more powerful, since it was explicitly mandated to submit evidence of illegal activities directly to the prosecutor's office.[15] Claude Wetta, a later president of Ren-lac, acknowledged that the ASCE's annual reports brought to light new details about state corruption, but since the head of the agency was appointed by the government it did not have "much autonomy or room for manoeuvre" and hardly any of its revelations led to judicial action.[16] (Once the political blockages of the Compaoré regime were later removed and an activist was named to head the ASCE, the agency was finally able to demonstrate its potential effectiveness.)

## LOCAL GOVERNMENT AND CONTESTATION

At the local level, the evolution of the southern town of Pô could serve as a microcosm of the Burkinabè state. In March 1985 this writer found a town of 10,000 inhabitants that had the legal status of a municipal commune but only a rudimentary administration. That began to change with the advent of the Sankara government, which brought defence committees to each of Pô's six sectors. According to Jean Baptiste Natama, who was sent to Pô as a political mobilizer, the previous town authorities never discussed anything publicly. "Now the people are linked to the government. When we do something, we call a meeting." But facilities remained limited. Natama had to work out of a dilapidated stone building originally constructed for French administrators in 1922 and his sole telephone was almost as old: a wooden box that one had to crank to connect with an operator in the capital.[17]

In 1995, eight years after the end of the revolutionary era, Pô got its first taste of elected local government. As elsewhere in the country, Compaoré's CDP dominated. Not only was the party able to rely on the traditional chief, the Popê, to turn out the vote, but five years later actually chose him as mayor. When some local youths joined the protests against Zongo's assassination, the Popê sent irregular militiamen against them. After a youth was mortally beaten at the royal court, national outrage forced the Popê to resign as mayor.[18] Popular contestation continued, however, eventually weakening the CDP in Pô. After several of its councillors defected to the opposition in 2006, Henri Koubizara, a local leader of the leftist PAI, secured the mayoralty. A heavy-handed intervention to restore the local CDP to power in Pô subsequently backfired, enabling Koubizara to remain as mayor. Burkinabè researchers cited Pô as the first instance of a serious breakdown in the CDP's municipal dominance, yielding "a laboratory of local democratic *alternance*."[19] At the next election in late 2012, the local CDP was reduced to less than a fifth of Pô's councillors.[20]

Usually with less drama than in Pô, towns and rural communes across Burkina Faso gained their own experiences with the government's particular brand of decentralization: formal electoral mechanisms that suffered the same maladies as at the national level, patronage forms of management, fierce factional conflicts, and inadequate financial resources or autonomy to effectively serve local communities.

The national authorities first turned their attention to local institutions in the early 1990s for two reasons: to extend their control throughout more of the territory and to please international donor agencies, which saw decentralization as an ingredient of "good governance" and a way to justify austerity at the centre. The first local elections took place in 1995 in the thirty-three towns that then had official municipal status.[21] The next year provinces were further divided, from thirty to forty-five, in the process upgrading the new provincial capitals to the status of full municipalities. The 2000 local elections were again held only in urban communes (then numbering forty-nine). But in 2006 rural voters for the first time also elected councillors to 302 rural communes (each covering groups of adjacent villages). Those deputies in turn selected from among themselves mayors to head the town and rural communes, as well as councils to oversee the thirteen regions. The authorities presented this as capping a process of "complete decentralization," in which selected administrative functions and basic services were devolved to local authorities in all territorial units, not just urban municipalities.[22]

This expansion created a new framework for the development of citizen consciousness and popular protest. Initially, like most others in Africa, the Burkinabè state was built from the centre. Citizens could only direct grievances at central state institutions in Ouagadougou and a few other large towns. But with the increase in local government bodies, many more people now had targets closer to home. The process in Burkina Faso was thus a reverse of what happened in Great Britain from the mid-eighteenth to the mid-nineteenth centuries, where, as the British state acquired a stronger central executive and Parliament, the forms and targets of popular contention shifted from primarily local ones to those of a national scope.[23]

The supremacy of the national CDP was usually replicated at the local level. As a result, most grievances were directed at the ruling party—and also reflected within it. Numerous factional conflicts erupted among contending wings of the CDP, sometimes leading to violence and even deaths. The authorities' overly ambitious municipal "modernization" schemes also stirred unrest, in turn deepening cracks within local government bodies and party chapters.

In Ouagadougou, a new zone devoted solely to administrative and business facilities in the city centre entailed the displacement of pockets of "substandard" residential housing and informal markets. Residents, many of them Muslim and poor petty traders, staged numerous major protests in 2000–2003, some turning violent, with road blockades, damage to public buildings, and skirmishes with riot police. The authorities ultimately contained the unrest with police repression and concessions to pay more compensation for those relocated.[24]

Arbitrary efforts to regulate, manage, tax, and relocate marketplaces were another recurrent source of conflict. The most dramatic involved Rood Woko, Ouagadougou's large central marketplace, much of which was destroyed by a severe fire in 2003. As rumours spread that the mayor's office intended to use the tragedy to force the market's relocation, merchants—many of them supporters of the CDP—called a mass general assembly in February 2004 to press for Rood Woko's reopening. But riot police broke up the assembly, injuring several. For four days angry merchants set up roadblocks and disgruntled youths in poor districts attacked symbols of government or municipal authority. Burkinabè journalists likened the protests to an "intifada," after the Palestinian uprising.[25] The authorities ultimately gave in and promised to rebuild Rood Woko, although it took more mass protests before the work actually began in 2007.

In informal, unplanned and poorly serviced neighbourhoods across the country, the authorities favoured an urban development strategy centred on granting official land titles. This was welcomed virtually everywhere, since residents saw possession of an official title as giving them greater security of tenure and a marker of their status as city dwellers.[26] But the initial enthusiasm frequently gave way to frustration and anxiety, as land titling exercises were poorly run or bogged down in corruption. The anti-corruption Ren-Lac network highlighted particular problems of fraudulent land operations in Bobo-Dioulasso, leading to confrontations.[27] In a country where rural-to-urban and urban-to-urban migration is common, competing claims over land titles inevitably also spurred divisive discourses of "indigenous" primacy, in which established communities sought to limit the acquisition of land rights by perceived outsiders, contributing to inter-ethnic violence. In the western town of Gaoua local Lobi residents attacked Peulh herders and Mossi gold miners in 2012, causing several deaths.[28] Municipal councillors and local administrators sometimes sought to mediate such conflicts.

With the enhanced role and size of municipal governments, the resources available to even small towns rose markedly. Between 1995 and 1999 alone, the combined budgets of thirty-four municipal councils more than tripled, from

CFA4.3 billion to CFA15.4 billion. Bobo-Dioulasso's budget grew more than five-and-a-half times between 1995 and 2008, and that of the small town of Zorgho in the Central Plateau region by four times.[29] That growth helped finance more municipal services, but also provided new opportunities for patronage, embezzlement, and other improprieties. In 2000, Ren-Lac's survey ranked the urban municipalities as the second most corrupt of ten institutions (after the police and gendarmes), although their standing subsequently improved, fluctuating over the next five years between fifth and eighth place.[30] As popular concerns about municipal corruption grew, so did dissension within municipal councils.

Despite the shortcomings, many mayors and municipal councils acquitted themselves relatively well, providing services as best they could with limited budgets. When confronted with criticism, they often responded with appeasement, compromise, or offers to relay grievances to higher authorities. As local government officials gained more experience dealing with the varied challenges of meeting citizens' needs and expectations, a number saw the wisdom of explaining their policies better or using conciliation rather than force. In Ouagadougou, the mayor, Simon Compaoré, organized public hearings to allow people to air complaints about problematic land titling operations. But not many municipal authorities engaged in regular, systematic consultations with their constituents. One handicap hindering improvements in local government bodies was the wider context. In a national political system marked by semi-authoritarian tendencies, patronage, corruption, and partisan factionalism, there were serious limits to how "good" governance could become at the local level.

## BATTLING FOR JUSTICE

The judicial system provided an especially revealing view of the contradictions in the state apparatus. Its official responsibility was to uphold the rule of law and combat injustice. In certain respects, a judge "was not a dependant of the state, but the state itself, in one of its constitutional organs, the judiciary," commented Guy Hervé Kam, a former judge.[31] Yet the judiciary could not fulfil its assigned role. Poor suspects often felt the harsh reality of the police, courts, and prisons, but those at the top usually enjoyed impunity, breeding popular antipathy towards the judicial system. In 2000, amidst the protests against Zongo's killing, demonstrators burned down the courthouse in Koudougou, Zongo's hometown, and then used the ashes to smear slogans on the remnants, including: "In Koudougou, there is no justice."[32]

The constitution of 1991 had promised something quite different: a modern, professional judicial system. The People's Revolutionary Tribunals of the previous era had already been shut down.[33] In 1995 the Supreme Court was sub-divided into several entities: one to monitor the constitutionality of legislation and certify elections, e to oversee public finances, an appeals court, and finally a high court to try the president and other government officials (which was only installed after Compaoré's downfall). Next in importance were the Tribunaux de grande instance (TGIs) to judge major criminal infractions, commercial disputes, and civil actions. Below them were lower courts for departments and arrondissements to rule on minor infractions.[34] There were also a variety of administrative and labour tribunals, military courts, and courts for children and juveniles. On paper, the judicial apparatus appeared well-developed. But in fact only a few courts functioned in major cities. During the 2000s, the number of TGIs increased from eleven to twenty-five.[35] Yet inefficiency, red tape, and numerous other deficiencies remained. Judicial corruption was cited most often. Ren-lac's anti-corruption surveys ranked the judiciary between the fifth and ninth most corrupt state sector during the first half of the 2000s.[36] The public image of the courts became so tarnished that even the Conseil supérieur de la magistrature (CSM), which regulated court affairs and was chaired by the president, devoted a special session to court corruption.[37]

Alongside corruption and inefficiency, high-level impunity was especially glaring. The most notorious example was the official response to the Zongo assassination. An independent commission of inquiry identified six "serious suspects," all from the elite RSP.[38] In 2000, three RSP members, including Warrant Officer Marcel Kafando, the former commander of the president's personal security detachment, were found guilty in a related case, but during Compaoré's rule, no one was ever charged with Zongo's killing. Nor was there any action on the assassination of Sankara. Lawyers representing the widow, Mariam Sankara, petitioned the courts to open a murder inquiry, but the Supreme Court rejected the request in 2001.

Public disgust over the failings of the justice system was echoed by some legal professionals. In 1997, the national leadership of the bar association drafted a law to standardize the rights and obligations of lawyers. When the government struck out any reference to the profession's "independence" and tried to subject lawyers to regulation by the Ministry of Justice, the president of the bar, Mamadou Savadogo, resigned in protest, followed by the rest of the association's governing council. The lawyers' resistance eventually succeeded in blocking the government's version of the bill, leading to enactment of the bar's own text.[39]

Judges also chafed at government's attempts to undermine their autonomy. According to Guy Hervé Kam, who became a judge in 1996, the judicial system included many "competent judges, honest judges."[40] While some older judges had accommodated themselves to the system's constraints, many younger ones pushed back. In the larger courthouses in Bobo-Dioulasso and Ouagadougou, noted the lawyer Apollinaire J. Kyélem de Tambèla, "it is not rare to find young judges who are motivated, dynamic, and notably more competent than their elders."[41] Those generational differences were partially reflected in the professional associations representing judges. The first had been SAMAB, originally launched in 1983. It suffered a minor split in 1990 that gave rise to the Syndicat des magistrats du Burkina (SMB). In 1999 many younger judges set up the Syndicat burkinabè des magistrats (SBM), with Guy Hervé Kam as its first general secretary.

The SBM became not only the largest judges' union, but also the most active. It conducted a week-long strike in March 2001 to protest at the "pauperization" of judges, despite long-standing regulations prohibiting judges from striking.[42] The SBM accused the authorities of promoting judges who were "corrupt, incompetent, unworthy, and servile," and challenged the executive's dominance of the CSM.[43] In 2003, the SBM was able to gather the signatures of more than 100 judges (out of 300) on a petition pressing for a revision of the CSM statutes to ensure "real independence" for the judiciary.[44]

The authorities refused to budge. Disillusioned, two former SBM leaders, Guy Hervé Kam and Séraphin Somé, resigned their positions as judges at the end of 2006. (Kam and Somé both remained active in the legal profession, as lawyers and consultants on human rights and democracy. Kam and Savadogo, the former bar association president, helped lead a judicial ethics centre to promote integrity in the legal profession.) Kam later explained that he had resigned his judgeship "out of love for the judiciary. I could no longer bear the moral crisis that continues to affect it." Although he and other judges had pressed for change, he ultimately concluded that "the problem with the justice system is not conjunctural, but above all structural. The administrative organization within which they are embedded does not allow judges any chance."[45] In other words, genuine reform of the judiciary would require political change at the top.

Kam's successors in the SBM nevertheless continued to fight, as judges, against government interference, for greater judicial independence, and to insist that high-level perpetrators be brought to trial. Responding to accusations that the SBM was too combative, René Bagoro, the union's second general secretary, said, "To say that we are radicals, hardliners, is relative. We have an ideal, to denounce any irregularity. If that's being radical, then we accept it."[46] In 2012 those judicial radicals scored a rare victory when the then minister of justice, Jérôme Traoré, was forced to resign after ordering the police to detain and beat a young mechanic following a traffic altercation. The resulting public outcry included a joint call by the SBM and SAMAB for Traoré's removal, leading Compaoré to bow to the pressure and dismiss him.[47]

## "KALASHNIKOV CONCERTS" AND COUP PLOTS

Burkinabè in uniform faced many of the same problems as other citizens: high prices, injustice, subordination to corrupt and incompetent superiors, and, if they dared complain, empty promises or repression. But because of the institutional secrecy that surrounded the army, gendarmes, and police, few of their grievances were aired publicly. Only rarely, during sporadic outbursts, could one glimpse the tensions within the security forces or the existence of dissidents who aspired to political alternatives.

The military's long involvement in political affairs left an armed forces that was far from unified and coherent, despite surface displays of discipline and loyalty. As elsewhere in the state administration, some revolutionary minded individuals had survived the purges of the late 1980s and bridled at the country's conservative direction.[48] A few, such as retired Colonel Charles Lona Ouattara, thought the basic problem was the army's politicization, whether before, during, or after the revolutionary era.[49] Some, including Emile Ouédraogo, another retired colonel and former security minister (2008–11), argued for subordinating the army to elected civilian control and combating corruption and favouritism within its ranks.[50]

The way the Compaoré government used the military generated strains among different units, and between the security forces and the public. The clandestine nature of the government's early military support for rebels in Liberia and Sierra Leone not only bred corruption but also resentment over the fact that soldiers who were killed or wounded there were not openly recognized. The special privileges, weaponry, and advanced training of the RSP stirred its own discontents. The suspected role of RSP members in Zongo's assassination reverberated within the military, as some soldiers and officers joined the protests. Among numerous anti-government tracts at the time, one, issued by "a group of officers," condemned military involvement in Zongo's murder and complained that the army, like the CDP and state administration, was afflicted by parallel centres of decision-making, "even civilian ones." To make rehabilitation of the armed forces possible, the statement continued, "the army has to separate itself" from partisan interference.[51]

The next decade saw sporadic protests by soldiers, police, gendarmes, and other uniformed personnel, often over economic or service grievances. In 2005 hundreds of police officers and trainees startled residents of Ouagadougou by marching in protest, in their khaki uniforms, to the national police academy and central police headquarters. They demanded unpaid bonuses, better crime-fighting equipment, and the right to form a union. For challenging the authorities, the trainees were expelled and scores of active-duty police were detained. But public sympathy was squarely on the side of the police and all the labour federations defended them, obliging the government to later reinstate the trainees and release those in detention.[52]

The next eruption, in December 2006, turned deadly. Just before Christmas regular army soldiers fought pitched battles with police and gendarmes in Ouagadougou, after members of the elite Compagnie républicaine de sécurité (CRS) beat a soldier at a music concert. Rank-and-file soldiers attacked the police and CRS headquarters, the offices of Ouagadougou's mayor, the home of Security Minister Djibrill Bassolé, and the central prison, allowing many prisoners to escape. By the time the troops returned to barracks, two police and four soldiers were dead. Within less than a week a series of armed demonstrations swept military bases in Ouagadougou, Kaya, and Bobo-Dioulasso. In addition to firing their weapons into the air—known as "Kalashnikov concerts"—some soldiers submitted written grievances complaining about high prices, the enrichment of their officers, and corruption in the selection of troops for special assignments.[53]

Soldiers renewed their protests in October 2007. Four times that month active-duty and retired soldiers rallied in Ouagadougou and Bobo-Dioulasso, both in uniform and out. The final rally, in Ouagadougou's large 4 August Stadium, drew participants from army bases across the country and included explicit criticisms of the head of the RSP, Gilbert Diendéré. Perhaps most alarming to the authorities, at a rally in Ouagadougou's central square, one soldiers' delegate chanted the trademark slogan of the Sankara era, "La patrie ou la mort," and was answered by his comrades with the traditional response, "Nous vaincrons!" (Homeland or death. We will win!)[54]

The largest and most widespread army protests erupted in March 2011, inspired to some extent by wider protests then sweeping the country (see Chapter 12). The first mutinies, in Ouagadougou and Fada N'Gourma, were initiated by soldiers incensed that some of their fellows were tried by civilian courts for beatings and rape. They not only freed their colleagues and attacked the courthouses, but engaged in widespread pillaging. In the capital they severely beat the mayor, Simon Compaoré, and looted the home of businesswoman Alizéta Ouédraogo, the mother-in-law of François Compaoré. From the end of that month into April, other "Kalashnikov concerts" or mutinies shook Gaoua, Kaya, Koupéla, Pô, and Tenkodogo. There also was a brief but dramatic uprising by rank-and-file soldiers of the RSP itself. They burned down Diendéré's house and fired rockets at the presidential palace, obliging Compaoré to flee the capital. After a month' pause, more mutinies hit army bases in six cities, for the first time including Bobo-Dioulasso, the country's commercial centre. There the uprising turned especially violent, as soldiers looted, shot into the air, and terrorized civilians in both the central business districts and outlying residential neighbourhoods. The government sent in a combined force of the RSP, paratroopers from Dédougou, and a mobile gendarme force to suppress the Bobo-Dioulasso revolt, killing six rebel soldiers. That crackdown, followed by the detention or dismissal of hundreds of mutineers (mostly from military units other than the RSP) succeeded in quelling the army mutinies.[55]

The soldiers' revolts had no central leadership, and the initiative appeared to come primarily from the ranks. The mutinies spread from one base to another largely by example, sometimes after rebellious troops contacted each other by mobile phone. Their grievances were never clearly articulated, but could be gleaned from their actions: looting, which reflected the economic desperation felt by many ordinary troops, and attacks on corrupt or unpopular officers and some political authorities. Public opinion, which initially included some sympathy for the soldiers, faded as the looting and indiscriminate shooting in civilian areas spread. After the first mutinies, Compaoré held closed-door consultations with representatives of the ranks, non-commissioned officers, and officers of all military units. Participants later revealed that the grievances included housing and food allowances, high prices, and problems of command and internal functioning. Compaoré promised to address the complaints and shuffled the commanders of the army, air force, and gendarmerie. The government emphasized the soldiers' economic concerns.[56] The political implications of the uprisings were nevertheless evident to many observers: even the repressive bulwarks of the Compaoré regime were seriously fractured.

More explicitly than in the soldiers' protests, the political cleavages afflicting the armed forces came out during a "coup plot" trial several years earlier, in April 2004. The supposed plot was first announced the previous October, when more than a dozen individuals were detained for questioning, ranging from two commanders and two captains down to several sergeants and ordinary soldiers (mostly former RSP members), as well as two civilians, a Protestant preacher and a prominent opposition figure, Norbert Tiendrébéogo, head of a Sankarist party. From the beginning there was widespread public scepticism, given the country's history of fabricated coup plots, the strange amalgam of defendants, the death in detention of one of the accused, and the fact that the supposed ringleaders had almost no troops under their command. Some saw the case as an attempt to politically smear the opposition, others as a convenient justification for getting rid of General Kwamé Lougué, a relatively popular professional officer who was dropped as minister of defence in a January 2004 cabinet reshuffle because of his ties with some of the accused. The trial itself featured many irregularities: the head of the military court was yet another of Compaoré's cousins and several defendants testified that Diendéré put pressure on them to falsely implicate Tiendrébéogo and Lougué.[57]

On the witness stand, Captain Luther Diapagri Ouali and Sergeant Babou Naon admitted that they had indeed wanted to organize a coup. But since Ouali had left active military service in the 1980s and none of the other defendants held any strategic command positions, the "plot" appeared to be more an idea than an actual plan, let alone a real attempt, as the prosecution charged. As to motivation, Ouali, Naon, and several others cited repeated instances of corruption in the armed forces, as well as in the political system more generally. Some of their grievances stemmed from the military interventions in Liberia. Naon and Corporal Bassana Bassolet had both fought there, with Naon noting that his own brother's body was never recovered and Bassolet accusing Diendéré of "eating" the soldiers' bonuses. Captain Ouali was an early champion of the Liberia veterans' cause.[58]

Most dramatically, several defendants voiced antipathy towards the government's repressive policies and its efforts to use the RSP and other military units against political critics. Naon testified that he was in the RSP at the time of Zongo's killing and that he had directly confronted the president's brother François about it. Captain Ouali said that his hostility to the Compaoré regime began earlier, with the assassination of Sankara in 1987. It then deepened with Zongo's murder. Ouali took part in Zongo's funeral, and as the mourners walked to the cemetery, they prayed for Compaoré's overthrow. "I was in the crowd, in tears, and it was then that the idea came to me to respond to the people's plea … It was a patriotic duty to chase President Compaoré from his armchair."[59]

When the military court issued its judgment, it was a mixed verdict. Reflecting the weak nature of the government case, six defendants were acquitted outright, Tiendrébéogo among them. Three received suspended sentences. Ouali got the most severe sentence, ten years in prison. Another captain received six years, as did Naon, while Bassolet got five.[60] Politically, however, many media commentators and opposition activists regarded it not so much a trial of the defendants as a "trial of the regime."[61] And in their eyes, the government lost badly. Throughout the proceedings audience sympathies were clearly with the defendants, and on several occasions the crowd in the courtroom or listening through loudspeakers outside cheered when the accused told of their desire to overthrow the government.[62] The audience erupted in thunderous applause when Captain Ouali, in his closing statement, referred to his aim to oust Compaoré as a "noble idea."[63]

# 12
# CONTENTION IN THE STREETS

The most explicit and sustained opposition to the Compaoré regime played out in Burkina Faso's streets, schools, markets, and workplaces. Protesters were motivated largely by their own grievances and reacted against perceived injustices spontaneously or following calls to action by trusted leaders and organizers. But they did not mobilize in isolation. Expressions of weakness or indecision by those in authority encouraged potential challengers to turn out in greater numbers than might otherwise have been the case.

Scholars of social movements have often examined how the occurrence, intensity, growth, and outcomes of protest are influenced by the wider political and social context. A regime may be more solid or disunited, closed or open, permissive or repressive, setting broad "political opportunities" that influence the scope available to potential challengers. Assuming that movement organizers carefully weigh the likely benefits or costs of their actions, analysts generally believe that greater repression usually dissuades protest.[1] But indiscriminate or particularly egregious repression might also have an opposite effect, by provoking reactive opposition.[2] Both results were evident in Burkina Faso. The very repressive first decade of the Compaoré regime saw few overt protests, even after the inauguration of a constitution that theoretically provided some space for public expression. Then followed several major waves of protest, often provoked by particularly shocking military or police killings. For the central authorities, cracking down hard became increasingly risky. And dissension within the police and military demonstrated dramatically that they could not even depend on their own security forces. However much they may have wished to suppress dissent, the institutions at their disposal did not always have the necessary coherence or capacity.

Interactions between states and social movements flow in both directions. State capacities and policies set the broad parameters within which activists operate. Yet such political structures may also be weakened or otherwise altered by the "agency" of political actors and movements, including what activists do and how effectively they are able to mobilize large followings.[3] Such dynamic relations constitute a "contentious politics" that shapes the overall and constantly changing political balance.[4]

This politics of contention is also conditioned by historical and cultural factors.[5] Burkinabè have repeatedly drawn inspiration from their particular culture of rebellion, from the 1966 insurrection to the 1983–87 revolutionary era and subsequent struggles. Revolt "is our heritage," commented Fousséni Ouédraogo, a civil society activist who participated in the anti-Compaoré movement. "Whenever someone threatens the people's interests, there are always those who react and say, 'No!'"[6]

The immediate economic, social, and external environments likewise matter. At certain points, abrupt shifts in economic conditions prompted the unions to be less accommodating and generated new grievances among other social sectors, while at the same time depriving the authorities of resources to sufficiently placate or buy off challengers. In the 2000s, with the rise of ethnic tensions and civil war in Côte d'Ivoire, hundreds of thousands of Burkinabè living there fled home. In the short term that enabled Compaoré to whip up nationalist sentiment in his favour, but eventually brought new demands for economic and social support and sharpened conflicts over land rights in western Burkina Faso.[7] From further afield, Western donor officials, embarrassed by the regime's killing of journalists and students, applied some pressure on the Burkinabè authorities to exercise restraint. Meanwhile, as popular movements spread across North Africa in 2011, toppling authoritarian rulers in Tunisia and Egypt, opposition currents in Burkina Faso and across Africa drew encouragement for their own struggles.

On the ground, Burkinabè activists also learned lessons from their numerous failures and occasional successes. Participants in local struggles became aware that whatever their particular grievances—high prices, deteriorating schools, inaccessible health care, police brutality, corruption—those issues often overlapped or intersected. More came to believe that long-term resolution of their specific problems depended on basic changes in the overall political system.

Sometimes consciously, but often by trial and error, organizers and their supporters had to make uncertain choices amidst an often contradictory and shifting reality. How far and in what ways could they push before incurring repression? Who were their potential allies? What methods would yield greater success? Tactical and strategic considerations were often shaped by protesters' particular concerns and organizational forms. Students drew on a standard repertoire of actions, from class boycotts and schoolyard rallies to marches through the streets. Trade unionists declared strikes, staged sit-ins, and marched and rallied. Community members blockaded nearby roads and highways. Civil society groups held press conferences, circulated petitions, and organized public demonstrations.

Since the 1980s Burkina Faso's civic landscape has been marked by a proliferation of organizations. Even the strongest and most structured sector, the labour movement, was fragmented, comprising several competing federations and numerous autonomous unions.[8] With the greater openings provided by constitutional rule, thousands of community, professional, civic, and other social associations were officially registered. On one hand, the seeming cacophony made it easier for the authorities to deflect or ignore their critics individually. On the other, it complicated official efforts at control, co-optation, and repression and gave potential challengers some organizational flexibility. If some groups fell into decline, supporters could form new ones. Formal organizational structures were not rigid. Whatever their stated purpose, many groups took up multiple issues and engaged in varied activities, giving them the "rather hybrid nature" that is typical of social movements in Africa.[9] Nor did organizational boundaries keep groups perpetually divided. At certain junctures they came together in common alliances or fronts, a phenomenon that became especially pronounced as opposition to the government became more widespread.

## LOCAL AND NATIONAL

In Burkina Faso and other African countries where so much power is concentrated in the capital, national protest movements are obviously important. But eruptions of unrest beyond the shadows of national parties or civil organizations also often reveal ordinary citizens' specific concerns and the depth of their anger. As early as the mid-1990s some small-town conflicts grew serious enough to draw national media attention. In Réo villagers sacked and burned a police station after a farmer was shot and killed at a police roadblock.[10] In Fada N'Gourma, youths defied police repression by demonstrating days on end to demand the mayor's resignation over corrupt land allocations.[11] Through such struggles, activists acquired experience that could later carry over to national campaigns. As local agitation became more widespread, it further sapped the authority and legitimacy of the central state. Over time, activism became more geographically dispersed, with demonstrations, rallies, strikes, sit-ins, occupations, boycotts, and other forms of opposition occurring even in the smallest and most remote locations.

National challenges came from two sectors in particular: workers and students. Despite the unions' past militancy, most were nevertheless slow to react to the government's austerity policies, perhaps because some were linked to moderate political currents. Others had different political leanings and were more open to action, including teachers' unions, historically aligned with the oppositionist Joseph Ki-Zerbo. Of the federations, the newest was the Confédération générale du travail du Burkina (CGTB), formed in 1988 and comprising both public and private sector unions. Several top leaders, including the general secretary Tolé Sagnon, reputedly belonged to the clandestine PCRV. When the federation's health workers' affiliate struck in June 1997 over economic demands, Compaoré condemned it as a "political provocation" and ordered the union leaders' dismissal. That heavy-handed response backfired, provoking a national strike that won wide support and obliged the government to back down.[12] As the authorities continued to push austerity and threatened the right to strike, more unions stirred and began exploring common action.

University and secondary students were usually quicker to hit the streets. Unlike the unions, they were centrally organized. The largest university group was the Association nationale des étudiants burkinabè (ANEB). Many members appear to have been influenced politically by either the PCRV or Sankarist ideas.[13] A variety of associations existed in the high schools, but at least in Ouagadougou they operated under a single umbrella. That centralized capacity meant that official student protests could be called on short notice and mobilize impressive numbers. Sometimes students acted over their own grievances, sometimes in solidarity with others, as in 1995 when secondary students demonstrated in support of striking teachers. In that instance, two students were shot to death by police in Garango, prompting yet more protests. The University of Ouagadougou was shaken in 1996–97 by a bitter, two-month student strike, the longest ever, partly over aid cutbacks, but also against several killings of students and professors. Said one student activist: "We see that we are moving towards a total dictatorship ... The students know that if they don't react now, things will only get worse."[14]

## "ENOUGH IS ENOUGH!"

The most dramatic protests against state repression came the following year, in reaction to the assassination of independent newspaper editor Norbert Zongo. Public revulsion was captured by the movement's main slogan: "Trop, c'est trop!" (Enough is enough). Between Compaoré's original coup and his eventual fall from power, the crisis was the country's single most widely reported and analysed political development.[15] Many later referred to the situation "before" and "after" 13 December 1998, highlighting its pivotal role in altering the dynamics of political life. Although the regime was able to regain effective dominance for some time longer, it would henceforth remain weakened and unsure, incapable of asserting its power as arbitrarily and forcefully as before. Some regime allies distanced themselves, and more Burkinabè, among ordinary citizens and seasoned activists alike, became bolder in expressing opposition.

When the body of Zongo, his brother, and two colleagues were found in a burned and bullet-riddled vehicle near Sapouy, 100 kilometres south-west of the capital, the shock was immediate. Zongo was a prominent figure. His weekly *L'Indépendant* had covered popular struggles (such as the student strikes) and was celebrated for exposing misdeeds by the wealthy and powerful. When the driver of François Compaoré, the president's brother, died mysteriously in January 1998, Zongo's newspaper uncovered evidence that he had been tortured to death by the presidential guard, the RSP. After François Compaoré ignored a court summons stemming from the death, Zongo warned of a cover-up. Many Burkinabè thus quickly assumed that Zongo was the victim of a political assassination, a conclusion confirmed when an independent commission of inquiry later named six members of the RSP as "serious suspects."[16]

Zongo's murder was not an isolated case. The human rights group MBDHP issued a tally of 101 people believed to have been the victims of police or other politically motivated killings between 1989 and February 1999.[17] Coming less than a month after Compaoré's re-election, Zongo's killing led many to wonder: what would the authorities do if they felt truly threatened? Who could feel safe?

The assassination, coming on top of growing popular anger over deteriorating living conditions and high-level corruption, was simply "too much," MBDHP President Halidou Ouédraogo told this writer. "Everywhere, in all sectors, people in different conditions, even in the majority party, said, 'No.'"[18]

The initial reaction was largely spontaneous. Two days after the murder, demonstrations broke out in Ouagadougou and Koudougou, Zongo's hometown. They quickly spread, with students and other youths the first to turn out, soon followed by salaried employees, professionals, street vendors, and others. Over the next month and a half large and widespread demonstrations rocked the country, some involving tens of thousands. "People turned out in localities in which they never demonstrated before," observed Halidou Ouédraogo.[19] An opposition round-up of protests *on a single day*, 5 January 1999, cited demonstrations, strikes, or clashes with the police in eighteen different localities.[20] That month saw two three-day *ville morte* ("dead city") national protest strikes, the first one paralysing practically the entire country.

Most protests initially focused on state repression. In reaction to a police killing of an electrical worker in Bobo-Dioulasso in January, his comrades shut down the national power grid. In February several hundred intellectuals marched to condemn killings or dismissals of academics. They called on Burkinabè to "reject barbarism."[21] Women organized their own actions. In April, about 1,000 marched on parliament, dressed in dark mourning clothes and carrying banners reading "Impunity = too many widows and orphans."[22] Protesters raised other political and social grievances as well. Sugar workers in Banfora struck to demand higher wages. Unemployed graduates staged sit-ins for jobs. Uniformed soldiers marched through central Ouagadougou and briefly blockaded the army headquarters to demand housing subsidies.

Although youths spearheaded the movement, older activists and political figures eventually tried to give it some central direction. Opposition leaders spoke at protest rallies, but generally had little influence. The closest semblance of leadership came from a loose coordinating body called the Collectif d'organisations démocratiques de masse et de partis politiques (CODMPP). It included civil society organizations, an alliance of ten opposition parties, women's associations, media and lawyers' groups, student formations, a labour federation, and others, for a total of forty-seven groups by mid-March. One of the collective's most influential components was the MBDHP, the human rights group, which at a congress in May 1999 reported a total membership of 40,000 in chapters across the country.[23] Its main spokesman was Halidou Ouédraogo (who had been a founder of the PCRV, a judge during the Sankara regime, and an adviser to Compaoré shortly after the 1987 coup, before breaking with the regime in the mid-1990s). While the various groups in the collective had different interests, they agreed to focus on justice and rights.[24] Demonstrators' readiness to echo demands for the rule of law and defence of constitutional rights reflected the extent to which such concepts had penetrated Burkinabè society.

Initially, only one union federation, the CGTB, was active in the protest movement. As a CODMPP member, it threw its authority and organizational strength behind the national strikes. Although the five other federations denounced Zongo's killing and many of their members joined the protests, they did not officially endorse the early national strikes. Eventually, economic grievances drew all the federations into a common action, for the first time since 1975, in a two-day general strike in late June 1999 for higher salaries, an end to privatizations, and justice for Zongo. Many individual sectors or enterprises were also hit by labour actions, a veritable "epidemic of strikes" as a local newspaper called it.[25] Teachers, health workers, railway employees, and many others struck or staged sit-ins. After the Poura gold mine, the country's only large industrial mine, was shut down in August, almost the entire work force embarked on a 180-kilometre march to Ouagadougou, but were halted half way by riot police. On the first anniversary of Zongo's death, the CODMPP organized a new round of nationwide marches, rallies, and strikes. Some drew tens of thousands of participants. Periodic mobilizations continued well into the following year.

The actions were mostly peaceful, but sometimes turned violent, especially when security forces or armed CDP supporters attacked. Protesters retaliated by stoning or firebombing houses of CDP leaders and other symbols of power. The head of the anti-riot police wondered whether the country was heading towards an "urban guerrilla" situation.[26] The sheer scope of the protests made it difficult for the government to contain the unrest. Official bans on demonstrations and strikes were routinely ignored. Crackdowns often enflamed popular anger, leading the security forces to begin exercising some restraint.

Meanwhile, the government tried to defuse opposition with compromises and manoeuvres. In August 2000 several of the presidential guards implicated in the killing of François Compaoré's driver were sentenced to prison. Several opposition politicians who had worked with the CODMPP, most prominently Hermann Yaméogo, were given ministerial positions, lending the government a slight appearance of reform. By the second half of 2000, there seemed to be a slackening in the pace and size of the popular movement, especially with the government-ordered closure of most schools disrupting student mobilization.

## CULTURE OF PROTEST

After nearly two years of massive unrest, agitation did not return to its previous levels. An overall climate of endemic protest set in, encouraged by a perception that the ruling elites were vulnerable to popular pressure. Some analysts saw the emergence of a politicized civil society, although highly diverse in its composition and aims.[27]

The well-organized student and labour movements remained prominent national actors. Radical student organizations carried out successive demonstrations, strikes, and class boycotts at the universities of Ouagadougou and Koudougou, while their counterparts in the high schools held sporadic protests across the country, sometimes in conjunction with teachers' strikes. The main union federations now maintained a common front in their negotiations with the government. When talks broke down, the federations repeatedly organized national general strikes—a total of twelve between 2001 and 2007—mostly for higher salaries, an end to privatizations, and lower consumer prices. The latter demand won the unions wide public sympathy, as even the state media acknowledged.[28]

Whether unorganized or in their own local associations, merchants, urban youths, judges, police trainees, civil servants, and other social groups more often aired their grievances in the streets. Some of their leaders had participated in the earlier protests and transferred their knowledge to other issues and targets. Even those without first-hand experience learned from media accounts that public mobilizations could be effective for pressing grievances.

The patterns and practices of protest also spread geographically. While the movement against Zongo's assassination showed that issues of justice had national resonance, the persistence of unrest in small towns and remote localities demonstrated that diverse political, social, and economic grievances could also drive people to act. From 2001 through 2007, available reports in the Burkinabè media confirmed at least 156 protests in twenty-seven municipalities in all major regions, motivated mainly by local grievances and not directly initiated by organized national movements.[29]

Some were clearly prompted, as in Zongo's death, by public revulsion over police and army brutality. In October 2004 youths in Pô protested after a soldier severely beat one of their comrades. In October 2007 1,000 people demonstrated in the village of Pièla and nearby Bogandé over the summary police execution of three residents.[30]

In Banfora, Garango, Niangoloko, Tenkodogo, and other towns, land allocation operations provoked rallies, demonstrations, and marches because of municipal mismanagement, favouritism, or corruption. In Bobo-Dioulasso, where issues of ethnic identity and CDP factionalism were mixed in with land disputes, several lives were lost.[31] The dislocations of urban development also led to frequent agitation. In Banfora, Bobo-Dioulasso, Fada N'Gourma, Koudougou, and Ouagadougou, among other locations, retail merchants protested peacefully or engaged in destructive rioting in reaction to customs raids, new taxes and fees, or attempts to move their markets.

Along with other urban residents angered by high consumer costs, merchants were actors in the "food riots" of February 2008. Anonymous leaflets circulated in Bobo-Dioulasso and other cities urging merchants to strike on 20 February against high taxes and fuel prices. The city's central marketplace shut down as large crowds of petty traders, youths, and other urban poor poured onto the streets. Protesters attacked public buildings, traffic lights, a statue of Compaoré, and other symbols of authority. Almost simultaneously, merchants in the northern town of Ouahigouya closed the central market there and crowds of youths clashed with municipal policemen. The next day, as unrest continued in Bobo-Dioulasso, Banfora was paralysed by a general commercial shutdown. Then at the very end of the month, several poor neighbourhoods erupted in Ouagadougou during a *ville morte* strike against high prices. Protests then spread to Tenkodogo, Gourcy, and several other locations.

Seeking to better coordinate the popular agitation, the major union federations called countrywide demonstrations in mid-March, again drawing thousands onto the streets. There was almost no violence, since the unionists, supported by volunteer student marshals, prevented attacks on property or clashes with police.[32] Under union leadership, a new coordinating body was established, the Coalition nationale contre la vie chère (CCVC). It included opposition parties, human rights groups, and civil society organizations, partially overlapping with the composition of the earlier Zongo protest CODMPP. The CCVC explicitly linked the issue of food prices to other demands: higher salaries, more funding for education, press freedom, justice for victims of repression, and an end to corruption. As one analyst observed, "This framing succeeds in linking more or less all of the relevant issues and actors within Burkina Faso's social movements."[33]

In May 2008 the unions organized large May Day demonstrations around the country, followed two weeks later by another national general strike and mass protest marches that attracted participation from well beyond labour's own ranks. Many marches featured contingents of women banging on empty pots to dramatize their families' plight.[34] Melding political, economic, and social aims, the CCVC proved to be a lasting organizational force, as well as a bridge between the unions and wider currents opposed to the regime and its policies.

As activists gained more experience in the streets and started forging new organizational connections, other changes also strengthened civic activism. In particular, independent media multiplied and became bolder. Several privately run newspapers had already emerged in the early 1990s, ending the state's media monopoly. The popular movement provoked by Zongo's assassination then forced the authorities to permit greater public liberties, including freedom of the press, noted Lookman Sawadogo of the association of private press editors: "After all, it was a journalist who was assassinated, and as a result, the media had their revolution."[35] Over the next decade and a half the independent media grew dramatically: a dozen newspapers and magazines, more than a score of FM radio broadcasters, a television station, and a number of online news sites. However Internet access remained one of the lowest in the world, at less than 4 percent of the population, limiting social media to a small urban elite. Ordinary Burkinabè benefited much more from the explosion of mobile phones, whose number increased nearly fifteen times between 2006 and 2015, to more than 14 million.[36]

The more rapid spread of information and ideas had an impact on youth culture. One of the most notable developments was a resurgence of interest in the legacy of Thomas Sankara. Parties citing allegiance to Sankara's example were especially active in the 1998–2000 protest movement and as a result recruited many new members. In the 2005 presidential election, the largest of those parties, the UNIR/PS, fielded Bénéwendé Sankara, who was better placed than any other opposition candidate. In legislative elections, the UNIR/PS and other Sankarist parties together generally polled about 10 percent of the electorate.[37] On 15 October 2007, the twentieth anniversary of Sankara's death, many thousands turned out in Ouagadougou, most of them young. When the late president's widow, Mariam Sankara, appeared at the cemetery, the large crowd grew unruly. She remarked: "The ideal of Thomas Sankara is still here, through all these youth who are mobilized, all these people."[38]

A number of popular musicians frequently attended the annual Sankara commemorations, including the reggae artist Sams'K Le Jah and the rapper Smockey. Their songs often incorporated references to Sankara's views and addressed the critical issues that drove public protest. Through their music and public pronouncements they brought radical messages to constituencies that were not actively engaged in politics, in a language that resonated well with Burkina Faso's youth.[39] Popular musicians in Côte d'Ivoire, Senegal, and other countries also quoted Sankara in their songs; their recordings and videos circulated widely, adding a Sankarist element to the emerging regional youth culture.

In 2010 Smockey won a major pan-African award, the Kora, in the category for Africa's best hip-hop artist. When he accepted the trophy at a large ceremony in a Ouagadougou sports stadium, he dedicated it to "all those who have struggled, to the great fighters," specifically naming Thomas Sankara. Compaoré was seated in the front row.[40] That impertinence was surpassed a few years later when Smockey and other Burkinabè musicians and activists founded Balai citoyen (Citizens' Broom), a key component of the anti-Compaoré insurrection. The group chose Sankara as its "patron." The revolutionary leader, Smockey later told this writer,

> inspires us on several levels. On the personal level, his simplicity, modesty, and integrity were a model for anyone aspiring to manage public property. On the level of political struggle, we recall his courage and his determination to build a Burkina Faso of social justice and inclusive development that takes into account both the environment and future generations.[41]

## "BURKINA WILL HAVE ITS EGYPT!"

As the year 2011 opened, youth across Africa were in a state of high expectation. Within just a few weeks two long-entrenched autocracies in the north, Tunisia and Egypt, had been toppled by popular outpourings, firing imaginations not only across North Africa and the Middle East—giving rise to the imagery of an "Arab Spring"—but also south of the Sahara. Whether in their hundreds or thousands, disgruntled youths and democratic rights activists launched protest movements in Malawi, Uganda, Sudan, Mauritania, Djibouti, Swaziland, and elsewhere. In Senegal, a group of activist rappers, Y'en a marre (We've had enough), succeeded in initiating huge demonstrations that blocked the president from amending the constitution to entrench his rule. For a time—before these movements lost their wind and most of the changes in the Arab world bogged down in conflict and partial reversals—many wondered whether this was the beginning of an "African Spring" of resurgent popular mobilization and voice.[42]

Already unsettled by ongoing unrest, Burkina Faso erupted anew on the crest of that regional wave, starting with secondary school students. Their first demonstrations in Koudougou on 22 February 2011 reflected an obvious external inspiration. Common slogans included, "Burkina will have its Egypt!" "Tunisia is in Koudougou!" and "Jazmin revolution!" referring to the name given by Tunisian activists to their movement just a few weeks earlier.[43] But the deep resonance of their actions and demands flowed most immediately from Burkina Faso's own circumstances, in this instance sparked by yet another police killing.

Two nights before the demonstrations, Justin Zongo, a student at a private secondary school in Koudougou, died in his hospital bed. According to provincial authorities, the cause was meningitis. But family, friends, and local clinic records showed that he had succumbed to severe trauma from a police beating. Although the student was not known as a political activist, many recalled the fate of Norbert Zongo (no relation), also from Koudougou. The city was rocked by exceptionally large and militant protests by students and other youths, some of whom burned police stations, destroyed other symbols of government authority, and threw stones at security personnel. The protests first spread to other towns in the province, and then nationally, to Ouagadougou, Ouahigouya, and elsewhere. When tear gas and clubs failed to stem the unrest, police fired live rounds. Within a week another four students were dead, and a couple more protesters or bystanders were killed later. Those new deaths further inflamed anti-police and anti-government sentiments. Successive waves of student and youth protests reached areas that had not previously experienced serious political unrest. Over 7–9 March alone, local media reported student actions in more than twenty separate locations. University students, teachers, parents, opposition leaders, and many others backed the students' demands for justice over the death of Justin Zongo and prosecution of the police responsible for killing protesters. That wide public support came despite the violence of some students, who burned police stations, CDP headquarters, houses and businesses of party leaders and supporters, and even the home of the prime minister.[44] Researcher Lila Chouli commented, "the authorities' monopoly of violence was lost and shared out among important sectors of society."[45]

Those student actions set the opening scene of a complex series of outpourings that lasted for months and mobilized numerous other constituencies in a series of labour marches, merchants' protests, judges' strikes, army and police mutinies, farmers' boycotts, attacks on mining sites, and other forms of struggle.

A tabulation of protest events drawn from local media accounts identified 356 separate actions in 2011.[46] The bulk (more than two-thirds) took place in the five-month period from February to June. Although the initial spark was Justin Zongo's killing and mobilized students most of all, their example inspired other sectors to come out, sometimes to support the students but also to express their own grievances (see Table 12.1).

Compared with the movement against Norbert Zongo's assassination, in which the CODMPP played a central coordinating role, this time "discontent was not channelled by any political force, trade union or other organization. The protests developed in a very fragmented way, without leaders or a platform of demands."[47] There were local or sector-specific leadership structures, of course: student councils and other coordinating bodies among secondary students, the ANEB for their university counterparts, and the trade unions for workers. However, as Chouli noted, the national structures (ANEB and the unions) "only joined the movement relatively late," after several weeks of local student agitation.[48]

Labour protests followed their own pace throughout the year, but peaked during April–June, amidst the wider turbulence. Most workers' actions were organized or supported by their unions. The labour-led CCVC held large demonstrations in early April to demand lower prices and taxes, as well as justice for Justin Zongo. Separately, finance employees, tax collectors, health personnel, teachers, and other public employees held rallies, sit-ins, and

***Table 12.1 Selected 2011 protest events by social category***

| Sector | Number of protests | Peak period |
|---|---|---|
| Students* | 107 | Feb–May |
| Merchants | 20 | Feb–Nov |
| Soldiers, police | 29 | Mar–June |
| Labour | 80 | Apr–Jun |
| Farmers | 18 | Apr–Jul |
| Community** | 64 | Apr–Jun, Dec |

Notes: * Overwhelmingly secondary students. ** Not already included in other categories.
Source: Author's database of Burkina Faso protest events.

strikes. Workers at several private gold mines also took action, on their own or as part of community mobilizations. In a few locales communities accused mining companies of harming the environment or not recruiting enough local workers.[49] When the unions were involved, labour protests were generally disciplined, with little violence. But union leaders could not always control their followers. At a sugar plantation and refinery near the western town of Banfora, seasonal workers armed with machetes and clubs blockaded a national highway to press for higher pay. Said a union representative, "The delegates weren't able to contain the crowd. It was a spontaneous movement that surprised the delegates, who were still in negotiations."[50]

The most leaderless actions appeared to be the soldier and police uprisings (see Chapter 11), which began in March and culminated with the suppression of the Bobo-Dioulasso mutiny in early June. The rebellious troops did share information by mobile phone, but aside from following each other's example, exhibited no real coordination. The result was not just vague expressions of anger against their officers, but also frequent looting and indiscriminate shooting, leading to a number of civilian casualties. Charles Lona Ouattara, a retired colonel, later speculated that the authorities may have allowed the mutinies to persist for more than two months in order to frighten the population and "neutralize" the student protests.[51]

Student unrest did subside by the end of May. Whatever the possible impact of the soldiers' mutinies, other factors were probably more influential. After the initial flurry of police shootings only provoked greater resistance, police and gendarmes largely pulled back and in some small towns simply withdrew. The August trial and imprisonment of three police officers in relation to Justin Zongo's death also dissipated the students' immediate anger. More generally, Compaoré's dismissal of his cabinet and constitution of a new one under Prime Minister Luc Adolphe Tiao, who introduced a number of economic and social concessions and repeatedly promised dialogue, seemed to suggest to many that the authorities might finally be amenable to reform.

Protest, however, did not end with the government reshuffle and the mutinies. Merchants, mainly small-scale retailers, repeatedly mobilized, sometimes violently and partially in reaction to the losses caused by pillaging solders. In communities across the country, local residents driven by their own specific concerns marched, rallied, blocked highways, and sometimes clashed with riot police. Municipal and other state authorities were usually their main targets, but occasionally so were other social sectors (such as merchants, contractors, or private companies).

Particularly noteworthy was the spread of agitation to a sector that had little previous history of organized protest: cotton farmers. Since their association, the UNPCB, was a 30 percent owner of the large state-owned cotton ginning company, Sofitex, cotton farmers generally accepted the prices offered for their cotton, albeit sometimes reluctantly. When a new price was announced in May, many considered it far too low, given a well-publicized increase in world cotton prices at the time. Individual UNPCB members and some provincial chapters thus demanded a doubling of the offered price, as well as lower costs for fertilizer and pesticides. Sofitex officials rejected the demands and UNPCB President Karim Traoré dismissed them as "utopian."[52]

Angry cotton farmers responded with demonstrations in Bobo-Dioulasso, Dédougou, and other locations, directing their anger at both Sofitex and the national UNPCB leadership, which was closely aligned with the CDP. Several general assemblies of farmers called for an unprecedented boycott of the new planting season. As the protests escalated, especially in the regions around N'Dorola, Dédougou, and Houndé, some boycott proponents destroyed the fields and equipment of farmers who continued to plant. Scores of rebellious farmers and supporters were arrested and the police sometimes acted quite violently and indiscriminately. At least one cotton farmer was killed, apparently by a vigilante force opposed to the boycott. As elsewhere during the 2011 protests, the repression further inflamed tensions. Some villages experienced virtual insurrections, as in Yaho, where in July "thousands" of residents, including farmers, family members, and youths, physically attacked local UNPCB officials opposed to the boycott and disarmed and chased away gendarmes sent in to quell the rebels.[53]

Although the farmers' revolt subsequently died down, other social agitation and local community protest continued for the rest of the year and throughout 2012. The issues were as diverse as the constituencies. But only rarely were there explicit anti-government political demands. Of course, the initial protests over the police killing of Justin Zongo and half a dozen demonstrators were highly political, focused primarily on calls for justice. And as the analysts Hilgers and Loada pointed out, it was possible to detect a political thrust behind the wider unrest: "Despite the disagreements and absence of coordination, the aims of the different groups converged on an appeal for better political management."[54]

Yet at the time few activists who were not members of the small opposition parties denounced Compaoré by name or called for regime change. The reggae artist Sams'K Le Jah did release a new song, "Le Président," calling on the incumbent to "leave" and was cheered by his audiences. But demands for Compaoré's departure had surprisingly little public resonance, despite the anger and passions so evident on the streets. One factor may have been a perception that Compaoré's exit was just a matter of time: He had been re-elected in November 2010 for his last constitutionally permitted term in office, and according to the law would have to step aside in 2015. Another factor was the evident mistrust that many activists had of the official opposition leaders, some of whom had records of compromise and betrayal. At one major protest called by the radical ANEB university student association, the group sternly called on party activists to refrain from circulating their own declarations: "This is a march and meeting of students, not political parties."[55]

The most dramatic indication of the parties' marginal role in the 2011 mobilizations came on 30 April of that year. An impressive list of thirty-four parties supported an appeal by Bénéwendé Sankara, then official head of the opposition, to demonstrate in central Ouagadougou to demand Compaoré's resignation. "Compaoré, dégage!" (Get out!) was the slogan, adapted from the democratic uprisings in Tunisia and Egypt. But the turnout that Saturday was derisory. The most generous estimates placed the crowd at around 1,000 or so.[56] Evidently the sponsoring parties were not able to mobilize even their own members in the capital.

Within two years that situation would turn around dramatically, with calls for Compaoré's departure moving to the forefront of national political life.

# 13
# FROM CONFRONTATION TO INSURRECTION

When President Blaise Compaoré was inaugurated in December 2010 for his fourth elected mandate, he and his closest colleagues were already considering ways to circumvent the constitutional clause making it his last five-year term. Although public sentiment was clearly against a further prolongation of his tenure, already one of the longest in Africa, Compaoré and his entourage persisted. Rather than secure an extension, however, their efforts stirred such a backlash that Compaoré could not even complete his existing mandate. An unprecedented popular mobilization cut it short by a full year, and launched Burkina Faso onto a new political path.

As the decade opened, a few prescient oppositionists already saw the end of Compaoré's rule. Louis Armand Ouali, a veteran leftist, stated just before the election that "our country is at the end of a cycle" and illustrated his assessment with a Dioula proverb: "The canoe has run onto the sands," suggesting that Compaoré had no real options left.[1] But for most political actors that was not yet apparent. Publicly, Compaoré was evasive about his plans. That led both the authorities and their opponents into a series of political skirmishes to test each other's capacities and prepare for a showdown that was possible but not certain. Until the stakes became clearer, many ordinary Burkinabè watched attentively from the side-lines, unsure about the costs of joining anti-government mobilizations or the ability of Compaoré's critics to alter the country's political direction. Many hoped that Compaoré would abide by the constitution, averting a confrontation.

During his re-election campaign in 2010, Compaoré left any suggestion about altering the constitution to his subordinates. Various CDP figures argued that the constitution's Article 37 setting the presidential term limit denied voters the option of electing whoever they wanted, however often. Roch Marc

Christian Kaboré, then still with Compaoré as CDP president, maintained that any term limit was "anti-democratic in principle."[2] If such comments were intended to test reactions, they succeeded in provoking a firestorm of criticism. A dozen opposition parties hastily formed a coalition to defend Article 37.[3] Many civil society groups came out strongly against amending the clause. Four prominent activists, including Guy Hervé Kam, a former high court judge, and Augustin Loada, executive director of the respected CGD, successfully collected 30,000 signatures on a public petition demanding that Article 37 be made constitutionally inviolate.[4] The trade unions added an explicit defence of Article 37 to their standard grievances over the high cost of living, unemployment, and taxes.[5] An episcopal conference of Catholic bishops warned that amending Article 37 would mark a "step backward" that could lead to "the same turbulence" that followed Zongo's killing.[6]

Under the circumstances, Compaoré's 2010 re-election was not an opportune moment to openly declare his intentions. In three major public speeches that December, he spoke only in general terms about political reforms. The massive protests that wracked the country in 2011 made it even harder to publicly advocate modifying Article 37. But in a flanking manoeuvre, proponents of an amendment hoped to use a new Conseil consultatif sur les réformes politiques (CCRP) to advance their cause. Its ostensible aim was to overcome the crisis of 2011 by achieving consensus across the political spectrum on various reforms. Some had been raised previously by regime critics or were relatively uncontroversial. But included in the mix was Article 37. Distrustful of the authorities, the radical opposition parties and many activist civil society groups refused to participate in the CCRP, so as to lessen its legitimacy. Yet despite the absence of the most vocal defenders of Article 37, proposals to amend it secured surprisingly little traction within the consultative mechanism. Among those rejecting any change was the ADF-RDA, a key presidential ally that was then the second largest parliamentary party and had ministers in the government. Even some CDP representatives favoured retaining the existing clause. As a result, the CCRP's final report categorized amendment of Article 37 as a "non-consensual" recommendation,[7] effectively preventing the authorities from using the consultative body to justify a change. Yet the matter was far from settled. On the closing day of the final national CCRP discussion in December, Compaoré affirmed that even the non-consensual reform proposals "remain no less important for deepening democracy" and thus warranted further consideration.[8]

## RECOMPOSITION, ABOVE AND BELOW

Meanwhile, the political landscape was starting to shift. At the summit of power, the approach of Compaoré's last constitutionally permissible term in office touched off disparate reactions, with those closest to the president anxiously searching for some way to prolong his tenure, but others starting to consider alternative, post-Compaoré scenarios. Inevitably, those contradictory tendencies came into conflict.

The CDP, a composite "mega party" that held together disparate factions, patrons, and power brokers, had long been plagued by dissension and occasional split-offs. A constellation of pro-Compaoré parties and associations that operated outside the formal confines of the ruling party only complicated matters, especially with the emergence in 2008 of the FEDAP-BC. Although it claimed to be a "non-political" civil society group, its patronage by Compaoré's younger brother François and funding by many of the same merchants who financed the CDP's election campaigns automatically made it a weighty political force, and to some extent in competition with the main CDP leadership.[9]

Those tensions burst dramatically into the open the following year. In July 2009, just two weeks before a scheduled CDP national congress, Salif Diallo, the party's first vice-president and long-time Compaoré confidant, gave a provocative interview that was carried in the foremost independent daily newspaper, *L'Observateur Paalga*. In it, Diallo echoed criticisms previously raised only by opposition currents and independent thinkers. He declared that the country's stability required a "profound reform of its political institutions" in order to give "equal chances to all political parties." He called on "all socio-political currents" to draft a new constitution to establish a parliamentary regime (in place of the existing presidential system), with the opposition brought into the government to help oversee the transition. Such a radical shift was necessary to prevent a further "patrimonialization of the state," a pointed critique of Compaoré's overall methods of rule and the growing influence of his brother François.[10]

A week later, the CDP control commission suspended Diallo from all party positions. To avoid outright expulsion, Diallo submitted a "self-criticism" several months later. But rumours of leadership dissension did not fade. Most dramatically, Roch Marc Christian Kaboré announced at the beginning of 2012 that he would not seek re-election as CDP president at a party congress set for that March. Then as if to confirm Diallo's argument about patrimonialization, that congress brought a sweeping overhaul of the CDP. Most long-time leaders (including Kaboré and Diallo) were relegated to the side-lines as "political advisers," while François Compaoré, his closest colleagues, and several other presidential confidants came into the central party leadership. Analysts saw it as a takeover by the FEDAP-BC, in preparation for a new attempt to abrogate the presidential term limit or groom François as a successor.

Meanwhile, activists were reorganizing their own ranks. Disillusioned by the main opposition's failure to make any real headway in the electoral arena, many sought new ways to reach wider sectors of the population. They came from different constituencies: civil society groups devoted to promoting democracy and human rights, prominent intellectuals, leaders of smaller opposition parties, and a few former "insiders" who had broken with the CDP. Although with diverse interests and political perspectives, most agreed on one central goal: *alternance*, or a change in government leadership. As long as Compaoré remained in office, they reasoned, no fundamental reforms or major expansion of democratic rights were possible. According to Fousséni Ouédraogo, president of the Mouvement burkinabè pour le développement et le civisme (MBDC), formed in 2005, "No democracy exists without *alternance*. Here, it's always the same person. That's not normal. It's not a democracy."[11]

That problem animated a May 2009 Forum des citoyens de l'alternance (Citizens' Forum on Alternance). The approximately 250 participants came from across the political spectrum, the trade unions, civil society groups, human rights associations, media houses, and other formations. The forum's main initiator was Zéphirin Diabré, a minister in several CDP-led governments in the 1990s, then a high-level UN official in New York, and finally a top executive in the French nuclear energy company Areva. After returning to Burkina Faso in 2006, he gradually became openly critical of the CDP and the government. The other organizers were largely academics. Only two had overt party positions, including Louis Armand Ouali, then a member of parliament from a small party. Some Sankarist figures attended. The gathering's aspiration, Diabré stated at its opening, was to initiate an "informal mass movement" that extended beyond the participating parties and civil society groups.[12]

The participants' critiques of the regime included denunciations of the use of public office for illicit personal gain by government ministers, parliamentary deputies, directors, and other top dignitaries. Such shady financial dealings were facilitated by the president's "monarchic" tendencies, the "familial influence" of his relatives, and the government's "clan-like military character," various forum reports emphasized. "Any democracy remains incomplete as long as it does not produce a political changeover," Diabré argued, elaborating afterwards that such *alternance* did not mean a change in the leadership of the CDP, the presidential majority, or a dynastic succession, but the assumption of power by parties clearly in the opposition.[13] The forum concluded by urging the creation of a "broad citizens' coalition" of parties and civil society groups to counter any subversion of the constitution.[14]

In major respects, the forum presaged the opposition party–civil society front that would emerge a few years later. For the moment, however, the participants focused on building the separate sides of that alliance. A majority decided to maintain their status as non-partisan civil society activists. They continued the forum's consultative dynamic through the Forum des citoyens et citoyennes pour l'alternance (Focal, a more gender-inclusive variant of its original name). The group organized similar gatherings in 2011 and 2013, chaired by Luc Marius Ibriga, a law professor, assisted by Loada's pro-democracy think tank, the CGD.[15]

A minority of forum participants chose instead to create a political party to fight for a "republican and citizens' democracy" through electoral means, explained Ouali, head of the forum's political commission.[16] In early 2010, those party proponents formed the Union pour le progrès et le changement (UPC), headed by Diabré. Although it was a presidential election year, Diabré emphasized first building up the party's structures before considering an electoral run. The party identified with "the camp of the republican opposition" and rejected any attempt to amend the presidential term limit. Diabré referred to himself ideologically as a free-market liberal and never disclaimed the structural adjustment programme he implemented as Compaoré's minister of finance. But the party itself was a "big tent." It proclaimed that it was "beyond ideologies," of the left or the right.[17] Ouali, its deputy secretary-general, openly avowed communist beliefs.[18]

After the widespread demonstrations and mutinies of 2011, the UPC was well-positioned to attract disillusioned supporters of the established opposition, as well as former backers of the CDP, thanks partly to Diabré's background and connections. The December 2012 legislative and municipal elections catapulted the UPC into the leadership of the opposition. The party secured nineteen deputies in an expanded National Assembly of 127 members, the second-greatest number (after the CDP).

As leader of the largest opposition party, Diabré became the new Chef de file de l'opposition politique (CFOP), taking over from his predecessor in that post, Bénéwendé Sankara of the UNIR/PS, which had four parliamentary deputies. While praising Sankara's previous stewardship, Diabré adopted a more moderate tone. If the opposition was ever to win, he argued, it had to offer a "responsible" alternative, capable not just of criticizing but also of governing. Diabré nevertheless sought to represent the views of the opposition as a whole. As of 2013, forty-four parties were formally affiliated to the CFOP. As Diabré described it, this was a "plural" opposition, ranging from liberals and centrists to social democrats, socialists, communists, and Sankarists.[19]

Some UPC militants also chose activism outside the parliamentary arena. Marie Madeleine Somda, who had been elected a UPC municipal councillor in Dissin, in the south-west, helped launch the Collectif des femmes pour la défense de la constitution (Cofedec) in 2012. While women had belonged to "mixed" organizations before, she explained, they usually occupied only secondary roles, so Cofedec opted to become "a rare women-only association dedicated to fighting for democracy."[20]

## BURYING A SENATE

For Compaoré supporters looking to extend his mandate, the 2011 upsurge, impasse at the CCRP consultations, and 2012 election results limited their options. By law, Compaoré had the authority to call a constitutional referendum at any time. Although many believed the authorities would be able to prevail through their usual dubious electoral methods, a referendum could still entail a major risk. Another possible avenue was by parliamentary vote, but only with the support of more than three-quarters of the deputies, a threshold the CDP could not breach without the ADF-RDA's eighteen deputies.

The authorities thus explored an alternative: introducing a Senate as a second chamber of parliament. A Senate had been one of the "consensual" reforms discussed at the CCRP and its creation as a largely unelected institution was approved by parliament in June 2012. Critics decried the Senate as a costly waste and worried that it could open a back door for amending Article 37: sitting together in a common session (called a "congress"), the Senate and National Assembly could theoretically give backers of an altered presidential term limit the three-quarters majority they lacked in the National Assembly alone.[21]

After some delays, the CDP majority in the National Assembly finally approved the implementing legislation for the Senate in May 2013, setting the stage for a major test of strength with Compaoré's opponents. These now included not only Diabré and other opposition leaders, but also a number of new, more openly militant civil society formations.

According to rap musician Smockey, a handful of activists who had previously been active in the protests against Zongo's assassination began informal discussions in 2010. Smockey and his colleagues concluded that elections "served no purpose" except to keep Compaoré in power. By 2013 they launched a new movement, Balai citoyen (Citizens' Broom), a name suggested by Smockey and the reggae artist Sams'K Le Jah. It aimed to "sweep out bad governance at all levels" and sensitize young Burkinabè to the importance of becoming active citizens. "We're a political movement, even though we're not a political party," Smockey explained to this author, emphasizing the organization's role as a civil society pressure group. Balai citoyen had "no organic links" with the opposition parties, seeing them rather as "partners of circumstance" with common goals, such as preserving the presidential term limit.[22] The ability of Smockey and his comrades to speak the language of disaffected youth brought rapid growth. Within two months Balai citoyen had affiliated "clubs" in all Ouagadougou neighbourhoods and most major cities.[23]

Another group was the Mouvement 21 avril (M21), named for the day in 2013 it was created. According to Marcel Tankoano, its president, the movement was primarily occupied with improving conditions in agriculture, health, education, and democratic rights, drawing inspiration from Sankara's legacy. But even practical changes were impossible because the authorities did not listen. "Since we could not have discussions with it, this regime had to go." Tankoano maintained that the M21 was the first group to explicitly call for Compaoré's removal. It soon won members in nine of Burkina Faso's thirteen regions. "The opposition parties knew we activists were very, very strong, so they were obliged to work with us."[24]

Towards the end of June 2013, following the National Assembly decision to set up the Senate, some individual senators were nominated and local government councils prepared to select others. Before the Senate could become a fait accompli, Diabré appealed for national demonstrations on 29 June against the Senate and in defence of Article 37. He invited participation "by citizens outside parliament, many of whom do not belong to parties."[25]

The demonstrations exceeded expectations and marked the opening salvo of a new wave of popular contestation. In the capital alone, as many as 50,000 poured into the central Place de la nation, or, as some called it, "Ouagaoudou's

Tahrir Square." In addition to slogans against the Senate and revision of Article 37, there were recordings of Sankara speeches from the podium and shouts of "Trop c'est trop!," echoing the movement against Zongo's killing. Some demonstrators explicitly called for Compaoré's removal. Smockey and Sams'K Le Jah were cheered when they arrived wielding brooms. They warned party leaders to "not sell out" and to keep on mobilizing "until the regime falls."[26] Similar demonstrations were held in Bobo-Dioulasso, Koudougou, Ouahigouya, and more than a dozen other cities, with crowds ranging from hundreds to thousands.[27]

July revealed cracks in government control over the state media. Angered by the intervention of Ministry of Information officials to minimize coverage of the protests, state media workers staged sit-ins and rallies in Ouagadougou, Bobo-Dioulasso, and Gaoua, chanting "No to censorship!," "Trop c'est trop!," and "Y'en a marre!"[28] According to Guézouma Sanogo, then a radio reporter, state media employees simply wanted to practise their profession by normal journalistic standards of fairness and objectivity.[29] As their union, affiliated to the militant CGTB federation, put it, "journalists are refusing to be partisans of the CDP."[30]

A few days later, twenty-one civil society groups came together to launch a broad alliance, the Front de résistance citoyenne (FRC). Its members included Focal, CGD, MBDC, Cofedec, and other associations. The FRC's demands included rejection of the Senate and support for the presidential term limit, as well as grievances against corruption, high prices, unemployment, poor education, and so on. The statement made no mention of the opposition parties, implicitly asserting civil society's own autonomous role in the growing agitation.[31]

The Mouvement ça suffit (Enough Movement), formed that same month, was also suspicious of the political parties. Since party leaders only acted in their own partisan interests, any collaboration was likely to be "an alliance of circumstance," said Aziz Sana, the movement's president. He spoke from experience. For nearly a decade Sana had belonged to the ADF-RDA, rising to become secretary-general of its youth wing. But the party's ambiguous relationship with Compaoré eventually led him to resign and become a civil society activist instead.[32]

The trade unions were even more insistent on asserting their distinct identity. Despite invitations, union leaders declined to officially endorse the parties' protests. While union spokesperson Mamadou Nama acknowledged that the parties and unions had many demands in common, "there is a difference": The unions represented workers' interests, whatever the regime in place, but the parties were guided by short-term political considerations and had a history of abandoning joint action in return for minor concessions.[33] The unions thus held their own demonstrations on 20 July under the banner of the CCVC. Many thousands turned out for rallies and marches in Ouagadougou, Bobo-Dioulasso, and dozens of other cities to protest against high prices, unemployment, and corruption. Demonstrators also rejected the Senate, arguing that its budget could be better used for social needs, reflected in the slogan, "One midwife is worth more than eighty-nine senators."[34]

On 28 July, a month after the opposition's initial anti-Senate mobilizations, the parties called another national action. Once again Ouagadougou's Place de la nation was packed, and large marches took place across the country. This time, civil society representatives were accorded a more prominent place, with Balai citoyen activists very visible in the Bobo-Dioulasso action and Smockey and Sams'K Le Jah invited to speak from the main podium in Ouagadougou. Some demonstrators wielded portraits of Sankara, Che Guevara, and other youth heroes. Clashes erupted between protesters and security forces in Ouahigouya and Bobo-Dioulasso, when some, ignoring the organizers' insistence on peaceful action, tried to physically prevent municipal councillors from voting for Senate representatives.[35]

By that point, certain traits of the movement were becoming evident. Most obvious was the variety of organizational spheres—political parties, civil society groups, and labour unions—each with its multiplicity of constituent organizations. Such fragmentation could have led to dissipated energies or enabled the authorities to deal with different sectors separately, as they did with the uncoordinated protests of 2011. But this time many activists were united by an overarching objective: a change in government. Whatever their particular outlooks, they agreed that Compaoré could not remain in office indefinitely. That common purpose in turn helped activists partially overcome their organizational divisions, a rare conjunctural occurrence for such a diverse range of opposition currents and interests. Although the unions still marched largely under their own banners, the opposition parties and civil society groups drew closer together in joint campaigns. That coordination was reflected in the disciplined action of many demonstrations, with professional sound systems, precise itineraries, and squads of volunteer marshals to maintain order. But differences did not disappear. While the main protest speakers usually focused on ensuring that Compaoré's current term would be his last, some among the ranks were ready to see him gone now, as expressed in signs such as "We are tired of the Compaoré regime" and "Compaoré, game over." The party leaders were scarcely able to contain the pressure for more forceful action, and probably were pushed further and faster than they intended to go.

Confronted with a growing, better coordinated protest movement, Compaoré's initial reaction was to stand fast. The authorities closed the universities to hinder student mobilization and promoted a new Republican Front of small pro-government parties to back the Senate. But the process of selecting senators was already in trouble. The trade unions and Catholic Church refused to name their allotted representatives, Protestant denominations hesitated, the ADF-RDA remained equivocal, and several prominent ex-regime figures spoke out against it. By mid-August Compaoré gave the first sign of softening by ordering a "review" of the Senate, followed by offers to reduce it in size and cost. As the months passed, it appeared that the Senate, while not officially buried, was nevertheless still-born.

For this, activists credited the massive citizens' mobilizations. Meeting in November for the third Citizens' Forum for Alternance, they declared that any change in Article 37 would constitute a "constitutional coup" and vowed to resist it with "civil disobedience" if need be.[36] The opposition parties pledged to remain on alert in case Compaoré tried to prolong his tenure in other ways.

## "BATTLE OF THE STADIUMS"

The president's opponents did not have long to wait for his next move. On 12 December, Compaoré for the first time explicitly declared that if there was no consensus on amending Article 37, "the people will have to say what they think ... by referendum."[37] Compaoré's use of that word immediately electrified the political atmosphere. Three days later an emergency meeting of leaders of thirty-eight parties accused the president of planning a "constitutional coup," the term previously used by civil society activists. They established a new crisis coordination committee and called on citizens to be ready for fresh mobilizations.[38]

More surprising were the repercussions within the ruling party. In early January 2014 some of the CDP's historical leaders announced their collective resignation and explicitly rejected the Senate and any modification of Article 37.[39] The party had lost a few top figures before, but this was an unprecedented split. A quarter of the party's 400 national political bureau members left, including Roch Marc Christian Kaboré, an ex-prime minister and party president, Salif Diallo, a former party vice-president, and Simon Compaoré, the long-time mayor of Ouagadougou until the year before. Kaboré publicly apologized for his earlier position favouring amendment of Article 37.[40]

Any doubts about the extent of the dissidents' break were alleviated by their participation in opposition protests against Compaoré's referendum call on 18 January. Diabré arrived at the main rally in Ouagadougou with Kaboré prominently in tow, to considerable applause. In his speech Diabré warmly welcomed the ex-CDP leaders to the opposition, but added, "The people will be watching you closely." The new actions were significantly larger than the previous year's turnouts. Independent estimates placed the Ouagadougou rally at 70,000 or more, with some 30,000 in Bobo-Dioulasso and tens of thousands in Koudougou, Fada N'Gourma, Dédougou, Kaya, and most other regional capitals. Many signs openly demanded Compaoré's removal: "Blaise bye-bye," "Liberate Kosyam" (the presidential palace), and, playing on the CDP acronym, "Compaoré doit partir" (Compaoré must go). Reflecting the parties' growing reliance on non-party activists, Smockey was invited as the first speaker at the Ouagadougou rally.[41]

The dramatic rift in Compaoré's own party and the dissidents' decision to shift over to the opposition clearly encouraged many more ordinary Burkinabè to join the protest movement. As elsewhere in the world, an open split within the elites was a major factor that would signal the approach of a potentially revolutionary situation.[42]

More politicized civil society groups also emerged. The demonstration in Bobo-Dioulasso featured many young people dressed in the bright red T-shirts of the new Mouvement en rouge, Faso kunko (Movement in Red, for the Nation's Cause).[43] A few weeks later, the Collectif anti-référendum (CAR) was formed. Hervé Ouattara, its president, explained that Compaoré:

> had committed himself to ensuring that the laws of Burkina were respected. So when he said that he was going to modify the constitution, we said: "That's enough!" We were kids when Blaise Compaoré took power. Today we're grown and have children of our own, and he was still in power. Was he trying to insult the memories of Burkinabè? We said, "No!"[44]

The CAR initially drew together 365 associations and was structured geographically, at first in Ouagadougou's fifty-five sectors, with about 100 "sentinels" per sector. It eventually built up a national structure with comparable groups in twenty-five of the country's forty-five provinces. During the anti-referendum campaign, the CAR drew especially close to Balai citoyen. It formally affiliated with the opposition parties, but "watched them carefully," said Laurent Monné, its secretary-general, since the parties had previously "played a double game."[45]

That scepticism mirrored the unions' attitude. According to Bassolma Bazié, the general secretary of the CGTB federation, the unions found the party-led protests "insufficient," since they did not pay enough attention to high prices and other worker grievances.[46] To press such issues, the unions carried out a national general strike on 4–5 February. It was called by a new union alliance, the Unité d'action syndicale (UAS), comprising thirty-three unions and union federations, effectively bridging the labour movement's historical fragmentation.

In early April, those who had split from the CDP held the founding congress of their own party, the Mouvement du peuple pour le progrès (MPP). Its very name, as Salif Diallo pointed out, suggested that the MPP's aspirations were not strictly electoral, but also activist, "the people in movement." The MPP labelled itself "social democratic" and criticized Compaoré's CDP for its "ultra-liberal" economic policies and support for monopolistic business practices. The closing rally packed the 25,000-seat Municipal Stadium, with an atmosphere of a protest meeting.[47]

A week later, in direct reply to the MPP and the rest of the opposition, pro-referendum forces organized their own large rally in a stadium in Bobo-Dioulasso. Together with various meetings and rallies around the country by Compaoré and his surrogates, those actions sought to shore up the morale of government supporters and through their belligerent speeches remind opponents that they had the power to unleash violence. Several attacks followed against anti-referendum activists, as well as the mysterious killing of Salifou Nébié, a Constitutional Court judge reputedly close to several MPP leaders. According to Diabré, the threats made it essential to organize a massive "citizens' resistance." The opposition coalition then launched a new round of anti-referendum rallies on 31 May in Ouagadougou's 4 August Stadium, which seats some 50,000. The rally featured an iconic moment when Arba Diallo, a former Sankara government minister, recalled the late president's anti-imperialist rallies in the same stadium and concluded that it was now time for Compaoré to leave the game, symbolically brandishing a soccer referee's red card, to wild and sustained applause.[48]

The same day the CAR and other civil society groups organized a large march through the streets of Bobo-Dioulasso.

Several weeks later the CDP also filled the Ouagadougou stadium, in what local media called a cyclical tit-for-tat "battle of the stadiums" with each side mounting shows of strength.[49] Although their efforts also featured open rallies and street marches, those claimed turnouts were harder to verify, while attendance in closed stadiums with known seating capacities were more easily corroborated.

One reason for the competing public mobilizations was that each side was addressing not only national constituencies, but also the country's main donors. Opposition leaders approached foreign embassies to portray Compaoré as anti-constitutional and anti-democratic, in violation of the rule-of-law precepts that most Western powers espoused. Compaoré, by contrast, painted himself as a force for long-term stability, a key player in the West's regional "war on terror," and still a popular figure at home. The president's supporters wagered that even though some donor officials warned against amending the term limit, they would ultimately acquiesce if Article 37 were altered through a "democratic" referendum. For more than two months the opposition eased up on its mobilizations, apparently hoping that Compaoré's attendance at a summit meeting of US and African leaders in Washington in August would bring further pressure from President Barack Obama, who previously had declared that Africa needed strong democratic institutions, not "strong men." But at the summit the US president instead avoided political issues, while Compaoré defiantly claimed there "will not be strong institutions unless there are strong men" leading them.[50]

With pressure from abroad limited, the opposition renewed its domestic campaign. For some civil society groups, the experience of the previous months indicated the need for a tactical shift. According to Hyppolite Domboué, a leader of the Cadre de réflexion et d'actions démocratiques (Framework for Democratic Reflection and Action), activists argued with opposition leaders to "leave the stadiums," since "the only way to overthrow this regime is in the streets." He saw the opposition's organization of another large demonstration in Ouagadougou on 23 August as a sign the activists were being heard.[51]

The action was very big. Organizers claimed 100,000 or more participants, and most media accounts labelled it the largest demonstration yet. The protest was also notable for its discipline, with demonstrators marching eight kilometres without a single scuffle with security forces or damage to property. Directly refuting Compaoré's comments in Washington, the marchers chanted, paraphrasing a Sankara slogan, "When the people stand up, strong men tremble!" They waved Balai citoyen's brooms and Arba Diallo's red penalty cards. Protest signs proclaimed, "No to strong men, we don't want them."[52]

## COUNTDOWN TO AN UPRISING

The next two months were relatively calm on the streets. While many activists wanted to push harder, the opposition leaders' central strategy was to pressure Compaoré into abandoning his referendum plan. When in late September Compaoré urged Diabré and the CDP leadership to engage in "dialogue," the opposition saw a sign that the president might be wavering and agreed to talk. After a brief suspension because of the death of Arba Diallo, a member of the opposition delegation, the discussions resumed on 6 October. But that session broke down after barely an hour. With the CDP apparently unwilling to budge, opposition leaders finally concluded that the dialogue may have been just a ploy to mask referendum preparations.

On 21 October an extraordinary meeting of government ministers, chaired by Compaoré, decided to send a draft bill to the National Assembly to authorize a public referendum. Since the constitution gave Compaoré that authority, why ask the legislature to do it? The answer soon emerged: Secret talks with the ADF-RDA had apparently induced that party's leadership to reverse its position and back modification of the presidential term limit after all.[53] The CDP's own deputies, those of several small pro-government parties and the ADF-RDA's legislators added up to ninety-nine votes, enough to directly amend the constitution, without a referendum.

The reaction was immediate. That evening and into the next day hundreds of angry youths began blocking major roads in at least half a dozen different areas of Ouagadougou. Spontaneous demonstrations continued into 23 October, when protesters used tree trunks and burning tyres to barricade the national highway between the capital and Ziniaré, Compaoré's hometown, others criss-crossed the capital on motorbikes, chanting against the "constitutional coup d'etat," and yet more blocked traffic on the Tanghin bridge and Koulouba Avenue.[54] A new, broader grouping of civil society organizations was formed. The representatives of Balai citoyen, CAR, FRC, and ten other groups appealed for massive resistance by unions, students, and the population at large. "Compaoré has crossed the line," a spokesperson declared, adding that Burkinabè should now cross the line as well, using any means possible.[55] The opposition parties called a national day of protest for Tuesday, 28 October, to launch an "ongoing campaign of civil disobedience."[56] Balai citoyen did not wait, and in its own name called for a week of civil disobedience from 24 to 30 October, the day on which National Assembly deputies were scheduled to vote.[57]

Nor did women activists want to wait until 28 October, deciding instead to hold their own demonstration the day before. The initiative came from two groups: the civil society association Cofedec and prominent opposition party women led by Saran Sérémé. Sérémé was a political veteran, having been an active supporter of Sankara's revolutionary government who was arrested and tortured for protesting at Compaoré's coup.[58] Although she joined the ruling party years later, and was even elected as a CDP deputy to the National Assembly, she split from it in 2012 to launch her own small party. According to Marie Madeleine Somda, the president of Cofedec, the activists and party women organized their action in less than forty-eight hours. Somda raised the idea of carrying spatulas, long wooden spoons frequently used to stir pots of porridge and a symbol, common to most ethnic groups, of women's determination to defend their homes. "It's not a good sign for a woman to brandish a spatula at a man."[59]

On Monday 27 October, that man was Compaoré. Many hundreds of women assembled first outside Ouagadougou's Maison du peuple, waving spatulas and brooms and chanting, "Liberate Kosyam!" After Sérémé joined them, the ever-growing crowd of women marched towards a main traffic roundabout several blocks away. Sams'K Le Jah, who was part of a Balai citoyen caravan circulating through the city that same day, stopped by in support. A riot police contingent tried to block the marchers, but after a brief exchange took down their barricades and allowed the women to pass. They then held a rally with more chants and speeches. Besides calling on Compaoré to withdraw his referendum bill, Sérémé appealed to soldiers and police: "Don't turn your arms against the people."[60]

The women's action went beyond a display of numbers and determination. According to a later analysis of women's role in Compaoré's downfall, "Elders saw in this march a coup de grace, because in human history, especially in African tradition, when a conflict reaches the stage where the 'mother of society' is in the streets half naked or wielding symbols of rupture, there are only two outcomes: divorce or the final solution." Moreover, seeing women risking themselves in the streets "gave courage to men to continue mobilizing."[61]

The following day, men and women alike assembled in unprecedented numbers in Ouagadougou and across the country. That Tuesday, the capital's central Place de la nation was packed to its limits and beyond. Organizers claimed a million participants. The national press agency and French daily *Le Monde* estimated hundreds of thousands, certainly the biggest single action ever held in Burkina Faso. Many thousands more rallied and marched in Bobo-Dioulasso, Koudougou, Ouahigouya, Kaya, Dédougou, Dori, and other locations. Diabré, in his advance instructions to demonstrators, insisted that the action remain perfectly peaceful and that the main demand should be to drop the referendum bill. While the demonstration in Ouagadougou was in fact quite peaceful, there were also transgressive moments. Many protesters chanted "Twenty-seven years is enough!" and called for Compaoré's removal, not just the withdrawal of a piece of legislation. Hundreds deviated from the official march route, threw stones at police, dodged tear gas canisters, and barricaded a national highway. In Bobo-Dioulasso demonstrators toppled a statue of Compaoré—and left a nearby one of the late Libyan leader Qaddafi standing. Protesters in Koupéla blocked national highways for hours, sacked a CDP office in Fada N'Gourma, and clashed with government supporters outside the CDP headquarters in Ouahigouya. Sensing the anger of the crowd, Diabré himself adopted an uncharacteristically belligerent tone in his rally speech. The opposition, he said, was giving Compaoré a "last warning" to withdraw his bill. "Our struggle is entering its final phase. Change is now or never." He concluded with the revolutionary slogan, "Homeland or death!"[62]

After Tuesday's outpouring, coordinated workers' marches and rallies the following day paled by comparison, even though they attracted thousands of protesters of their own. Called by the CCVC, the action's main focus was against the government's education policies, although most speakers also denounced the referendum bill. While demonstrations were also held in Bobo-Dioulasso, Banfora, and Dédougou, the largest was in Ouagadougou. At one point, marchers reacted in anger to riot police who blocked the road to the National Assembly, but union security marshals intervened to forestall any physical confrontation.[63] That would be the last time protesters held back.

## "UPROOTED BY THE PEOPLE"

Up to the eve of the scheduled National Assembly vote on 30 October it was the opposition parties that largely set the pace. But as it became evident that the strategy of pressing Compaoré to drop the referendum bill was not working, party leaders had difficulty outlining a new goal. The most militant activists, however, were not only keen for more forceful methods, but also to simply bring down the regime. Diabré "wanted to do things in a republican way," observed the CAR's Hervé Ouattara. "We activists understood that that approach would not force Blaise Compaoré out. We had different methods and different visions."[64]

Earlier in the week, Balai citoyen had already issued directives about what to do if the authorities did not back down: mass outside the National Assembly.[65] The evening of 29 October, as leading activists in Bobo-Dioulasso were being arrested, the CAR sent out mobile phone text appeals urging people to "to liberate your country." Some activists spent the night in central Ouagadougou waiting, and by 5:00 am there were already thousands assembled at a roundabout several hundred metres from the legislature. Hervé Ouattara and Laurent Monné of the CAR were in the first group to move towards the National Assembly, but at that point there were fewer than a dozen protesters and "police everywhere with barricades," recalled Monné. One particularly courageous youth approached the barricades with raised arms, and the police fired tear gas, scattering the protesters. But half an hour later, as the crowd swelled at the roundabout, many more headed towards the parliament building, throwing stones and dodging tear gas canisters. By around 9:00 am, after hours of skirmishing, the police ran out of tear gas. When warning shots failed to deter the crowd, the police retreated. Youths broke down the National Assembly gates, rushed inside past fleeing deputies, and sacked and burned part of the building. "The National Assembly in flames," a group of student researchers later commented, "was a powerful symbol of defeat for the regime and victory for the demonstrators."[66]

As young Burkinabè streamed in from the capital's outlying districts, the demonstrations grew and marches and clashes spread in different directions. Shortly after the clashes at the National Assembly, a large group surged further up the street to seize and sack the headquarters of the national radio and television network, shutting down official transmissions. Since protesters normally received only limited coverage in the state-owned media, noted Ouattara, they had already become accustomed to relying on alternative methods of communication, including social media, text messaging, and private FM radio stations. Social media and texting were especially important for reaching out to members of the security forces. Activists, said Aziz Sana of the Mouvement ça suffit, sent texts or other messages to soldiers they knew, urging them not to set a "bad example" by opposing the protesters. And in return, "some soldiers sent social media messages that they supported us." According to Ouattara, the collaboration was also direct: "There were soldiers in civilian dress among us. Even the soldiers had become convinced that Blaise had to go. We were able to push through the barricades because police and gendarmes knew they could not stop the crowd."[67]

Other soldiers, however, especially members of the elite RSP, tried to halt the marchers. As one group approached the mansion of François Compaoré, just across from the university, troops in vehicles fired into the crowd without warning, killing at least one and injuring several. Enraged, protesters broke through to the mansion and sacked it. The image of that first slain youth quickly circulated on local social media sites, further enflaming the popular mood.[68]

Elsewhere in Ouagadougou the homes and businesses of various government ministers, local mayors, CDP leaders, and Compaoré in-law Alizéta Ouédraogo were stormed, pillaged, and burned. In Bobo-Dioulasso crowds of protesters, some of whom were shot, torched the mayor's offices and the CDP headquarters, the homes of ministers and other dignitaries, and the businesses of prominent financiers of the ruling party, including Djinguinaba Barro. A hotel and home of a former prime minister, Ernest Paramanga Yonli, were reduced to ashes in Fada N'Gourma. In retaliation for its last-minute decision to support the referendum bill, various ADF-RDA buildings and the home of its leader, Gilbert Ouédraogo, were destroyed in Ouahigouya. Similar violent protests were reported from Bagassi, Dédougou, and other provincial towns.[69]

As more demonstrators were shot—later tallies put the number of protesters killed nationally at about thirty—the divisions within the armed forces deepened. Many soldiers were revolted by the actions of the RSP. Thousands of civilians rallied outside Camp Guillaume, near the Place de la nation, appealing to the troops to assume their "responsibility," interpreted by some as not joining the repression and by others as actually ousting Compaoré. Among those who looked for some form of military intervention, many shouted the name of General Kwamé Lougué, regarded as a relatively honest officer, whose reputation had been enhanced by his dismissal as defence minister in 2004 because of purported links with the coup plotters imprisoned that year. Support for Lougué increased further when he told a foreign radio station that it was important for "the army to side with the people" and said he was considering joining a column of protesters marching towards Kosyam, the presidential palace.[70]

That march had begun shortly after noon, with Hervé Ouattara in the lead contingent. He first addressed a crowd that had gathered outside the residence of the Mogho Naaba, the Mossi emperor. "I told people that it was time to finish off President Compaoré." They then set off towards Kosyam, several miles away in an area called Ouaga 2000. Repeatedly, soldiers, mostly from the RSP, fired into the crowd, killing a number of them. "Even though some had fallen, we continued forward, and asked people to raise their hands" to show they were unarmed. Despite the casualties, the march came within 400 metres of the presidential palace. At that point, Diendéré, in charge of the RSP, agreed to bring Ouattara and two other march leaders into the palace to talk with Compaoré. According to Ouattara, Compaoré initially took an ironic tone, saying "that he understood that we wanted his departure. I said yes, that's true, since there have already been so many deaths." Compaoré then offered to stand aside at the end of his current term in November 2015. Ouattara and his colleagues replied that he had to resign now. By the end of the meeting they believed they had extracted a vague agreement from Compaoré to step down that evening.[71]

Compaoré did not make things that simple. He issued two contradictory declarations over a private TV channel (since the state network was still down). In the first he rescinded the referendum bill, dissolved the government, and declared a national "state of siege" to be administered by the army chief of staff, General Honoré Traoré. His second declaration repeated some of the same points, but withdrew the state of siege. In neither statement did he mention resignation, implying that he intended to remain in power through a political transition. Confusing matters further, in between Compaoré's two declarations, General Traoré issued a decree in his own name dissolving the government, imposing a curfew, and appealing for consultations with all parties to establish a transitional administration, without specifying who would head it.[72]

Confusion was also evident among government opponents. As some leading activists seemed to welcome a possible military intervention against Compaoré, Diabré suggested calling off the demonstrations after the president publicly dropped his referendum bill. Protesters assembled outside his offices reacted angrily. "You are giving Blaise more time," one shouted. "We cannot accept that our comrades died in vain," another declared. Hervé Ouattara reiterated that Compaoré had to go. Louis Armand Ouali, a top leader of Diabré's own party, said he warned him that if he called for an end to the protests, "the people will march over us." Finally, under popular pressure, Diabré issued a declaration on behalf of the opposition demanding that Compaoré resign immediately and calling for continued occupations of all public spaces until he did. As night fell, Ouagadougou's Place de la nation remained packed with demonstrators.[73]

The morning of Friday 31 October started out much like the day before, with huge crowds of protesters assembling in Ouagadougou's central square, in front of the army headquarters, and in numerous provincial cities. As demonstrators prepared for another march on the presidential palace, the security forces appeared incapable of maintaining even a semblance of order. Looting spread throughout the capital's commercial districts. Although a World Food Programme warehouse was among the facilities sacked, most pillagers went after politically connected targets: the homes of current or former government officials and businesses belonging to members of the Compaoré family or those who had financed the CDP.[74]

Only a few hours later, Compaoré fled Ouagadougou to the military base in Pô, and from there was whisked away to exile in Côte d'Ivoire. French President François Hollande later admitted that he had authorized French troops to assist the escape and prevent Compaoré's possible death.[75]

Citing the power vacuum, General Traoré promptly declared himself interim head of state, much to the consternation of activists who regarded him as too close to Compaoré. "Remain vigilant and on high alert," Sams'K Le Jah tweeted to Balai citoyen's followers, "so that no one steals victory from the sovereign people." With large numbers of protesters still occupying much of Ouagadougou, the pressure of a mobilized citizenry deepened divisions within the officer corps. It soon became evident that Traoré's bid was opposed by some of his own colleagues. The clearest sign came early that afternoon when a little-known officer, Lieutenant Colonel Yacouba Isaac Zida, appeared before the crowd at the Place de la nation to publicly announce Compaoré's departure. Flanked by Smockey and other prominent activists, he declared:

> From today, Blaise Compaoré is no longer president of Burkina Faso. Your national army has heard your appeal, and we are here to tell you that power henceforth belongs to the people. From now on, the people will decide their future. This Place de la nation will be the headquarters of Burkina Faso's government.

Zida made no mention of Traoré, and it would not be long before the rest of the military command lined up behind Zida instead.[76]

While Burkina Faso's immediate future remained uncertain, the atmosphere in the streets was for the moment celebratory. As the news spread that Compaoré had fled, many danced and cheered. "I'm very happy," said one protester. "My children are going to know another president." A civil servant commented, "The big baobab [tree] has fallen, uprooted by the people."[77]

# 14
# A TROUBLED TRANSITION

The euphoria over the Compaoré regime's downfall was soon diminished by wrangling over the country's political direction. Many Burkinabè had hoped for a clear path towards constitutional rule, but they soon realized that the removal of an individual and his small coterie still left in place many pillars of an embedded political structure. "We were aware that the Compaoré system was not dead," observed Laurent Monné of the CAR. "Blaise was in power for twenty-seven years, not twenty-seven days. There were people who did not accept that they had lost."[1]

Meanwhile, the popular movement revealed its weaknesses. The existence of scores, even hundreds, of parties, student groups, unions, civil society associations, and other organizations had been highly effective in mobilizing major sections of the population. But the plethora of groups and interests also made it difficult to stay united once the common enemy was gone. Some activists remained devoted to pushing for greater democracy and citizens' rights, but others appeared more interested in improving their personal circumstances or launching party political careers. "Now that the elephant has been slain," commented civil society activist Fousséni Ouédraogo, "everyone comes with his knife to cut off his own piece."[2] Ultimately, it was the readiness of key activist networks and ordinary citizens to mobilize again when necessary that made it possible over the following months to overcome both the old order's resistance and the shortcomings and mistakes of the new transitional authorities.

As soon as Compaoré left, the question of succession was posed. Most party leaders and activists believed in following the constitution, but the document offered no guidance for the circumstances. It specified that if the president was unable to perform his duties, the head of the National Assembly would assume interim executive authority until new elections. Yet the National Assembly president had himself fled and the legislature was no longer functioning. The opposition leaders were visibly unprepared to offer an alternative. As political analyst Siaka Coulibaly noted, Compaoré's sudden flight "was a surprise to the party leaders. They were focused on the withdrawal of the [constitutional amendment] bill, but not the overthrow of Blaise Compaoré."[3] And once a political transition was clearly on the agenda, the party leaders were less interested in vying for office on an interim basis than in preparing for the next elections. Even the radical Sankarists, who were more engaged with the popular movements, saw no clear solution. Bénéwendé Sankara, leader of the UNIR/PS, noted: "There was no vanguard party capable of saying, 'This revolution belongs to us.'"[4] Overall, civil society and labour would push for reforms, but did not view themselves as players in the formal political arena.

The resulting institutional vacuum led a number of military officers to consider stepping in, as had happened so often before. The first was General Honoré Traoré, who met immediate rejection from demonstrators. The second was Lieutenant Colonel Yacouba Isaac Zida, deputy commander of the RSP, who received the endorsement of the military command on 1 November. Some leading activists were willing to temporarily accept that outcome, out of fear that continuing divisions among the security forces could open the way to armed clashes, uncontrolled looting, and wider chaos. But that did not mean they supported military leadership. Guy Hervé Kam, Balai citoyen's spokesman, explained the distinction: "Wanting the army to take power to avoid a bloodbath and wanting the army to run the government are two different things."[5]

Fearing prolonged military involvement, however, the opposition parties called a protest in Ouagadougou the day after Zida became interim president. Thousands turned out against army attempts to usurp the popular insurrection, as everyone called the events of 30–31 October. The rally was notably smaller than those against Compaoré just a few days earlier, and ended in deadly clashes with troops and confused attempts by sections of the crowd to unilaterally proclaim other individuals as head of state (Saran Sérémé and General Kwamé Lougué). The demonstrators' message of opposition to a military-led transition was nevertheless echoed by France, the US, the United Nations, the African Union, and other international bodies. Bowing to the pressure, Zida pledged that same day to start consultations on a broadly acceptable transition.

After Zida met with opposition parties, religious leaders, civil society groups, trade unions, business associations, and the Mogho Naaba, they all agreed on the principles of a civilian-led government and year-long transition. But it took another week for negotiators to finalize a detailed Charter of the Transition. Seen as an addendum to the constitution, the charter specified that an electoral college choose a civilian president, who in turn would name a prime minister to form a cabinet. Legislative authority would rest with a ninety-member Conseil national de la transition (CNT), composed of thirty opposition party representatives, twenty-five from civil society, twenty-five from the military, and ten from the CDP and its allies. The charter stated clearly that no military officer could be president or head the CNT, although they could be government ministers. To ensure that high-level transition officials could not use their power unfairly in the next presidential and legislative election, the president, all government members, and the head of the CNT were barred from running.[6]

The charter was a delicate compromise. An earlier draft by opposition and civil society representatives reserved only ten seats for the military in the transitional legislature, an allotment that military negotiators promptly amended upward.[7] There had also been differences over the transitional administration's basic functions. According to Issaka Traoré, an activist who participated in the talks, party leaders wanted the transition to focus mainly on preparing new elections. "For us, civil society organizations, we said, 'No.' We overthrew Blaise Compaoré because we did not have a true democracy. So before going to an election, we needed a lot of rules and laws that would strengthen our democracy." The activists thus succeeded in inserting clauses requiring the transitional authorities to initiate political, institutional, and constitutional reforms, combat corruption, and review the electoral code, among other measures.[8]

Shortly after the charter's adoption, a committee of two dozen party, civil society, religious, and military figures began considering presidential nominees. Civil society representatives advanced three names. Only one of them, newspaper editor Chériff Sy, made it to the final shortlist, which also included Joséphine Ouédraogo, a minister in Thomas Sankara's revolutionary government, and Michel Kafando, a retired diplomat. Early on 17 November, the committee settled on the seventy-two-year-old Kafando, whose name had been put forward by the military. The next day Kafando took the oath of office and Zida relinquished his position as interim president.[9] Zida was not gone for long. Kafando promptly appointed him prime minister, ensuring the military a prominent place in the transition. When Zida subsequently named the rest of the cabinet, he appointed three more military officers to ministerial posts.

Several prominent activists were also named, including Augustin Loada as labour minister and Luc Marius Ibriga as head of the main anti-corruption agency. Joséphine Ouédraogo became justice minister.[10]

The political influence of the "insurgents" was most evident in the legislative CNT, established in late November. Activists picked their own representatives for the twenty-five civil society seats. Most came from groups identified by areas of activity, including economic development, human rights, people with handicaps, and so on. Several came from organizations that were especially active in the insurrectionary movement, including Hervé Ouattara (CAR), Aziz Sana (Mouvement ça suffit), and Sylvie Drabo (Mouvement en rouge).[11] Overall, the CNT was the youngest legislature in the country's history. Although female activists like Marie Madeleine Somda initially hoped that one-third of the deputies would be women, there were only twelve, or 13 percent. Somda believed the problem was not gender bias by her male colleagues, but that not enough women "had the courage" to step forward.[12]

In their first plenary session, CNT members overwhelmingly chose Chériff Sy, the editor of the independent newspaper *Bendré*, as president of the legislature. A self-described Sankarist who had actively opposed Compaoré's 1987 coup, Sy was on the radical end of the political spectrum. Just a few days before, he had argued that the insurrection's goal was not just to remove Compaoré, but to "destroy" his entire system of rule, including by bringing to trial former dignitaries suspected of major financial and "blood" crimes.[13]

## CONTRADICTORY PRESSURES

The transitional government was initially greeted with mixed public reactions. Some civil society critics were especially severe. The first problem, said Marcel Tankoano of the M21, was that "the person who took power was not an insurgent." The second was that many Compaoré supporters were still in their old positions, and those who left the country had been able to take their stolen assets with them.[14]

Although some activists were open to military involvement, others saw a usurpation. One concern was Zida's specific place in the military: he was not just any officer, but the second-in-command of the feared RSP. Since he was now prime minister, some concluded, his goal must be to preserve the old system as much as possible. Zida moved quickly, however, to dispel such worries. He publicly expressed admiration for Sankara, prompting UNIR/PS leader Bénéwendé Sankara to urge tolerance of the "Sankarists in the army."[15] Whether genuine or not, Zida's stance acknowledged the popularity of radical views. President Kafando, seen as a political moderate given his long career in the diplomatic corps, similarly echoed such sentiments. In a speech during Zida's formal handover of the presidency, Kafando referred positively to the development model and ideals "advanced by the revolution of 1983." In that spirit, he declared: "No more injustice, no more waste, no more corruption."[16]

Lingering suspicions about the orientation of the transitional government, and Zida in particular, were further dissipated on 13 December, the anniversary of Norbert Zongo's assassination. That day, thousands again packed Ouagadougou's central square in response to a call by the CODMPP collective that had organized the original protests against Zongo's murder and the union-led CCVC coalition. Many speakers demanded that Zongo's killers be brought to justice and the RSP itself dissolved. When Zida arrived on the margins of the rally, people demanded that he speak. From the podium, he began, "I'm here to listen to what the people want." He was answered with chants of "Justice!," "Dissolve the RSP!," and "Nationalize the enterprises!" owned by Compaoré cronies. Dressed not in uniform but in a Faso dan Fani outfit popularized during the Sankara era, Zida punctuated his points with a clenched fist in the air. He promised: "Justice will be given to Norbert Zongo. Justice will be given to all those who fell to the bullets of Blaise Compaoré's assassins." Two enterprises irregularly ceded to Compaoré loyalists under the privatization programme would be nationalized, he said, and the RSP would no longer ensure presidential security but be attached instead to the regular army.[17]

The transitional authorities came under pressure from the streets on numerous other occasions. Two ministers were forced to resign shortly after their nomination because of opposition by their ministries' employees. From the day after Compaoré's downfall through to the end of March 2015, a period of five months, the local media reported just over 100 protest actions of various kinds. About a third were labour demonstrations, sit-ins, and strikes, including a widely followed two-day general strike in February organized by all the union federations to demand reduced fuel prices and trials of former officials suspected of corruption and rights abuses. Reflecting the continued *national* scope of protest, actions were held in small towns across the country, often for electricity, water, and other services, as well as at gold sites by mine workers and members of surrounding communities. One Burkinabè journalist called it a "season of strikes and protest movements" that reflected a "quasi-institutionalization of governance by the streets."[18]

Despite the agitation, the transitional government could still focus on its primary task: organizing new elections. That undertaking was made easier by the existence of a credible electoral commission. With almost everyone agreed that the CENI did not need major overhauls, the authorities were able to quickly initiate consultations to work out a suitable timetable. They selected 11 October 2015 as the date for presidential and legislative elections and soon began registering new voters.

There was resistance, however. Despite the dissolution of all municipal and regional councils and limited purges of the most prominent Compaoré loyalists nationally, many stalwarts of the old order remained in place and did what they could to fight the momentum for reform. RSP commanders feared that their dominant position in the military could be diminished, stoked by Zida's perceived "betrayal" and Kafando's decision to remove General Gilbert Diendéré as head of presidential security. On 30 December, defiant RSP units demanded that the regiment be maintained and that two of its commanders be appointed to key security positions—or else that Zida step down as prime minister. They did the same on 4 February, provoking cancellation of a cabinet meeting amidst fears of a coup. Kafando and the military command negotiated a compromise in which the RSP pledged support for the transitional government, the authorities accepted its command nominations, and a commission was established to study reorganization of presidential security.

Activists were less accommodating. A score of civil society groups, including those most active in the rebellion, denounced the RSP threats as an attempt to sabotage the transition. On 7 February thousands again filled the capital's main square (as well as central Bobo-Dioulasso), chanting "RSP get out!" and "No to the army within the army!" Civil society and party speakers criticized the government's compromise, warning that the RSP's real goal was the ultimate return of Compaoré. "We won't let our insurrection be stolen," vowed Luc Marius Ibriga.[19]

Reinvigorated by such popular support, the transitional government and parliament moved ahead with the reforms envisaged by the charter. The legislature created a national reconciliation and reform commission, headed by Archbishop Paul Ouédraogo, to propose institutional reforms, promote national unity, and seek "truth and justice" over past crimes. Although Balai citoyen had previously declined to accept any posts in the government or CNT, its spokesperson Guy Hervé Kam agreed to head the new body's sub-commission on constitutional, political, and institutional reform.[20]

In March an "estates general" of the justice sector agreed on numerous reforms, including ending the president's chairmanship of the magistrates' council and other measures to enhance judicial independence, and strict sanctions for judges who accepted bribes.[21] Major cases that had long languished under Compaoré came to life: a reopened judicial investigation of the Zongo murder, a new military court inquiry into Sankara's assassination, and a trial of the former customs director, Ousmane Guiro, on bribery charges.

Then in April CNT deputies voted by a big majority to amend the electoral code. Its most controversial aspect was a prohibition from the upcoming elections of any party leader or ex-government official who had supported dropping the presidential term limit. Officials of the CDP and its allies protested vigorously, claiming that barring them was partisan. Civil society activists and some party leaders countered that it was a logical follow-up to the insurrection. Chériff Sy noted that the electoral code was approved by virtually all deputies of the former opposition parties, military, and civil society, and thus reflected the "deep aspiration of the people for change." Besides, he pointed out, no particular party was barred from the elections, only individuals who supported an "anti-constitutional" amendment. Eighty-three civil society groups warned that "confederates of the old regime," with encouragement from abroad (presumably Compaoré), were threatening to physically disrupt the transition.[22]

## ANOTHER SHOWDOWN

Political tensions mounted as pro-Compaoré parties attempted to stage public protests against the new electoral code, and some of their leaders were arrested as a result. Ultimately, the Constitutional Court ruled that nearly fifty prospective candidates of the CDP, ADF-RDA, and other parties could not run for election because they had actively backed efforts to overturn the presidential term limit, thereby provoking the insurrection. Others from the same parties, however, were allowed to place their names on the ballot.[23]

The transitional authorities meanwhile moved cautiously to reform the army. In early June CNT deputies approved a new armed forces code, much of it devoted to recruitment, promotions, training, the conditions for female soldiers, and similar service matters. The code explicitly stipulated that any member of the armed forces wishing to be politically active had to first resign from the military. After decades in which officers held high political positions, this was a notable change, supported by virtually all deputies, including those from the military. Hervé Ouattara, speaking for the civil society deputies, praised the code for promoting "a republican army, an army at the service of the Burkinabè nation."[24]

Sectors of the RSP resisted such moves. Amidst reports of a plot to kidnap Zida and direct threats against several private radio stations, RSP dissidents again demanded Zida's resignation. Although Kafando refused to remove Zida, he tried to placate the RSP by dropping from the cabinet the minister of territorial affairs and security Colonel Auguste Barry, a Zida ally.

Diendéré and his loyalists ultimately led the RSP into open revolt. On 16 September troops burst into a cabinet meeting and seized Kafando, Zida, Loada, and René Bagoro, a former activist judge who was now minister of housing. The following day they announced that Diendéré was president of a new governing junta, styled the National Council for Democracy, and proclaimed the dissolution of the transitional government and the CNT. To justify their action, the plotters cited the "exclusionary" electoral code, the new armed forces statutes, and other measures.[25]

The coup attempt elicited immediate condemnation from abroad, as France, the US, the African Union, and others threatened to cut off aid and urged that the transitional government be restored. Most significant, however, was the domestic reaction, marked by the largest, most widespread mobilizations since the insurrection.

That popular resistance was organized by the same activist networks that had brought down Compaoré. As the coup began, CAR leaders were meeting at their Ouagadougou headquarters. "We called Balai citoyen, and then decided to convene at Revolution Square," recalled Monné. Thousands quickly gathered there and at 4 pm decided to march on the presidential palace at Kosyam. "That day, I was proud to be a Burkinabè," said Monné. But then they reached a blockade of RSP troops who warned the marchers that anyone who kept going would not leave alive. When evening fell, "the RSP went out and began shooting everywhere," he said. "We dispersed, since we were empty-handed."[26]

The labour unions, through their UAS coordinating body, immediately called an indefinite general strike, paralysing most administrative and economic activity nationwide.[27] Chériff Sy, president of the CNT, played an especially pivotal role.

With the detentions of Kafando and Zida, he was the highest-ranking transitional figure at large. On the day the RSP struck, Sy appealed for national mobilizations by "the entire Burkinabè people to defeat this operation."[28] Speaking from hiding via local and international radio stations, he subsequently declared himself interim president and urged the regular army to stand with the transitional authorities.[29]

Over the following days large crowds tried to assemble in downtown Ouagadougou, but repeatedly faced RSP gunfire, that eventually took an official toll of eleven dead and more than 100 wounded. Since public gatherings were too risky in central Ouagadougou, activists focused on the poorer outlying districts, where they erected barricades of burning tyres, large rocks, and tree branches to keep out RSP vehicles. "This is our district, we know all the hiding places," said a twelve-year-old at a barricade in Paglayiri, in southern Ouagadougou.[30]

The street skirmishing was echoed by a "war of information," as Smockey called it.[31] Most newspapers, even the state-owned *Sidwaya*, continued to report on the resistance. Although RSP units attacked journalists and burned Radio Omega, a popular FM station, activists countered with Citizens' Resistance Radio, broadcasting from a secret location. They circulated declarations and photos of the demonstrations over Facebook and other social media sites.[32]

Since the RSP had little presence outside the capital, anti-coup protests spread virtually unhindered in the provinces. On the first day, hundreds of mostly young protesters surged through Yako, Diendéré's hometown in the north-west, where they burned his house, as well as the home of the CDP leader. In Koudougou, protesters overwhelmed pro-Compaoré militants and commandeered the offices of the provincial high commissioner for their "citizens' struggle" coordinating committee.[33] Similar scenes were repeated in Ouahigouya, Kaya, Banfora, Fada N'Gourma, and other towns.

The provincial protests won acquiescence and open support from police and gendarmes. In cities with army garrisons, protesters assembled outside and urged them to back the transitional government. The commander of the second military region in Bobo-Dioulasso assured demonstrators that his troops would not confront them.[34] Thousands of women marched to the Bobo-Dioulasso army base, many of them carrying spatulas—to hit Diendéré, one of them told a reporter. They challenged the troops to prove they were men by moving militarily against the RSP.[35] Young soldiers were especially sympathetic towards the resistance. "We were their big brothers," noted Marcel Tankoano. "We were their little brothers. Some had children of their own in the streets. In all regions, the army mobilized to support the people."[36] However, as later inquiries revealed, some officers in the army and air force initially provided the putschists with logistical support, while the generals of the high command refrained for several days from condemning the coup, apparently fearing to cross the RSP should its takeover succeed.[37] But younger corps commanders eventually took the initiative to move against the coup-makers. One young officer explained, "There was popular pressure. For our honour, we couldn't just stand around and do nothing."[38] With more junior officers already taking the lead, the army head, General Pingrénoma Zagré, finally authorized their movement towards Ouagadougou. As three army columns from the west, east, and north rolled towards the capital, large crowds of protesters cheered them on.

Eventually surrounded at the main RSP base in Ouagadougou, Diendéré tried to negotiate a compromise. But many ordinary RSP troops and officers had already surrendered or fled, leaving him no hand to play. As the army moved in to occupy the base, Diendéré slipped out, but within a few days was forced to surrender.

Even before Diendéré was in custody, the transitional authorities resumed their duties on 23 September. In his first declaration, Kafando credited the "national clamour" against the coup with helping restore him to office. The popular resistance to the takeover, he said, demonstrated "that the heightened consciousness that guided the insurrection has not diminished, to the contrary."[39]

## RUSH TO REFORM

For most party leaders and foreign donor officials, the central task was getting the elections back on track, and they were soon rescheduled for 29 November. But the attempted coup convinced many that this was not a time for reserve. Encouraged by the countrywide mobilizations, activists and reformers in the government, legislature, and judiciary felt they now had sufficient support to push more sweeping action. And unsure how enthusiastically the new elected government would maintain the reformist drive, they also wanted to accomplish as much as possible *before* the handover.

The obvious first step was to definitively eliminate the military threat. Endorsing a decree issued by Sy during the coup attempt, a cabinet meeting on 25 September officially dissolved the RSP, a bold stroke compared with the government's earlier timid responses. It still took a few more days to complete the army's occupation of the RSP base and fully disarm the rebels. Most RSP officers and soldiers were then reassigned to other branches of the army, to peacekeeping missions abroad, and to the military's anti-terrorist contingents operating along the northern borders. Diendéré and the bulk of the coup ringleaders were detained, but several dozen more ex-RSP members remained at large for a while longer. The regiment's presidential security functions were later assigned to an inter-army group drawn from different branches of the military.

The coup attempt also stirred judicial action. Diendéré and eighty-four others were indicted by a military court on charges of murder, treason, conspiracy, crimes against humanity, and related charges.[40] At the time of writing in 2017, most suspects were in custody, although a few had fled the country. A majority were military personnel, but a number of civilians from the CDP and other pro-Compaoré groups were also under investigation. Although a military court had already begun investigations into the assassination of Sankara in March and reopened inquiries into the Zongo murder, the abrupt apprehension of so many RSP suspects gave an unexpected boost to those cases. Three RSP soldiers were eventually accused of participating in Zongo's murder. Diendéré and thirteen others were formally charged in Sankara's killing, with international arrest warrants issued for two others who had fled the country: Compaoré and Hyacinthe Kafando, the presumed leader of the assassination squad.[41]

There also were repercussions in the electoral arena. The earlier controversy over the exclusion of leading candidates of pro-Compaoré parties was muted when a number, including former interior and foreign minister General Djibrill Bassolé, were detained for complicity in Diendéré's action. Although most detained leaders denied involvement in the coup attempt, their parties ultimately decided to stay in the legislative election with alternative candidates.

A number of particularly important laws were passed during the last months of the CNT, with civil society deputies taking the most active lead. That was partly because the political parties, less concerned with the transition than the upcoming elections, had refrained from nominating their most experienced people; with a few exceptions, the party legislators played a mainly supportive role. The deputies from the military were similarly reserved. As a result, the civil society representatives, led by their energetic president, Chériff Sy, were frequently in a position to champion new legislation.

For these activists, their part in the CNT was an extension of their role in the popular mobilizations. They soon found, however, that they needed to function quite differently. "We were new and had no experience in managing the state," recalled Aziz Sana of the Mouvement ça suffit. To understand how to draft laws and operate as legislators, Sana and his colleagues drew on the knowledge of former deputies and parliamentary assistants. Nevertheless, Sana added, the activists had a great asset: their "political conviction." That enabled them not to get lost in parliamentary details but to maintain a focus on the central reforms that people wanted.[42] Marie Madeleine Somda, a key women's activist, found herself as chairperson of the legislature's finance committee, the first time a woman had ever held that post.[43] For Hervé Ouattara, who became head of the civil society caucus, the biggest adjustment was learning the appropriate forms of speech. "It was sometimes frustrating, because I had learned how to conduct myself differently in the streets, to pose problems clearly," he said. But in the CNT, "we had to use language that was oblique, diplomatic. We had to address people as 'honourable'!"[44]

During the legislature's first half-year, CNT deputies had already adopted a number of signature pieces of legislation, including the revision of the armed forces statutes, the new electoral code, a stronger anti-corruption law, and a mining code that reduced tax breaks for companies, strengthened environmental safeguards, and ensured that both local communities and the central treasury benefited more from mining operations. The CNT set up a special commission of inquiry to review the financial accounts of the Compaoré government's last three years. Its work was interrupted by the abortive coup, but then resumed. Its report in October revealed that the government had lost $250 million through tax and customs fraud and was owed another $75 million in unpaid loans, of which nearly $7 million was soon recovered.[45] (The stronger anti-corruption legislation approved by the CNT later facilitated exposure of questionable practices by some officials of the transitional government itself, most prominently Zida.)

The CNT's crowning work came on 5 November, when it amended the constitution. Earlier that year some deputies had started consultations for a new constitution, to inaugurate a Fifth Republic. But with all the other challenges facing the transition, that proved unworkable. The legislature instead took up several basic and widely accepted amendments. Foremost was the presidential term limit, which the deputies "locked in" as a permanent feature of the constitution, beyond the possibility of modification. They also stripped from the constitution all clauses on the Senate, enshrined judicial independence, allowed independent candidates in all elections, permitted any citizen to challenge a law's constitutionality, and gave constitutional authority to the national anti-corruption agency. Sy, representing the amendments' authors, termed their adoption "a decisive step towards the consolidation of the gains of the popular insurrection and the people's resistance to the failed coup."[46]

The CNT did not stop there. Even with the intense focus on the elections of 29 November, the deputies continued their work for another month longer, before the new National Assembly was inaugurated. By the time the CNT completed its work on 28 December it had approved a total of 110 laws, an unprecedented output nearly twice as high as any other recent legislative session.[47]

## TOWARDS ELECTORAL LEGITIMACY

For more than a year, political legitimacy in Burkina Faso rested mainly on expressions of popular power. Transitional government ministers and parliamentary deputies, all unelected, claimed their authority directly from "the people," whether mobilized in the streets or represented by loose political and civil society networks. Decades of Compaoré's semi-authoritarianism and periodic electoral charades made that exceptional situation possible. But almost no one thought it should last. Even radicalized youths alienated from the party elites or inspired by Sankara's revolutionary example knew that the time had come for a return to constitutional rule.

Every step towards the elections generated public enthusiasm. Many new voters registered, reaching a total of 5.5 million, 70 percent more than in the last presidential election in 2010 and nearly half of them under thirty-five years old. Even after several prospective old-regime candidates were knocked out of the running there were still fourteen contenders for the presidency. The legislative election was even more competitive, with nearly 7,000 candidates standing for 127 National Assembly seats, from eighty-one political parties and nineteen groups of independents. With no one from the transitional government allowed to run, the race, for the first time in the country's history, was also free of candidates who could wield the undue influence of state incumbency.

Candidates, religious leaders, traditional chiefs, government officials, legislators, media commentators, and civil society figures called on voters to turn out massively for an election billed as vital for Burkina Faso's future. The activists of Balai citoyen urged young people previously disillusioned by party politics to go to the polls, under the slogan, "After your revolt, your vote."

A new network emerged, the Convention of Civil Society Organizations for Observing Domestic Elections. Headed by Halidou Ouédraogo (leader of the collective that protested against Zongo's killing), it comprised more than 100 groups and mobilized 6,000 volunteers to guard against election fraud. Other organizations provided 10,000 more monitors, mostly Burkinabè but also from the European Union and neighbouring West African states.[48] Activists and intellectuals appealed to the candidates and parties to refrain from violence or ethnic or religious appeals.

With no ruling party to dominate the campaign or tamper with the process, the electoral field was theoretically wide open. Yet in reality certain candidates and parties had a considerable advantage. Zéphirin Diabré was clearly a leading contender, in part based on his UPC's performance in the last legislative election in 2012 and his own role in heading the alliance that brought down Compaoré. The UPC, however, had difficulty projecting a clear direction. On some occasions Diabré cited his ideological commitment to free-market liberalism, raising alarm on the left and in the unions. Yet during the campaign's closing days, Diabré played to radical youth by pledging to "complete the work that Sankara began."[49]

Like Diabré, Roch Marc Christian Kaboré was also once a Compaoré regime insider, although he broke with it far more recently. The origins of his MPP had disadvantages and advantages. MPP candidates encountered suspicions that they were opportunists who had abandoned the Compaoré regime when it was already sinking and would ultimately replicate similar governing policies and practices. But Kaboré, as a former prime minister and parliamentary president, could by the same token highlight his experience in managing the affairs of state. Most significantly, because the MPP came out of the CDP, its candidates could tap some of the same patronage networks and sources of financing. Although overt appeals to ethnicity were prohibited, the fact that Kaboré was Mossi (compared with Diabré, who came from the much smaller Bissa) was seen by some analysts as an attribute, especially in helping mobilize support from Mossi traditional chiefs. Finally, the MPP presented itself ideologically as "social democratic." The party distanced itself from Compaoré's embrace of crude IMF liberalization policies (and by implication, Diabré's role in them) and pledged to increase both state investment and popular social programmes, a stance that attracted support from a number of leftist parties.

When the votes were counted, Kaboré had 53.5 percent, a bare majority, but enough to avoid a second-round runoff. Although Kaboré's percentage score was well below Compaoré's habitual totals of 80 percent or more, the larger pool of voters meant that he actually received a quarter more votes than Compaoré did in 2010. Diabré, Kaboré's closest challenger, secured 29.6 percent. Diabré's prompt concession to the winner, monitors' overwhelming certification of the election's transparency, and the absence of any major challenges to the results ensured that the poll was accepted as legitimate, both domestically and internationally.

In the legislature, Kaboré's MPP fell short of an outright majority, winning just fifty-five seats out of 127. To get enough other deputies to secure a working majority, the party negotiated with some of the thirteen other parties that won seats. Ultimately, the MPP gained the backing of eight other parties, with a total of fifteen deputies, including the Sankarists' UNIR/PS with five legislators. With the support of that MPP-led majority, Salif Diallo was elected as National Assembly president. The UPC, with thirty-three seats, chose to remain in the opposition. Although that left Diabré in the same position of official opposition leader that he had held before, this time it came with a rather awkward alliance: The opposition now included the CDP, which with eighteen deputies had survived as the third largest party in the legislature.

After Kaboré was officially sworn in as president on 29 December, his new government was dominated by MPP figures and technocrats, including Simon Compaoré as security minister. It also had ministers from three allied parties, two of the ministers from the UNIR/PS. For the first time since the 1960s, no military officers were appointed to the cabinet.

The political line-up in the legislature reflected the continued influence of money politics. The non-governmental anti-corruption network Ren-lac enumerated several hundred instances of election code violations: giving out money, fuel, T-shirts, and other goods to draw people to campaign rallies, plastering public spaces with more campaign posters than allowed, and persuading traditional chiefs to sway the vote. Three parties accounted for the bulk of the violations: the MPP with about half of all instances, followed by the UPC and CDP. "Money remains the most important means for winning elections in Burkina Faso," Ren-lac concluded.[50] Bénéwendé Sankara, reflecting on the UNIR/PS' modest performance, admitted to this writer that some voters lacked confidence in parties that had never held power before, but also cited the bigger parties' utilization of traditional chiefs and the persistence of "electoral corruption" that left smaller parties "lacking the logistical and financial means to wage a campaign."[51] The local government elections of May 2016 were similarly skewed. By a margin wider than in the legislative poll, the MPP gained 59 percent of the local councillors for Burkina Faso's 365 municipalities, arrondissements, and rural communes, perhaps reflecting the MPP's position now as a governing party able to promise patronage favours to communities supporting it.

For those who had looked forward to a sharp break with the past, the election outcome was somewhat sobering. Many were of two minds. While the voters' choice had to be respected, said Boureima Ouédraogo, editor of the respected independent fortnightly *Le Reporter*, he nevertheless expressed scepticism that it would be possible "to build something new with something old."[52] Sams'K Le Jah of Balai citoyen saw the election as "historic" and a "sign of change," yet added, "We have the impression that Blaise Compaore's system is still here."[53]

Uncertainties about the character and direction of the new government were temporarily overshadowed when Ouagadougou experienced its worst ever terrorist attack on 15 January 2016. That evening three fighters loyal to Al-Qaeda in the Islamic Maghreb (AQIM), who had infiltrated across Burkina Faso's northern borders, slaughtered more than thirty foreigners and Burkinabè at a hotel and restaurant in the heart of the city. Burkinabè troops and gendarmes, supported by French special forces, killed all the assailants. A week later, compounding the sense of insecurity, fugitive soldiers of the former RSP attacked an armoury, although most were soon captured.

While the RSP remnants reflected only a residual threat, the AQIM attack was a worrying new development. For years, the country had escaped the sort of insurgent activity by AQIM and other groups that had long plagued Mali, Niger, Algeria, and Libya. At the time, Compaoré served as a West African mediator in various regional conflicts and Diendéré maintained close ties with the insurgent leaderships, reportedly helping arrange ransom payments to free European hostages. Some analysts detected a kind of "non-aggression pact," while President Kaboré termed it "collusion."[54] Whatever the appropriate term, that arrangement came to an end with Compaoré's overthrow and Diendéré's imprisonment, leaving the country now vulnerable to an unexpected new source of insecurity.

Other attacks followed the one in Ouagadougou, but mostly in the remote northern provinces along the country's long and porous border with Mali and Niger. The majority seemed to be the work of AQIM and similar groups that were especially active in Mali's protracted conflict. But in November 2016, for the first time, a Burkinabè "jihadist" group also entered the fray. Ansarul Islam ("defenders of Islam"), led by a radical Islamic preacher from Burkina Faso's northern town of Djibo, carried out a dramatic assault against a Burkinabè military post in Nassoumbou, killing a dozen troops. The group, which called for the establishment of a separate Peulh emirate, also assassinated local municipal councillors and teachers, spreading panic in several provinces and demonstrating the limits of the Burkinabè army's ability to ensure protection of the population.[55]

## NO "HONEYMOON"

The rise of an active insurgent threat won the government a degree of patriotic support. Some activist groups even organized demonstrations in solidarity with the armed forces' battle against the jihadists or muted their usual criticisms of the presence of French special forces in the country. Many Burkinabè accepted the need for enhanced security, from a stronger military presence at the borders to armed checkpoints, metal detectors, and frequent patrols around key public locations.

The authorities, however, did not receive a blank cheque for governing. None of the country's underlying social and economic problems were resolved by the change in government. Although Kaboré and other officials promised to tackle poverty and the legacies of corruption and poor governance, and even launched important initiatives to improve health care and education, people remained impatient for tangible change. Teachers, health care employees, miners, students, community residents, and even judges marched, rallied, barricaded highways, or staged sit-ins to press their demands. Whether addressing their grievances to the national government or local officials, Burkinabè expected a response.

Civil society activists continued to articulate popular grievances and pledged to hold the authorities to account. "We are not giving them any honeymoon," said Ismael Diallo, spokesperson of the FRC civil society coalition. "We have to be vigilant."[56]

The Ren-lac anti-corruption network urged concrete measures against corruption and appealed to ordinary Burkinabè to help expose financial abuses. The union-led CCVC demanded reduction of consumer prices, more jobs, improved working conditions, and trials of former officials suspected of political and economic crimes. When Prime Minister Paul Kaba Thiéba met civil society representatives, they pressed him on a range of issues, including youth unemployment, corruption, and high prices. Most also raised concerns about the absence of a clear government policy towards the emergence of hundreds of informal local self-defence groups, commonly called Koglwéogo ("protectors of the bush" in the language of the Mossi), which were hailed for combatting armed banditry in remote rural areas but also criticized for sometimes engaging in abuses.[57]

With the aim of institutionalizing societal oversight, some civil groups launched an initiative called "Présimètre" (president metre), to periodically track how well Kaboré fulfilled his promises. Inspired by similar undertakings in Nigeria, Senegal, and France, the proposal to launch the Présimètre was first conceived in February by the civil society election monitoring network, the Centre pour la gouvernance démocratique, and other organizations. Its proponents sent a delegation to inform Kaboré that they would be monitoring his performance. "He said he likes the idea," Diallo reported shortly after. "But even if he doesn't like it, we will do it."[58]

Présimètre was largely an online communications tool, utilizing a website (www.presimetre.bf), text messages, social media posts, and other means to publicize its conclusions and solicit reactions. Its initial opinion survey, marking Kaboré's first 100 days in office, was scathing. Of the more than 2,000 people who responded by answering questions disseminated online and by cell phone, only 43 percent expressed confidence in the government's overall direction.[59] To signal his openness to criticism, Kaboré appeared on a live national television broadcast, "Citizens' Dialogue," sponsored by Présimètre a few days later. For the first time, a sitting president subjected himself to questions from ordinary citizens on a range of issues posed directly by phone, text message, or online.[60] Many viewers later expressed appreciation of the exercise, although some wondered whether Kaboré's media performance would be followed by concrete deeds. At a minimum, said Rasmané Ouédraogo, an unemployed graduate, Kaboré had to know that he now "faced a watchful population, a mobilized youth."[61]

There were only limited indications that such vigilance would be enough to spur the authorities to more conclusive action, however. In October 2016, the second anniversary of the anti-Compaoré insurrection, many activists complained that those in power were dragging their feet on essential reforms and failing to address people's pressing economic and social problems. Balai citoyen joined with six other civil society groups to form the new Coalition Ditanyè (the name of the national anthem). They accused the government and opposition alike of "demonstrating their incapacity to pursue our people's profound aspirations for real change."[62] Guy Hervé Kam, Balai citoyen's spokesperson, warned that if the authorities disregarded those aspirations, citizens knew how to remind them: "Insurrection is rooted in the DNA of the Burkinabè people."[63]

# 15
# A NEW BURKINA FASO?

It was common for top leaders in both the transitional administration and the Kaboré government to cite the memories of the "national martyrs" killed by security forces during the October 2014 insurrection. As for the insurrection itself, while transition officials readily cited it as the source of their authority, President Kaboré and his colleagues usually traced their own legitimacy to the elections. Yet the two sources of authority were not counter-posed, argued the transitional president, Michel Kafando, echoing views prevalent among civil society activists. Legitimacy, he said on the first anniversary of the insurrection, involved "above all a clear understanding that one must serve the country at the call of its people." Rejecting "the false thesis and rhetoric that sees legitimacy as only coming from the ballot box," he told the deputies of the transitional legislature that "no one is more legitimate than you, since you were the direct and spontaneous emanation of the people's will."[1]

Both sources of legitimacy continued to animate political discourse and practice for some time. The open and democratic character of the elections did give the members of the Kaboré government greater *constitutional* authority than either the ousted Compaoré regime or the administrators of the transition, who had been chosen in a rather ad hoc manner by relatively small circles of politicians, civil society, and military figures. The "international community," principally France, the US, the European Union, and the African Union, likewise equated the election outcome with the restoration of legal authority. Yet Kaboré, sensitive to criticisms that he and his closest colleagues had come out of the old system, also sought to tap into popular legitimacy, pointing to his party's role in weakening the Compaoré regime at a crucial moment and from time to time lauding the insurrection itself. In March 2017, the government appointed as Kaboré's "high representative" Chériff Sy, the former president of the transitional parliament and a hero to many activists for his role in blocking the coup attempt by Diendéré's presidential guard.[2]

Those activists, meanwhile, remained the foremost standard bearers of "insurgent citizenship." They upheld the power of the streets in part because they lacked confidence in the new authorities' promises, but also out of a deep conviction that democracy required the conscious and sustained engagement of ordinary people. "It's important to maintain some form of counter-power, to force the government to respect its commitments," said Smockey of Balai citoyen. "If this balance is allowed to disappear, there will be a risk of the old ghosts coming back."[3]

Although Smockey and his comrades drew inspiration from the revolutionary ideals of the Sankara era, their immediate experience had been forged in a battle to defend the constitution of 1991. That meant acceptance of representative democracy, complete with its emphasis on formal institutions. Yet they did not limit themselves to upholding established constitutional norms. They constantly pushed for more active citizen engagement and an expansion of rights, including in the social sphere: against inequality and exclusion, for jobs and gender advancement, for recognition of young people's initiatives. While government officials bemoaned the frequent strikes, sit-ins, community agitation, and other protests as disruptive, activists generally saw them as signs of a vital new era of popular movement and mobilization.

Although some saw the new order as at least partially a continuation of the old, there were nevertheless significant differences. The most repressive and interventionist sector of the military, the RSP, was gone, and the rest of the armed forces had moved to the political side-lines, at least for the time being. Political life, especially in the electoral arena, still reflected the influence of money politics, but there existed many more "horizontal" forms of citizen participation to counteract the weight of patronage. Urban elites continued to dominate official institutions, yet politics and protest were more *national* than ever, involving more ordinary citizens and extending into remote corners of the country.

## UNFINISHED REFORMS, NEW CHALLENGES

The year following the insurrection was an especially heady one, animated by an urgency to pursue structural reform. The post-election authorities, however, adopted a more measured pace. Critics often accused them of dragging their feet. "Hesitation, fumbling, and procrastination" was the way Hervé Ouattara summarized the government's performance.[4]

The need for further reform of the security sector was glaringly obvious, given both the increase in attacks by Islamist insurgents and the spread of armed banditry in poorly patrolled areas of the countryside. After his election, President Kaboré met several times with his army command to urge wider restructuring of the rest of the armed forces, and initiated a five-year (2017–21) military reform plan to upgrade the army's capacities and improve training in "asymmetrical warfare" against small groups of mobile insurgents. Some concrete measures were initiated: army reinforcements sent to the north and more all-terrain vehicles were acquired as well as helicopters to provide air support for ground troops. Some 800 Burkinabè peacekeeping troops were to be recalled home from a UN–African Union peacekeeping force in Sudan's Darfur region, and a portion of another 1,700-troop force serving with a UN mission in Mali was to be redeployed closer to the Burkina Faso border.

Reform of the army's command structures was less evident, however. While a number of abusive and inefficient officers were removed with the dissolution of the RSP, noted retired colonel Charles Lona Ouattara, others who had long "benefited from corruption and disorder" under Compaoré still remained in the military hierarchy.[5] Exasperated by the failure of the armed forces to halt insurgent action in the north, Balai citoyen called for a "clean-up" of the officer corps, declaring that the Burkinabè people and their army "deserve better than this politico-bureaucratic and bourgeoisified command."[6] At the end of 2016 Kaboré finally dismissed the army chief-of-staff General Pingrénoma Zagré, and replaced him with Major Colonel Oumarou Sadou, a seasoned veteran originally from the north.

Justice system reforms were initiated during the transition, but subsequently moved into a slower gear. Despite the constitutional amendments to enhance judicial independence, many believed that the courts, police service, and prisons still needed major changes in personnel and practices. According to human rights lawyer Apollinaire J. Kyélem de Tambèla, some judges were still corrupt: "Criminals who were captured and sent to the courts have bribed judges and were free a week later. That's why people are demanding more integrity in the justice system."[7]

To some extent, the era of impunity, in which high-level perpetrators escaped any accounting, appeared to be ending, however slow the judicial process. Numerous suspects were at last in detention facing charges over the assassinations of Thomas Sankara and Norbert Zongo. While such high-profile cases were emblematic, Burkina Faso's history is littered with many other abuses, often committed against ordinary citizens. For impunity to be truly over, many Burkinabè agreed, those victims also deserved justice. One step in that direction was the establishment, during the last weeks of the transitional government, of a new High Council for Reconciliation and National Unity. Officially installed in March 2016, its principal task was to expedite action on 5,065 unresolved cases of economic and "blood" crimes dating back to Burkina Faso's independence in 1960.[8]

Fighting corruption was also an ongoing process. During the transition, the government's main anti-corruption agency, the Autorité supérieure de contrôle de l'Etat et de lutte contre la corruption (ASCE-LC), was strengthened and placed under the leadership of Luc Marius Ibriga, a prominent activist, who was kept at its helm following the election. At the ASCE-LC's request, the courts launched formal anti-corruption inquiries against Compaoré, his brother François, and former finance minister Lucien Marie Noël Bembamba.[9] In one among several signs that the courts were also beginning to tackle "ordinary" instances of corruption more systematically, a district health manager in the provincial town of Diébougou was condemned in August 2016 to ten years in prison for embezzling funds under both the transitional administration and the elected government.[10] To discourage future malfeasance, all members of the new government (including President Kaboré) were required to provide full public listings of their assets and incomes, to make it easier to later highlight excessive wealth acquired while in office. The idea dated back to the asset declarations introduced by Sankara in 1987, but was then abandoned after Compaoré's coup.

Other reforms had also been raised in the years of contestation against the CDP regime and after its downfall. A National Commission on Reconciliation and Reform, created during the transition, summarized many of the most widely accepted proposals in a report released just before the elections: strengthening financial transparency in government institutions, political parties, civil society groups, and other entities; barring civil servants from establishing party "cells" in their places of work; reinforcing the independence and capacities of the judiciary and private media; bolstering parliamentary and judicial controls over the executive; and ensuring that traditional chiefs do not use their authority to sway voters or otherwise support particular parties. There were also a variety of economic and social recommendations, from general admonitions to reduce social inequalities and injustices to specific policies such as allocating set percentages of mining revenues to new investments, developing solar energy as a national priority, creating new mechanisms to resolve land-tenure disputes, and promoting the use of locally made cotton fabrics (another idea revived from the revolutionary era).[11]

The commission envisaged that many of those proposals would be taken up in a new constitution. During the transition and in the election campaigns, most political and civil society leaders agreed that consolidating the gains of the insurrection would require not only entrenching the presidential term limit, but also going beyond other elements of the 1991 constitution by drawing up a charter for a new, Fifth Republic. Accordingly, a Constitutional Commission was sworn in at the beginning of June 2016. Named to head it was one of the country's most experienced jurists and activists, Halidou Ouédraogo, who vowed that the new constitution would reflect "the aspirations of the insurgents."[12] By the first months of 2017 a preliminary draft was ready. To a much greater extent than with the previous constitution, that draft was then submitted to the public for wide discussion. Beginning in late March, consultative sessions were held in all thirteen regions and among Burkinabè living in France and other countries. Some debates were heated: over the relative powers of the presidency and the legislature, the degree of judicial independence, abolition of the death penalty, women's right to land, and a variety of other issues. Taking into account the views expressed in the public consultations, the Constitutional Commission was then to prepare a final draft for government review, before voters decided on it in a national referendum.

Whatever the specifics of the new constitution or other reforms signed into law, many warned that official policies, proclamations, and texts could not by themselves guarantee citizens' rights and interests. For activists, the answer was obvious: ongoing popular organization and mobilization to ensure that reforms are actually implemented and preserved. Burkina Faso's turbulent history demonstrated, however, that pressure from below was only one essential element. A committed and uncorrupted state leadership willing to engage with diverse sectors of society would also be vital for generating lasting solutions to the country's many problems, current and future.

Potential new threats loomed on the horizon. How to balance newly acquired liberties with security and management concerns could prove especially delicate. Some authorities, citing the exigencies of state, questioned the prerogatives of the courts and the degree of press freedoms. A National Assembly decision in November 2016 to allow military officers to serve as cabinet ministers or as heads of state institutions (revising the armed forces statutes approved by the transitional CNT) raised some worries of a future revival of military involvement in political affairs.

Historically, religious tension had been minimal and the country's various faiths intermixed and cohabited relatively harmoniously (the population is about 60 percent Muslim, 25 percent Christian, and 15 percent followers of traditional beliefs). Still, as one detailed study pointed out, while the peaceful coexistence of religions "remains robust," it nevertheless "is beginning to erode around the margins."[13] One reflection: Muslims have become more aware of their underrepresentation among the political and administrative elites and more vocal about perceived favouritism towards Christians in education and development financing. If ignored or unaddressed by the central authorities, resentments could go in dangerous directions.

Ethnic relations were also marked by relatively low levels of conflict, especially in comparison with some of Burkina Faso's immediate neighbours. Yet worrying signs have emerged. The population has been growing rapidly, with projections of an increase from 18.1 million in 2015 to 27.2 million by 2030. Besides spurring faster urbanization, that growth will heighten rivalry for access to fertile land. There already had been occasional clashes over land among farmers and between farmers and livestock herders, conflicts that sometimes turned more deadly when the contenders belonged to different ethnic groups. Electoral competition likewise exacerbated animosities when supporters of rival parties were primarily from one ethnic group or on the rare occasions when politicians sought to mobilize support through appeals to ethnic identity. After the rise of jihadist attacks in the north, Tuareg refugees from Mali and Burkinabè Tuareg alike were frequently stigmatized and sometimes subjected to open discrimination.[14]

Persistent poverty and the wide income gap combined to provide other potential sources of conflict. In 2014, according to the National Institute of Statistics, some 40.1 percent of all Burkinabè lived in poverty, a rate that reached 70 percent in the arid north. That was better than the 46.7 percent registered nationally five years earlier, but still left the country one of the poorest on the continent.[15] While educated urban youths generally fared better than their rural cousins, the high unemployment rate among secondary and university graduates fostered acute grievances among an especially active and occasionally volatile sector of the population. The participation of many young people in the transitional government and legislature gave youths some hope that their concerns might receive greater official attention. But subsequently no one under thirty-five was named to the new government and youths in general were pushed back "into the shadows," noted Fayçal Traoré, project coordinator for the civil society organization MBDC. That shift away from inclusion was "an element of dissatisfaction for youth, who constituted 90 percent of those who marched, fought on the ground, and took the greatest risks."[16]

Popular anger was stoked further by the contrast between the conditions of the vast majority and the wealthy elites. Prime Minister Thiéba, citing a World Bank study, acknowledged that "the richest 10 percent of the population holds about a third of the national wealth," while the poorest 10 percent accounted for less than 3 percent.[17]

Burkina Faso's political regimes have dealt with social problems differently over time. During the first two decades after independence, poverty and other social miseries were virtually ignored, except for patchwork programmes by some religious orders and foreign aid groups. During the revolutionary era of the 1980s political and social interventions were closely linked, with state reforms matched by attempts to reallocate resources and incomes to the poor. The return to constitutional rule in the early 1990s not only brought halting results in the political arena, but with the introduction of externally directed austerity programmes also left most social interventions by the wayside, worsened by the "crony capitalism" of the Compaoré system. The breadth and tenacity of the protest movements against that regime owed much to popular dissatisfaction with economic and social conditions, even though the immediate rallying cry was forthrightly political: defence of the constitution. The subsequent transitional and elected governments promised many new economic and social initiatives against poverty and inequality, sometimes expressed in the revolutionary language of the 1980s. But liberal democracy's enforced separation of the political and social spheres and the authorities' continued adherence to internationally sanctioned policies based largely on the market place severe limits on targeted state interventions—with a high risk of continued popular dissatisfaction, social agitation, and conflict.

## BEYOND BORDERS

In dealing with Burkina Faso's current and future challenges, many Burkinabè have realized that they must rely largely on their own capacities and initiatives.

They succeeded against difficult odds in toppling an autocratic ruler, and that success left them on firmer ground for tackling the country's many other difficulties. Some problems, however, originated from the outside, requiring greater collaboration with others.

Although a local insurgency emerged in the far north in late 2016, the main immediate threat remained from the regional groups that were most active in Mali and often launched incursions into Burkina Faso. The government, as part of its broader security response, forged a new alliance with Sahelian neighbours Mali, Niger, Chad, and Mauritania. Known collectively as the Group of Five (G5), they agreed to enhance joint military training, intelligence sharing, and logistical infrastructure and form a unified military force to combat terrorism and drug-trafficking in the region. Whether as part of the G5 or through other initiatives, Burkina Faso also strengthened collaboration with the rest of the Sahel in a variety of fields to address the region's other common problems, including the severe impacts of climate change, economic disadvantages, rapid demographic growth, migrating populations, and changing social and cultural patterns.

Political actors—including some of Burkina Faso's activists—also increased their relations with counterparts across the region, and more widely in Africa. That was facilitated by Africans' enhanced interest in Burkina Faso, largely because of its dramatic insurrection, still a rare case in which popular mobilizations succeeded in toppling a sitting president. "A veritable democratic harmattan [desert wind] is sweeping Africa," commented Francis Kpatindé, an editor of the Paris weekly Jeune Afrique, originally from Benin. "People who have been stifled can now legitimately think that what was possible in Ouagadougou could also be in Brazzaville, Kinshasa, Banjul, and elsewhere."[18] Just two weeks after Compaoré's downfall, opposition representatives from seven African countries (Burundi, Central African Republic, Congo Republic, Democratic Republic of the Congo, Equatorial Guinea, Gabon, and Senegal) met in Paris to compare strategies for defending constitutional liberties. They hailed the "tsunami in Ouagadougou" as an example for Africa and believed that it might "inaugurate the end of an era of perpetual governments." Yet some also recognized that inspiration alone could not bring change and that much depended on the particular circumstances in each country. Mathias Dzon, an opposition leader from the Congo Republic (Brazzaville), acknowledged: "Burkinabè didn't go out into the streets spontaneously to change their president. We can't forget that some work went into it."[19]

Meanwhile, some African presidents exhibited fear that external inspiration might in fact tip the balance more in favour of their own domestic challengers. In the Democratic Republic of the Congo, which experienced intense opposition to efforts by President Joseph Kabila to prolong his tenure beyond the constitutional limit, security forces cracked down on expressions of pan-African solidarity with local critics. In March 2015 they detained members of a Congolese alliance called Filimbi ("whistle" in a local language) while they were meeting with activists from Senegal's Y'en a marre and Burkina Faso's Balai citoyen.[20]

Leading Burkinabè activists consciously saw themselves as part of a growing pan-African movement for democratic rights. The Collectif anti-reféréndum, one of the prime movers in the popular insurrection, in March 2015 renamed itself the Citoyen africain pour la renaissance (keeping its old acronym, CAR). Within a year it had set up chapters in the Central African Republic, Côte d'Ivoire, Mali, and Morocco.[21] Balai citoyen did not try to form chapters abroad, but rather sought to work directly with similar groups in Senegal, the Democratic Republic of the Congo, and other countries. "We succeeded in carrying out an insurrection, and we will share our experience of struggle with whoever wants," explained Smockey. Balai citoyen, he said, had a "pan-African vocation," alongside activists elsewhere. "We share the same visions and dreams for the continent."[22]

# NOTES

### *Chapter 1*

1 *L'Observateur Paalga*, 6 June 2016.
2 Anderson (1991).
3 Weber (1978), pp. 212–301; Zaum (2012), pp. 50–51.
4 Harsch (2014).
5 Loada (2010), p. 289.
6 Migdal, Kohli, and Shue (1994).
7 Boone (1992); Olukoshi and Laakso (1996).
8 Mamdani (1996).
9 *Sidwaya*, 4 August 2016.
10 Tarrow (1998).
11 Johnston (2011), p. 19; also see Holston (2008).
12 *L'Observateur Paalga*, 18 June 2014.

### *Chapter 2*

1 Tilly (1992).
2 Goody (1967); Savonnet (1976); Savonnet-Guyot (1986).
3 Duperray (1984), pp. 1–47.
4 Jacob (2001), pp. 18–19.
5 Curtin (1984).
6 Irwin (1981); Delmond (1953), pp. 21–38.
7 Zahan (1967), pp. 156–157.
8 Izard (1984), pp. 211–237; Goody (1964), pp. 177–189.
9 Skinner (1964), pp. 13–59; Savonnet-Guyot (1986), pp. 91–97, 103–105.
10 Le Moal (1967), p. 182.
11 Izard (1985a).
12 Boutillier (1963), p. 5.
13 Skinner (1964), p. 75.
14 Izard (1985b), p. 139.
15 Pacere (1981), p. 152.
16 Bretout (1976), p. 40.
17 Balima (1996), pp. 209–210; Gnimien (2016); Kambou-Ferrand (1993).
18 Massa and Madiéga (1995), p. 23.
19 Ki-Zerbo (1972), p. 436.
20 Delavignette (1946), p. 29.

21 Massa and Madiéga (1995), pp. 357–359.
22 Massa and Madiéga (1995), p. 151.
23 Balima (1996), p. 201.
24 Massa and Madiéga (1995), pp. 21, 90.
25 Kambou-Ferrand (1993), p. 347.
26 Skinner (1964), p. 162.
27 Massa and Madiéga (1995), p. 21.
28 Beucher (2009), pp. 18–21.
29 Duperray (1984), p. 203.
30 Gervais (1987), pp. 109–121.
31 Massa and Madiéga (1995), pp. 157–162; Bonnafé, Fiéloux, and Kambou (1982), pp. 132–136.
32 Marchal (1980), pp. 123, 139, 153–154.
33 Hodgkin (1957).
34 Thompson and Adloff (1969), pp. 30–35.
35 Massa and Madiéga (1995), pp. 435–438.
36 Cooper (2014).
37 Diané (1990), pp. 120–123; Massa and Madiéga (1995), pp. 430–431; Dicko (1992).
38 Skinner (1964); Balima (1996), pp. 280–281,
39 Balima (1996), p. 293.
40 Dicko (1992), pp. 97–98.
41 Balima (1996), pp. 294–295.

### Chapter 3

1 *Carrefour africain*, 3 June 1962.
2 Between 1960 and 1994 one French franc was equivalent to CFA50 and from 1994 to 1999 to CFA100. Subsequently, as a result of France's entry into the Euro monetary zone, the CFA franc was pegged at CFA656 to €1.
3 *Carrefour africain*, 21 March 1965.
4 Cabanis and Martin (1987), pp. 20–21; Skinner (1964), p. 203; *Carrefour africain*, 18 March 1962 and 10 May 1964.
5 *Carrefour africain*, 10 May 1964.
6 Marçais (1964), pp. 321–329; Cabanis and Martin (1987), p. 27.
7 *Carrefour africain*, 10 November 1963.
8 Zagré (1994), p. 55.
9 *Carrefour africain*, 17 June 1962 and 16 June 1963.
10 Guirma (1991), 128–132.
11 Guirma (1991).
12 Balima (1960), p. 361.
13 Balima (1996), pp. 305–206 ; Guirma (1991), pp. 135–139; Muase (1989a), pp. 68–70; Zagré (1994), pp. 58–61; *Carrefour africain*, 7–14 November 1965.

14 Skurnik (1970), pp. 67–71; Guirma (1991), pp. 139–147.
15 *Carrefour africain*, 3 September 1966.
16 *Carrefour africain*, 16 July and 3 December 1966.
17 *Carrefour africain*, 9 December 1967; Balima (1996), p. 307.
18 Zagré (1994), pp. 69-74.
19 *Carrefour africain*, 4 May, 25 May, and 9 November 1968; Balima (1996), p. 315.
20 *Carrefour africain*, 1–15 November 1975.
21 *Carrefour africain*, 24 August 1968.
22 *Carrefour africain*, 20 August 1976.
23 *Carrefour africain*, 11 May 1968.
24 Lippens (1972), pp. 34–35.
25 Damiba (1970).
26 *Carrefour africain*, 18 July 1970,
27 Lippens (1972), p. 35.
28 Yarba (1980), pp. 117–119; Lippens (1972), pp. 35–36.
29 *Carrefour africain*, 23 January 1971.
30 *Carrefour africain*, 10 July 1971.
31 Cross and Barker (n.d.), pp. 97–125.
32 Comité information Sahel (1974), p. 204.
33 Zagré (1994), pp. 90, 101; Comité information Sahel (1974), pp. 201–203.
34 *Carrefour africain*, 8 January, 6 May, and 21 October 1972 and 3 February, 21 April, and 16 June 1973.
35 Balima (1996), pp. 321–322.
36 *Afrique-Asie* (Paris), 13 December 1976; Zagré (1994), p. 98.
37 Cabanis and Martin (1987), pp. 25–26.
38 *Carrefour africain*, 13–27 July 1974.
39 Zagré (1994), p. 102.
40 Yarba (1980), pp. 120–121; Zagré (1994), pp. 100–101; *Carrefour africain*, 13–27 December 1975
41 Interview with Bassolma Bazié.
42 Zagré (1994), p. 102; *Carrefour africain*, 20 January–20 February and 12 March 1968, 14–28 January, 11 February, and 25 February–11 March 1977; *L'Observateur*, 2 February, 22 February, 2 March, and 4–6 March 1977.
43 Cadenat (1978), pp. 973–1088; Owona (1979).
44 Yarba (1980), pp. 124–125.
45 Interview with Louis Armand Ouali.
46 *Carrefour africain*, 20 April 1979.
47 *Carrefour africain*, 11 April 1980.
48 Guissou (1995b), p. 63.
49 Dumont (1978), pp. 270–271.
50 Dumont (1978), pp. 276–277.

51 *Demain l'Afrique*, 7 April 1980.
52 Balima (1996), p. 329.
53 *West Africa* (London), 17 November 1980.
54 *Carrefour africain*, 15 November–31 December 1980.
55 *Carrefour africain*, 15 November–31 December 1980; Zagré (1994), p. 109.
56 Zagré (1994), pp. 112–115.
57 *Carrefour africain*, 7 July 1982.
58 Zagré (1994), p. 119.
59 *L'Observateur*, 26–28 February and 2 March 1982; *Carrefour africain*, 6 March 1982; "Haute-Volta: Les raisons sociales d'un coup d'état" (1983), p. 86.
60 *L'Observateur*, 8 March 1982.
61 *Carrefour africain*, 3 April and 10 April 1982.
62 *Carrefour africain*, 6 March 1982.
63 *L'Observateur*, 28 December 1981.
64 Muase (1989a), pp. 157–162.
65 *L'Observateur*, 2 and 3 November 1981; *Carrefour africain*, 25 November 1981; Zagré (1994), p. 166.
66 *L'Observateur*, 23 December 1981; *Carrefour africain*, 20 January 1982; Muase (1989a), p. 164.
67 *L'Observateur*, 3 May 1982.
68 Muase (1989a), pp. 165–166; *L'Observateur*, 6 January, 15 April, 16 April, 30 April–2 May, 16–18 July, and 10–12 September 1982; *West Africa* (London), 11 October and 1 November 1982.

## Chapter 4

1 Author's informal discussions with Captain Thomas Sankara and other military officers, 1985–87.
2 *L'Observateur*, 26 April 1982; *Carrefour africain*, 18 May 1984; Andriamirado (1987), pp. 40–41.
3 *Carrefour africain*, 12 November 1982.
4 *L'Observateur*, 11 November 1982.
5 Englebert (1986), p. 70.
6 Andriamirado (1987), pp. 27–53.
7 *Carrefour africain*, 26 November 1982.
8 *L'Observateur*, 24 November 1982 and 13 July 1983.
9 "Haute-Volta: le coup d'état du 7 novembre 1982" (1982), pp. 23–24.
10 *Afrique-Asie*, 20 December 1982.
11 *L'Observateur*, 15 November 1982.
12 *Carrefour africain*, 31 December 1982.
13 Sankara (1983), pp. 90–92.
14 *L'Observateur*, 4 January 1983.

15 *L'Observateur*, 2 February 1983.
16 *Carrefour africain*, 1 April 1983.
17 *L'Observateur*, 5 May 1983.
18 *Carrefour africain*, 13 May 1983.
19 *L'Observateur*, 14 February 1983.
20 Andriamirado (1987), p. 55.
21 *Carrefour africain*, 22 April 1983.
22 *Afrique-Asie*, 14 March 1983.
23 *Carrefour africain*, 22 April 1983
24 *Carrefour africain*, 22 April 1983.
25 *Afrique-Asie*, 11 April 1983.
26 *Carrefour africain*, 11 March 1983; *L'Observateur*, 21 March 1983.
27 *Carrefour africain*, 1 April 1983.
28 *Afrique-Asie*, 6 June 1983.
29 *Carrefour africain*, 18 May 1984.
30 Andriamirado (1987), pp. 63–66.
31 *Carrefour africain*, 20 May 1983.
32 Englebert (1986), p. 75.
33 *L'Observateur*, 30 May 1983.
34 *L'Observateur*, 27 May 1983.
35 *L'Observateur*, 1 June 1983.
36 *L'Observateur*, 24 May 1983.
37 *L'Observateur*, 31 May and 1 June 1983.
38 *L'Observateur*, 30 May 1983.
39 Andriamirado (1987), pp. 74–80.
40 *Carrefour africain*, 17 February 1984.
41 Andriamirado (1987), pp. 80–86.
42 Sankara (2007), p. 67.
43 Jaffré (2007), pp. 203–204.
44 Somé (1990).
45 *Afrique-Asie*, 26 March 1984.
46 Englebert (1986), p. 123.
47 Sankara (2007), p. 81.

### Chapter 5

1 Sankara (2007), p. 93.
2 *Carrefour africain*, 11 October 1985.
3 Asche (1994), pp. 25–27.
4 Kambou (1988), pp. 379–389.
5 *Carrefour africain*, 25 November 1983.
6 Kambou (1988), p. 383.

7 *Africa* (Paris), September 1984; *West Africa*, 5 March 1984.
8 Kambou (1988), pp. 383–386.
9 *Sidwaya*, 29 November 1985.
10 *Sidwaya*, 23 July and 24 September 1985.
11 Kambou (1988), p. 387.
12 Roussillon (1987).
13 Nikiema (1983).
14 Zagré (1994), p. 133.
15 Azam and Morrisson (1999), p. 69; *Carrefour africain*, 9 December 1983.
16 Asche (1994), pp. 25, 43.
17 Augustin and Drabo (1989).
18 Ba (1989).
19 *Sidwaya*, 16 August 1985; *Carrefour africain*, 23 August 1985.
20 *Sidwaya*, 2 September 1985.
21 Conseil national de la révolution (1985a).
22 *Sidwaya*, 3 and 7 March 1986; *Carrefour africain*, 7 and 14 March 1986.
23 *Carrefour africain*, 26 September 1986.
24 Klitgaard (1988), p. 187.
25 Delouvroy (1987), p. 240.
26 Yonaba (1988), p. 369.
27 Skinner (1964); Meyer (1988); Bohmer (1978); Lampué (1979); Lamy (1989).
28 Conseil national de la révolution (1986), p. 25.
29 Yonaba (1988), pp. 365–374; *Carrefour africain*, 8 March 1985.
30 *Carrefour africain*, 14 August 1987.
31 *Carrefour africain*, 6 January 1984.
32 Meerpoel (1988), p. 303.
33 Interview with Ernest Nongma Ouédraogo.
34 Author's field notes from the 18th TPR in Ouagadougou, 9–11 March 1987.
35 Sankara (2007), pp. 113, 115.
36 *Carrefour africain*, 6 January 1984.
37 *Carrefour africain*, 20 January and 10 February 1984.
38 *Carrefour africain*, 4 August 1984.
39 *Carrefour africain*, 16 August 1985 and 10 January and 9 August 1986.
40 Conseil national de la révolution (1986), pp. 55–72.
41 Conseil national de la révolution (1986), pp. 61–62; *Carrefour africain*, 23 August 1985.
42 Conseil national de la révolution (1986), p. 57.
43 Jaffré (1989), pp. 113–117.
44 *Sidwaya*, 4 November 1986.
45 *Sidwaya*, 15 October 1985, and 24 June 1986; *Carrefour africain*, 15 November 1985.
46 Author's field notes, Maison d'arrêt et de correction de Ouagadougou, 7 March 1987.
47 *Carrefour africain*, 13 September 1985.

48 *Sidwaya*, 29 July 1985; *Carrefour africain*, 1 November 1985.
49 Syndicat autonome des magistrats burkinabè (1984), p. 39.
50 *Sidwaya*, 19 April 1984.
51 Syndicat autonome des magistrats burkinabè (1984), pp. 34–35, 45, 52–58, 66–68.
52 Martens (1989), pp. 37, 224, 228.
53 *Carrefour africain*, 7 December 1983.
54 World Bank (2000).
55 *Sidwaya*, 11 April 1986.
56 *Sidwaya*, 9 October 1985.
57 *Sidwaya*, 12 November 1985.
58 *Sidwaya*, 17 October 1985.
59 *Sidwaya*, 13 November 1985.
60 Interview with Thomas Sankara, 1984.
61 *Sidwaya*, 9 October and 12 November 1985 and 8 October 1986.
62 Interview with Thomas Sankara, 1984.
63 *Afrique-Asie*, 13 January 1986.
64 Englebert (1996), p. 154; International Court of Justice (1986); Queneudec (1988), pp. 29–41.
65 Interview with Pierre Ouédraogo, 1987.
66 *Afrique-Asie*, 13 January 1986.

## Chapter 6

1 Conseil national de la révolution (1985c), p. I.
2 FBIS, *Sub-Saharan Africa,* 27 July 1988.
3 Yonaba (1986), pp. 159–162 164–165, 170.
4 *Sidwaya*, 12 and 15 December 1986; *Carrefour africain*, 19 December 1986.
5 *Sidwaya*, 9 March 1987.
6 Saint-Girons (1987).
7 *Sidwaya*, 16 and 17 July 1986, and 6, 9, and 12 March 1987.
8 *Carrefour africain*, 31 May 1985.
9 *L'Intrus*, 23 May 1987; *Carrefour africain*, 5 June 1987.
10 Savadogo and Wetta (1992), p. 59.
11 *Carrefour africain*, 14 June 1985; *Sidwaya*, 13 January 1986.
12 Savadogo and Wetta (1992), p. 62.
13 International Monetary Fund (1992).
14 *Carrefour africain*, 12 February 1984.
15 Zagré (1994); Savadogo and Wetta (1992).
16 Azam and Morrisson (1999), p. 69.
17 Interview with Youssouf Ouédraogo.
18 Author's calculations from data in World Bank (1995), pp. 22, 49, 317.
19 Zagré (1994), pp. 164, 176.

20 Savadogo and Wetta (1992), p. 60.
21 Sankara (2007), p. 384.
22 *Afrique-Asie*, 24 October 1983.
23 *Carrefour africain*, 15 November 1985.
24 Conseil national de la révolution (1985b). p. 31.
25 *Carrefour africain*, 26 July 1985; *Sidwaya*, 1 July and 23 August 1985.
26 *Sidwaya*, 28 June 1985; *Carrefour africain*, 16 July 1985.
27 Meyer and Sawadogo (1986), pp. 35–62.
28 Lecaillon and Morrisson (1985), pp. 57, 65; *Carrefour africain*, 26 July 1985.
29 Novicki (1986); *Sidwaya*, 27 January 1986.
30 Conseil national de la révolution (1985c), p. 269.
31 *Sidwaya*, 20 August 1985.
32 Saul (1987), p. 92.
33 Author's field notes, Doundouni, Bazega province, 9 March 1987.
34 Secrétariat général national des CDR (1986), pp. 63–64.
35 *Sidwaya*, 4 July 1985; *Sidwaya*, 8 August 1985.
36 Labazée (1985), p. 17.
37 *Carrefour africain*, 17 August 1984.
38 *Lolowulen*, No. 2, February 1986.
39 Labazée (1985), p. 12.
40 Otayek (1985), p. 89.
41 Englebert (1996), p. 1
42 *Carrefour africain*, 5 September 1986.
43 Harsch (1987a).
44 Interview with Léonard Compaoré.
45 *Carrefour africain*, 29 December 1984.
46 Tallet (1985), pp. 65–67.

## Chapter 7

1 Sankara (2007), p. 67.
2 Interview with Aristide Compaoré.
3 *Carrefour africain*, 4 August 1984.
4 *Carrefour africain*, 4 August 1984.
5 Sankara (2007), pp. 97–98.
6 Conseil national de la révolution (1984), pp. 3–4, 10–27, 46–47.
7 Interview with Pierre Ouédraogo, 1985.
8 Martens (1989), pp. 94–95.
9 Secrétariat général national des CDR (1986), p. 22.
10 *Carrefour africain*, 6 January 1984 and 4 August 1984.
11 Jaglin (1995), pp. 243–250; *Sidwaya*, 7 April 1986.
12 Interview with Jean Baptiste Natama.

13 Banégas (1993); Otayek, Sawadogo, and Guingané (1996), pp. 10–11.
14 Diawara (1996), p. 239.
15 Faure (1991), pp. 102–109.
16 *Carrefour africain*, 17 August 1984.
17 *Carrefour africain*, 25 November 1983.
18 Bovin (1990), p. 35.
19 *Sidwaya*, 11 November 1985.
20 *Carrefour africain*, 30 May 1986.
21 Secrétariat général national des CDR (1986), p. 62.
22 *L'Observateur*, 11–13 November 1983.
23 *Carrefour africain*, 13 February 1987.
24 Secrétariat général national des CDR (1986), p. 66.
25 Harrison (1987), pp. 269–270.
26 Ministry of Health and UNICEF (1985), pp. 301–327.
27 Harrison (1987), p. 270.
28 Harsch (1987a).
29 Interview with Léonard Compaoré.
30 Kohler (1971), pp. 125–134.
31 Somda (1987).
32 Ouédraogo (1990).
33 Six S (1987), p. 32.
34 *Carrefour africain*, 15 May 1987.
35 Notes from author's field visit to Ouahigouya, 11 March 1987.
36 Six S (1987), pp. 69–70.
37 *Seeds*, August 1986.
38 *Carrefour africain*, 15 May 1987.
39 Koumba (1990), p. 6.
40 Hannequin (1990).
41 Kanse (1989), pp. 70–71.
42 Interview with Pierre Ouédraogo, 1985.
43 *Carrefour africain*, 4 August 1984.
44 *Carrefour africain*, 17 April 1987.
45 *Sidwaya*, 23 March 1987.
46 *Lolowulen*, "Semaine nationale de la femme burkinabè," special issue, 1985.
47 *Sidwaya*, 23 September 1985.
48 Harsch (1987a).
49 *Education nouvelle*, Ouagadougou (n.d.), special edition on the 13th Congress of SUVESS, Ouagadougou, 26–30 December 1984, pp. 32–33.
50 *Sidwaya*, 21 July 1986.
51 *Carrefour africain*, 4 November 1983.
52 Muase (1989a), p. 191.

53 *Sidwaya*, 10 July and 17 December 1985.
54 Muase (1989b), pp. 50–52; Muase (1989a), pp. 198–201; *Carrefour africain*, 20 April 1984.
55 Muase (1989a), pp. 201–203; *L'Unité*, 17 March 1987.
56 Martens (1989), pp. 31–35; Muase (1989a), pp. 207–210.
57 Martens (1989), p. 34.
58 Dumont (1986), p. 73.
59 *Carrefour africain*, 9 August 1985.
60 Secrétariat général national des CDR (1986), pp. 39, 41.
61 Jaglin (1995), p. 251.
62 *Carrefour africain*, 9 August 1985.
63 Secrétariat général national des CDR (1986); *Lolowulen*, June 1986.
64 Sankara (2007), pp. 281, 284–285.
65 Interview with Pierre Ouédraogo, 1987.
66 *Carrefour africain*, 10 and 17 April 1987.

### Chapter 8

1 Secrétariat général national des CDR (1986), pp. 67–68.
2 *Sidwaya*, 11 July 1986.
3 *Carrefour africain*, 11 October 1985.
4 *Sidwaya*, 7 January 1986.
5 Sankara (2007), p. 397.
6 *Carrefour africain*, 17 January 1986
7 *Sidwaya*, 5 January 1987; *Carrefour africain*, 16 January 1987.
8 Sankara (2007), pp. 396.
9 FBIS, *Sub-Saharan Africa*, 18 June 1984.
10 Personal letter to the author, Ouagadougou, 23 August 1987.
11 Guissou (1995a), p. 81; Guissou (1995b), p. 70.
12 Somé (1990), p. 30.
13 *Le Matin* (Paris), 17–18 October 1987.
14 Interview with Ernest Nongma Ouédraogo.
15 Englebert (1986); Martens (1989).
16 Somé (1990), pp. 109–120; Andriamirado (1989), pp. 50–52; *L'Observateur*, 22 May and 1–4 June 1984.
17 Andriamirado (1989), pp. 52–53.
18 Somé (1990), pp. 144–148; Andriamirado (1989), pp. 54, 61.
19 Martens (1989), pp. 39–40
20 Somé (1990), p. 149.
21 Labazée (1986), pp. 119–120; Andriamirado (1989), pp. 56–58.
22 *Sidwaya*, 20 May 1986.
23 Sankara (1991), pp. 267–277.

24 Somé (1990), pp. 87–90; Andriamirado (1989), p. 11.
25 Author's private conversation with Frédéric Kiemdé, Ouagadougou, 14 October 1987.
26 Jaffré (2007), pp. 199, 202–203.
27 *Carrefour africain*, 4 September 1987.
28 Andriamirado (1989), p. 88.
29 Author's notes, Ouagadougou, 10 October 1987.
30 Andriamirado (1989), pp. 86–89.
31 *Le Monde*, 13 March 2017.
32 Somé (1990), pp. 29–30.
33 Ellis (2001), p. 68.
34 Jaffré (2009).
35 Somé (1990), p. 30.
36 Andriamirado (1989), p. 80, 93.
37 Somé (1990), p. 29.
38 Somé (1990), pp. 13–14
39 Andriamirado (1989), pp. 29–33.
40 Martens (1989), p. 64.
41 Andriamirado (1989), pp. 98–99.
42 *Le Pays*, 28 October 2009; *L'Observateur Paalga*, 29 October 2009.
43 Drawn from the author's notes and own published news reports.
44 Harsch (1987b).
45 Somé (1990), p. 199.
46 Loada (1996), p. 293; *West Africa*, 31 October 1988; *Economist* (London), 21 March 2009.
47 Balima (1996), p. 388.
48 Loada (1996), p. 293.
49 Front populaire (1988b).
50 Front populaire (1988a).
51 Front populaire (1989), p. 5; Jaglin (1996), p. 265.
52 Jaglin (1996), p. 262.
53 Harsch (1989).
54 *Sidwaya*, 13 October 1988.
55 Englebert (1995), p. B10.
56 Somé [2015].
57 BBC, 19 May 1988.
58 *Le Monde*, 21 October 1987.
59 Harsch (1989).
60 Otayek (1989), p. 8.
61 *West Africa*, 25 January 1988.
62 *Le Monde*, 17 October 1988.
63 BBC, 3 and 4 August 1988.

64 *Carrefour africain*, 16 September 1988.
65 Front populaire (1988b), pp. 21, 23–24.
66 *Carrefour africain*, 12 August 1988
67 *West Africa*, 12 June 1989; Englebert (1996), p. 64; Mouvement des démocrates progressistes [1988], p. 3.
68 Yé (1995), pp. 17–18.
69 Harsch (1989).
70 Harsch (1989).
71 Englebert (1996), p. 63.
72 Englebert (1995), p. B12.
73 Englebert (1996), pp. 63, 65.
74 AFP, 20 September 1989.
75 FBIS, AFR-89-182, 21 September 1989; *Jeune Afrique*, 2 October 1989; *West Africa*, 2 October 1989.
76 FBIS, AFR-89-183, 22 September 1989; Englebert (1995), p. B12.

### Chapter 9

1 Bratton and van de Walle (1997), p. 7.
2 Mitterrand (1990).
3 Yé (1995), p. 12; Guion (1991), p. 63.
4 Compaoré (1990).
5 Yé (1995), p. 21.
6 Yé (1995), pp. 18–19.
7 Sawadogo (1996), pp. 314–315; Yé (1995), pp. 26–34.
8 Yé (1995), pp. 36–105, 192–225.
9 Sawadogo (1996), p. 319.
10 Yé (1995), p. 123; Sawadogo (1996), pp. 318–320.
11 Yé (1995), pp. 131–133.
12 *Marchés tropicaux et méditerranéens*, 11 January 1991; Englebert (1998), p. B18.
13 Kiemde (1996), p. 359.
14 Yé (1995), pp. 126–127.
15 Yé (1995), pp. 140–143.
16 Englebert (1998), pp. B15–B16; Yé (1995), pp. 143–147.
17 Kiemde (1996), p. 359; Englebert (1998), p. B14; Yé (1995), pp. 153–154.
18 *L'Evénement*, 12 April 2005; *Mutations*, 15 March 2014.
19 Yé (1995), p. 157.
20 Yé (1995), p. 160.
21 Kiemde (1996), pp. 360–362.
22 Yé (1995), p. 167; Kiemde (1996), pp. 362–363.
23 Kiemde (1996), pp. 362–363.
24 Hilgers and Mazzocchetti (2006), p. 11.

25 Loada (1998), p. 64; *Marchés tropicaux et méditerranéens*, 23 May 1997.
26 Loada (2010), p. 281.
27 Loada (1998), p. 64.
28 Loada (2010), p. 271.
29 Hilgers and Mazzocchetti (2006), pp. 15–16.
30 Lemarchand (1988), pp. 149–170.
31 Bayart (1979); Bayart (1993); Callaghy (1984); Joseph (1987); Theobald (1990).
32 Weber (1978), pp. 1010–1069.
33 Schmidt et al. (1977).
34 Migdal (1988).
35 Harsch (1998), pp. 636–637.
36 *L'Evènement*, 10 September 2011; *L'Observateur Paalga*, 10 August and 17 October 2011; *Le Pays*, 7–9 and 17 October 2011.
37 Assemblée nationale (2016a).
38 *Sidwaya*, 1 March 2000.
39 *Sidwaya*, 28 March 2000.
40 *L'Observateur Paalga*, 1 August 2003.
41 *Le Pays*, 25 April 2008; *L'Observateur Paalga*, 28 April 2008; *L'Evènement*, 10 May 2008; *San Finna*, 12–18 May 2008.
42 *Sidwaya*, 22 February 2001.
43 *Sidwaya*, 27 September 1998.
44 Beucher (2010), p. 47.
45 Beucher (2010), p. 49; Bieri and Froidevaux (2010), p. 78; *Sidwaya*, 23 April 2007.
46 *Sidwaya*, 27 May 2004.
47 Hilgers and Mazzocchetti (2006), p. 10.
48 *L'Observateur Paalga*, 14 June 2007; *Sidwaya*, 14 June 2007.
49 *Sidwaya*, 13 July 2000.
50 *Le Pays*, 6–9 March 2015.
51 Loada (1998), p. 73.
52 Martens (1989), pp. 67, 295–296.
53 *Sidwaya*, 9 January 2015.
54 *Sidwaya*, 6 July 2015.
55 Loada (2006), p. 21.
56 *Le Pays*, 1 July 2015.
57 Commission d'enquête indépendante (1999).
58 AFP, 1, 4, and 7 February 2002.
59 AFP, 13 December 2000; *L'Observateur Paalga*, 18 December 2000.
60 *Le Pays*, 12 June 2006; *Sidwaya*, 19 July 2006.
61 *Washington Post*, 4 February 2013.
62 United States (2005–2012).
63 *L'Indépendant*, 15 September 1998.

64 *Sidwaya*, 26 April 2006.

65 EIU, *Burkina Faso Country Report*, March 2004, p. 14; EIU, *Burkina Faso Country Report*, December 2005, p. 17.

66 EIU, *Burkina Faso Country Report*, December 2006, p. 14.

67 Loada (2006), pp. 26–27.

68 Dubus (2006), pp. 102–110.

69 Vaast (2010), pp. 58–59.

70 *Sidwaya*, 10 May 2005.

71 Hilgers (2006), pp. 42–62.

72 *Sidwaya*, 21 November 2005; *L'Observateur Paalga*, 21 November 2005.

73 *Journal du soir*, 14 June 1997.

74 Loada (2010), p. 281.

75 Tilly (1995a), p. 37.

76 McAdam, Tarrow, and Tilly (2001), p. 276.

### Chapter 10

1 Diabré (1998), p. 5.

2 Young (1991), pp. 1–2.

3 Mkandawire and Soludo (1999); Cheru (2002); Olukoshi (2003).

4 Englebert (1995), p. B20.

5 International Monetary Fund (2015), p. 24.

6 *Courier*, January–February 1997.

7 Harsch (1991), pp. 18–19.

8 *Jeune Afrique économie*, 1 July 1996.

9 Labazée (1988).

10 Ganne and Ouédraogo (1994).

11 AFP, 28 May 1996; *Sidwaya*, 16 May 2005.

12 EIU, *Burkina Faso Country Profile 2007*, p. 23.

13 EIU, *Burkina Faso Country Profile 2007*, p. 23.

14 Sneyd (2015), p. 55.

15 *Le Pays*, 3 May 2006.

16 *L'Observateur Paalga*, 14 May 2009; *Sidwaya*, 18 May 2009.

17 *Sidwaya*, 14 May 2009.

18 Zagré (1994), p. 39.

19 *Sidwaya*, 30 March 1998; AIB, 31 August 1999.

20 Assemblée nationale (2003); International Monetary Fund (2014b), pp. 25, 30.

21 *Sidwaya*, 3 December 2009.

22 International Monetary Fund (2014b), p. 22.

23 *Sidwaya*, 3 December 2009.

24 Assemblée nationale (2016b).

25 International Monetary Fund (2014b), pp. 5, 22, 24.

26 *Sidwaya*, 12 May 2010.
27 *Le Pays*, 9 June 2010.
28 *Le Pays*, 21 August 2007; *L'Observateur Paalga*, 21 August 2007; *Sidwaya*, 22 August 2007.
29 *Le Pays*, 15 and 21 September 2011.
30 AIB, 21 March 2012; *Bendré*, 28 March 2012; *Sidwaya*, 29 March 2012.
31 *Sidwaya*, 30 October 2015.
32 *Jeune Afrique*, 18 July 2012.
33 *L'Observateur Paalga*, 1 August 1995.
34 *Bendré*, 25 July 2012.
35 Assemblée nationale (2016a), p. 70.
36 Kevane (2014), p. 2.
37 *Le Journal du Dimanche* (Paris), 11 September 2011.
38 *Bayiri*, 16 July 2015
39 Assemblée nationale (2016b).
40 Assemblée nationale (2016a), p. 137.
41 Labazée (1988), pp. 177–181.
42 *Sidwaya*, 20 October 2011.
43 *L'Observateur Paalga*, 1 August 1995; *Journal du soir*, 3 May 1996; *Jeune Afrique*, 2 December 1997.
44 Ren-Lac (2012), p. 47.
45 *L'Observateur Paalga*, 13 April 2015.
46 *L'Observateur Paalga*, 5–7 June 2015; *Bayiri*, 25 June 2015; *Bayiri*, 16 July 2015.
47 *L'Observateur Paalga*, AIB, and *Le Pays*, 19 October 2015.
48 *Le Pays*, 23–25 October 2015.
49 Ren-Lac (2012), pp. 30–32; *L'Observateur Paalga*, 10 June 2015.
50 *Sidwaya*, 22 June 2015.
51 *Sidwaya*, 30 December 1994.
52 *L'Indépendant*, 20 June 1995.
53 *Journal du Soir*, 6 March 1997.
54 Ren-Lac (2012), pp. 15, 20.
55 Ren-Lac (2001), p. 66.
56 *L'Observateur Paalga*, 16 May 2001.
57 Englebert (1996), pp. 158–159.
58 Englebert (1996), p. 159; Sierra Leone (2004), Vol. 2, Chapt. 2, para. 380.
59 United Nations (2000b).
60 *Sidwaya*, 20 July 1998; *La lettre du continent*, 19 November 1998.
61 United Nations (2000a).
62 United Nations (2009).
63 Ministry of Economy and Development (2002).
64 International Monetary Fund (2014a), p. 8.

65 Ministry of Economy and Development (2006), p. 25.
66 United Nations Development Programme (1997), pp. 81–86; Ministry of Economy and Development (2006), p. 19; International Monetary Fund (2014a), p. 8.
67 Ministry of Economy and Development (2006).
68 United Nations Development Programme (1997), pp. 93–94.
69 Ministry of Economy and Development (2006), p. 75.
70 International Monetary Fund (2014b), p. 4.
71 International Monetary Fund (2014b), p. 5; International Monetary Fund (2014a), p. 8.
72 International Monetary Fund (2014b), p. 6; United Nations Development Programme (2007), p. 292.
73 *L'Observateur Paalga*, 4 November 2003.
74 Centre pour la governance démocratique (2012), pp. 25, 47.
75 *Sidwaya*, 1–2 March 1997.

### Chapter 11

1 Asche (1994), pp. 24–26.
2 Harsch (1998), p. 630.
3 Conseil des ministres (2015).
4 *Le Pays*, 23 June 2015.
5 Interview with Apollinaire J. Kyelém de Tambèla.
6 Compaoré (1999).
7 Somé (2016), Vol. 1, p. 231.
8 Collège de sages (1999).
9 Interview with Ismael Diallo.
10 *Sidwaya*, 14 September 2001.
11 *L'Observateur Paalga*, 2 August 2011.
12 EIU, Burkina Faso Events, 26 October 2012.
13 Natielsé (2009).
14 African Peer Review Mechanism (2008).
15 *Sidwaya*, 10 June 2008; *Sidwaya*, 1 June 2009; *L'Observateur Paalga*, 1 June 2009.
16 Interview with Claude Wetta.
17 Notes from author's visit to CDR headquarters, Pô, 16 March 1985.
18 *Le Pays*, 12 March 2001.
19 Centre pour la governance démocratique (2009), p. 20.
20 Commission électorale nationale indépendante (2012).
21 Sawadogo (2001), pp. 209–210; Ouattara (2007), p. 170.
22 EIU, *Burkina Faso*, June 2006, pp. 12–13.
23 Tilly (1995b).
24 Gosselin and Gomez-Perez (2011), pp. 273–309; Biehler (2006).
25 *L'Observateur Paalga*, *Le Pays*, and *Sidwaya*, 16, 17, and 18 February 2004.

26 Hilgers (2008).
27 Ren-Lac (2004), pp. 89–91.
28 *Le Pays*, 16 August 2012; *Sidwaya*, 16 August 2012; *L'Observateur Paalga*, 17–19 August 2012.
29 Author's calculations, based on annual budget data released by the Association des municipalités du Burkina Faso for the 1995–99 period, and on later figures from Bobo-Dioulasso (*Sidwaya*, 31 December 2007) and Zorgho (*Sidwaya*, 27 January 2007).
30 Ren-Lac (2000–2005).
31 *Le Pays*, 27 July 2007.
32 *Sidwaya*, 19 April 2000.
33 In the early 1990s, 151 individuals convicted by the TPRs filed appeals with the regular courts, and 43 succeeded in having their verdicts overturned, *Sidwaya*, 26 February 1998.
34 Lompo (1995).
35 Ministry of Justice (2001); *Le Pays*, 19 September 2006; *Sidwaya*, 11 January 2007.
36 Ren-Lac (2000), pp. 49–55; Ren-Lac (2005), p. 31.
37 *Sidwaya*, 11 May 2005.
38 Commission d'enquête indépendante (1999).
39 *L'Observateur Paalga*, 8 June 2015.
40 *Le Pays*, 13 October 2003.
41 *Le Pays*, 5 October 2006.
42 *L'Observateur Paalga*, 9 March 2001; *Sidwaya*, 16 March 2001.
43 *L'Observateur Paalga*, 1–3 July 2005; *Le Pays*, 30 March 2006.
44 *Le Pays*, 13 October 2003.
45 *Le Pays*, 27 July 2007.
46 *Le Pays*, 26 June 2006.
47 AIB, 23 February 2012; *Le Pays*, 24–26 February 2012; *L'Observateur Paalga*, 27 June 2013
48 Author's discussions with an active-duty army captain, Ouagadougou, February 1999.
49 Interview with Charles Lona Ouattara.
50 Ouédraogo (2014).
51 *La Lettre du continent*, 4 February, 1999.
52 *Le Pays*, 21 and 23 February and 13 April 2005; *L'Observateur Paalga*, 21 February 2005; *Sidwaya*, 21 March 2005.
53 *Sidwaya*, 21, 22, and 26 December 2006; *L'Observateur Paalga*, 21 December 2006 and 4 January 2007; *Le Pays*, 21 and 22 December 2006 and 4 January 2007.
54 *L'Observateur Paalga*, 8 and 10 October 2007; *Le Pays*, 8, 10, and 11 October 2007; *Sidwaya*, 10 and 12 October 2007.
55 EIU, *Burkina Faso,* May 2011, pp. 17–18; EIU, *Burkina Faso*, August 2011, pp. 16–17.
56 EIU, *Burkina Faso,* May 2011, p. 18; EIU, *Burkina Faso*, August 2011, p. 17.

57 Ouattara (2004), pp. 14, 16, 77, 161, 212; EIU, *Burkina Faso*, December 2003, pp. 9–12.
58 Ouattara (2004), pp. 28–29, 37–41, 70; EIU, *Burkina Faso*, May 2004, p. 11.
59 Ouattara (2004), pp. 30–31, 36.
60 Ouattara (2004), pp. 121–124.
61 *L'Observateur Paalga*, 19 April 2004.
62 *Sidwaya*, 8 April 2004; *L'Observateur Paalga*, 15 April 2004.
63 *L'Observateur Paalga*, 19 April 2004.

### Chapter 12

1 Tilly (1978); McAdam, McCarthy, and Zald (1996).
2 Gurr (1968); Gurr (1970).
3 Johnston (2011), p. 31.
4 McAdam, Tarrow, and Tilly (2001); Tilly and Tarrow (2007).
5 Foran (2005).
6 Interview with Fousséni Ouédraogo.
7 Banégas and Otayek (2003).
8 Muase (1989a).
9 Ellis and van Kessel (2009), p. 4.
10 Harsch (1998).
11 *L'Observateur Paalga*, 13–15 March 1998; *Journal du jeudi*, 19–25 March 1998.
12 *Sidwaya*, 26 June, 7 July, and 17 July 1997.
13 Mazzocchetti (2006), pp. 84, 92; Mazzocchetti (2010), pp. 206–208, 216.
14 Wise (1998), p. 32.
15 Hagberg (2002); Harsch (1999).
16 Commission d'enquête indépendante (1999).
17 *Le Pays*, 25 February 1999; Centre national de press Norbert Zongo (1999).
18 Interview with Halidou Ouédraogo.
19 Interview with Halidou Ouédraogo
20 "Permanences: Mardi 5 janvier 1999" (1999).
21 *Le Pays*, 26 February 1999.
22 Harsch (1999), p. 399.
23 AIB, 24 May 1999.
24 Collectif d'organisations démocratiques de masse et de partis politiques (1999).
25 *L'Observateur Paalga*, 12 August 1999.
26 *Sidwaya*, 13 April 2000.
27 Loada (1999).
28 *Sidwaya*, 19 July 2007.
29 Based on the author's dataset of Burkina Faso protest events.
30 *Sidwaya*, 6 October 2004; *L'Observateur Paalga*, 6 November 2007.
31 Sanou (2010).
32 EIU, *Burkina Faso Country Report*, May 2008, pp. 11–12.

33 Engels (2015).
34 *Sidwaya*, 15 and 20 May 2008.
35 Interview with Lookman Sawadogo.
36 International Telecommunications Union (2013); Central Intelligence Agency (2006).
37 Harsch (2013), p. 359.
38 *Sidwaya*, 16 October 2007.
39 Cuomo (2015).
40 *L'Observateur Paalga*, 12 April 2010; *Le Monde*, 16 April 2016.
41 Interview with Serge Bambara ("Smockey").
42 Harsch (2012).
43 *L'Observateur Paalga*, 23 February 2011.
44 EIU, *Burkina Faso Country Report*, May 2011, pp. 15–17.
45 Chouli (2012), p. 46.
46 Compiled by the author mainly from reports in the daily newspapers *Le Pays*, *L'Observateur Paalga*, *San Finna*, and *Sidwaya*, the AIB national news agency, the weeklies *Bendré* and *L'Indépendant*, and the fortnightly *L'Evénement*.
47 International Crisis Group (2013), p. 30.
48 Chouli (2012), p. 56.
49 Harsch (2016).
50 *L'Observateur Paalga*, 13 June 2011.
51 Interview with Charles Lona Ouattara.
52 *Le Pays*, 5 May 2011.
53 *L'Evènement*, 10 August 2011.
54 Hilgers and Loada (2013), p. 189.
55 *L'Observateur Paalga*, 14 March 2011.
56 *San Finna*, 2 May 2011; *Le Pays*, 3 May 2011; *Bendré*, 11 May 2011.

### Chapter 13

1 *L'Evénement*, 5 November 2010.
2 *Le Pays*, 8 February 2010.
3 *Le Pays*, 4 May 2010.
4 *L'Observateur Paalga*, 1 June 2010; *Le Pays*, 1 June 2010.
5 *L'Observateur Paalga*, 3 May 2010.
6 *Le Pays*, 1 March 2010.
7 *L'Observateur Paalga*, 18 July 2011.
8 *Sidwaya*, 12 December 2011.
9 *L'Evénement*, 25 April 2008.
10 *L'Observateur Paalga*, 8 July 2009.
11 Interview with Fousséni Ouédraogo.
12 *L'Observateur Paalga*, 4 May 2009.
13 *L'Observateur Paalga*, 4 May 2009; *Le Pays*, 22–24 May 2009.

14 *Sidwaya*, 22 May 2009.
15 Zongo (2011).
16 Interview with Louis Armand Ouali.
17 *L'Observateur Paalga*, 2 March 2010.
18 *Sidwaya*, 4 July 2006.
19 EIU, Burkina Faso Events, 9 July 2013.
20 Interview with Marie Madeleine Somda.
21 *Bendré*, 20 June 2012.
22 Interview with Serge Bambara ("Smockey").
23 *Jeune Afrique*, 13 September 2013.
24 Interview with Marcel Tankoano.
25 *Le Pays*, 25 June 2013.
26 AIB, 29 June 2013; *Le Pays*, 1 July 2013; *L'Observateur Paalga*, 1 July 2013.
27 *Sidwaya*, 1 July 2013.
28 AIB, 16 July 2013; *Sidwaya*, 17 July 2016.
29 Interview with Guézouma Sanogo.
30 *Le Pays*, 15 July 2013.
31 *Le Faso.net*, 19 July 2013.
32 Interview with Aziz Sana.
33 *Sidwaya*, 5 July 2013.
34 AIB, 20 July 2013; *L'Observateur Paalga*, 22 July 2013; *Le Pays*, 22 July 2013.
35 AIB, 28 July 2013; *Sidwaya*, 29 July 2013; *L'Observateur Paalga*, 29 July 2013; *L'Evénement*, 10 August 2013.
36 *Sidwaya*, 2 December 2013; *Le Pays*, 4 December 2013.
37 *Sidwaya*, 13 December 2013.
38 *Le Pays*, 17 December 2013.
39 *Sidwaya*, 6 January 2014.
40 *L'Observateur Paalga*, 8 January 2014.
41 *Sidwaya*, 20 January 2014; AFP, 20 January 2014; *L'Observateur Paalga*, 20 January 2014.
42 Tilly (1978).
43 *L'Observateur Paalga*, 20 January 2014.
44 Interview with Hervé Ouattara.
45 Interviews with Hervé Ouattara and Laurent Monné; *Le Pays*, 18 June 2014; *L'Observateur Paalga*, 18 June 2014.
46 *Sidwaya*, 3 February 2014.
47 *Sidwaya*, 7 April 2014; *L'Observateur Paalga*, 7 April 2014; AIB, April 7, 2014; *Le Pays*, 8 April 2014; *Le Pays*, 10 April 2014.
48 *Observateur*, 16–18 May 2014; AIB, 31 May 2014; *Sidwaya*, 2 June 2014. *L'Observateur Paalga*, 2 June 2014; *Le Pays*, 2 June 2014.
49 *Sidwaya*, 19 June 2014.

50 *Sidwaya*, 6 August 2014.
51 Bantenga [2015], p. 58.
52 AIB, 23 August 2014; *Sidwaya*, 25 August 2014; *L'Observateur Paalga*, 25 August 2014; *Le Pays*, 25 August 2014.
53 *Le Pays*, 21 October 2014; *L'Observateur Paalga*, 22 October 2014; *Le Pays*, 22 October 2014.
54 AIB, 22 October 2014; *L'Observateur Paalga*, 23 October 2014; *Le Pays*, 24–26 October 2014.
55 *L'Observateur Paalga*, 22 October 2014.
56 *Le Pays*, 23 October 2014.
57 *L'Observateur Paalga*, 24–26 October 2014.
58 Somé [2015], pp. 65–68.
59 Interview with Marie Madeleine Somda.
60 *L'Observateur Paalga*, 28 October 2014; *Le Pays*, 28 October 2014.
61 Ouédraogo and Yabré (2015), pp. 21–22.
62 AIB, 28 October 2014; *Le Monde*, 28 and 29 October 2014; *Le Pays*, 29 October 2014.
63 *L'Observateur Paalga*, 30 October 2014; *Sidwaya*, 30 October 2014.
64 Interview with Hervé Ouattara.
65 *Le Pays*, 28 October 2014.
66 Interview with Laurent Monné; Bantenga [2015], pp. 43–44.
67 Interviews with Hervé Ouattara and Aziz Sana.
68 Amnesty International (2015), pp. 15–19; Bantenga [2015], p. 44.
69 *Le Monde*, 30 October 2014; *L'Observateur Paalga*, 31 October–2 November 2014; *Le Pays*, 31 October–2 November 2014.
70 *Le Pays*, 31 October-2 November 2014; *Le Monde*, 31 October 2014; *L'Observateur Paalga*, 31 October–2 November 2014.
71 *L'Observateur Paalga*, 7–9 November 2014; interview with Hervé Ouattara.
72 *L'Observateur Paalga*, 31 October–2 November 2014.
73 *L'Observateur Paalga*, 31 October–2 November 2014; interviews with Hervé Ouattara and Louis Armand Ouali.
74 *Le Monde*, 31 October 2014; *New York Times*, 31 October 2014; *Le Monde*, 1 November 2014; *Le Pays*, 3 November 2014.
75 AIB, 5 November 2014.
76 BBC, 31 October 2014; *New York Times*, 31 October 2014; *Sidwaya*, 31 October 2014; *Le Monde*, 1 November 2014; *Le Pays*, 3 November 2014.
77 BBC, 31 October 2014; *Le Monde*, 3 November 2014.

### Chapter 14

1 Interview with Laurent Monné.
2 Interview with Fousséni Ouédraogo.
3 Interview with Siaka Coulibaly.

4 *Le Pays*, 21–23 November 2014.
5 *Le Pays*, 3 November 2014.
6 "Charte de transition" (2014).
7 *Sidwaya*, 11 November 2014; *L'Observateur Paalga*, 11 November 2014.
8 South African Broadcasting Corporation (2015).
9 Interview with Hervé Ouattara; *Le Pays*, 17 November 2014; *Sidwaya*, 17 November 2014; *L'Observateur Paalga*, 18 November 2014; *Le Monde*, 18 November 2014.
10 *Sidwaya*, 20 November 2014; *L'Observateur Paalga*, 24 November 2014.
11 *Burkina 24*, 26 November 2014.
12 Interview with Marie Madeleine Somda.
13 *L'Observateur Paalga*, 21–23 November 2014; *Le Pays*, 28–30 November 2014.
14 Interview with Marcel Tankoano.
15 *Le Pays*, 21–23 November 2014.
16 *Sidwaya*, 24 November 2014.
17 *L'Observateur Paalga*, 24 November 2014.
18 *L'Observateur Paalga*, 31 March 2014.
19 *Le Pays*, 6–8 February 2015; *Sidwaya*, 9 February 2015; *L'Observateur Paalga*, 9 February 2015.
20 *L'Observateur Paalga*, 26 January 2015; *Sidwaya*, 11 March 2015.
21 Etats généraux de la justice (2015).
22 *Le Pays*, 7 April 2015; *Sidwaya*, 8 April 2015.
23 Conseil constitutionnel (2015).
24 Conseil national de la transition (2015a), p. 124; *Le Pays*, 8 June 2015.
25 *Le Pays*, 17 September 2015.
26 Interview with Laurent Monné.
27 *Le Pays*, 17 September 2015;
28 Sy (2015a).
29 *Le Pays*, 18–20 September 2015.
30 *L'Observateur Paalga*, 20 September 2015.
31 *Le Monde*, 24 September 2015.
32 *The Guardian* (London), 24 September 2015.
33 *L'Observateur Paalga*, 21 September 2015; *Le Pays*, 21 September 2015.
34 *Sidwaya*, 18 September 2015; Reuters, 18 September 2015.
35 Interview with Ismael Diallo; Voice of America, 19 September 2015.
36 Interview with Marcel Tankoano.
37 *Mutations*, 1 May 2016.
38 *Le Monde*, 23 September 2015.
39 *Sidwaya*, 24 September 2015.
40 *L'Observateur Paalga*, 15 September 2016.
41 *Les Echos du Faso*, 11 December 2015; Reuters, 12 December 2015; *Le Pays*, 25 July 2016; *L'Observateur Paalga*, 25 July 2016.

42 Interview with Aziz Sana.
43 Interview with Marie Madeleine Somda.
44 Interview with Hervé Ouattara.
45 *Le Pays*, 19 October 2015.
46 Conseil national de la transition (2015c), p. 27.
47 Sy (2015b).
48 Jaffré (2015).
49 AFP, 26 November 2015.
50 *Sidwaya*, 12 January 2016; *L'Observateur Paalga*, 13 January 2016.
51 Interview with Bénéwendé Sankara.
52 *Le Reporter*, 1–14 February 2016.
53 AIB, 10 December 2015.
54 *Bayiri*, 18 January 2016; *L'Observateur Paalga*, 3 February 2016.
55 Harsch (2017).
56 Interview with Ismael Diallo.
57 *Sidwaya*, 25 March 2016.
58 Interview with Ismael Diallo.
59 *L'Observateur Paalga*, 20 April 2016; *Le Pays*, 20 April 2016; *Sidwaya*, 20 April 2016,
60 RTB, 25 April 2016; *Le Pays*, 3 May 2016.
61 *Bayiri*, 28 April 2016.
62 *Le Pays*, 28 October–1 November 2016.
63 *Le Pays*, 14 November 2016.

## Chapter 15

1 Conseil national de la transition (2015b), p. 5.
2 AIB, 10 March 2017.
3 AFP, 3 December 2015.
4 *Le Pays*, 26 September 2016.
5 Interview with Charles Lona Ouattara.
6 *Le Pays*, 20 December 2016.
7 Interview with Apollinaire J. Kyélem de Tambèla.
8 *Sidwaya*, 22 October 2015; *Le Pays*, 23 March 2016.
9 *Bayiri*, 16 April 2016.
10 *Bayiri*, 25 August 2016.
11 Commission de la réconciliation nationale et des reformes (2015).
12 *Le Pays*, 16 June 2016.
13 International Crisis Group (2016), p. 1.
14 *Le Monde*, 10 April 2017.
15 AIB, 11 January 2016.
16 Interview with Fayçal Traoré.
17 AIB, 20 June 2016.

18 *Le Soleil* (Dakar), 5 November 2014.
19 *Le Potentiel* (Kinshasa), 15 November 2014.
20 *Le Pays*, 16 March 2015; *L'Observateur Paalga*, 17 March 2015; *Sidwaya*, 17 March 2015.
21 Interview with Hervé Ouattara.
22 Interview with Serge Bambara ("Smockey").

# REFERENCES


African Peer Review Mechanism (2008) *Rapport d'evaluation du Burkina Faso*, Midrand, South Africa.

Amnesty International (2015) *"Just What Were They Thinking When They Shot at People?": Crackdown on Anti-Government Protests in Burkina Faso*, London: Amnesty International Publications.

Anderson, Benedict (1991) *Imagined Communities: Reflections on the Origin and Spread of Nationalism*, London: Verso.

Andriamirado, Sennen (1987) *Sankara le rebelle*, Paris: Jeune Afrique livres.

Andriamirado, Sennen (1989) *Il s'appelait Sankara*, Paris: Jeune Afrique livres.

Asche, Helmut (1994) *Le Burkina Faso Contemporain: l'expérience d'un auto-développement*, Paris: L'Harmattan.

Assemblée nationale (2003) *Code minier au Burkina Faso*, Loi N° 031-2003/AN, 8 May.

Assemblée nationale (2016a) *Rapport générale, Commission d'enquête parlementaire sur le foncier urbain au Burkina Faso*, September.

Assemblée nationale (2016b) *Rapport Ouagadougou, générale, Commission d'enquête parlementaire sur la gestion des titres miniers et la responsabilité sociale des entreprises minières*, Ouagadougou, September.

Augustin, Jean-Pierre, and Yaya K. Drabo (1989) "Au sport, citoyens!," *Politique africaine*, No. 33, March, pp. 59–65.

Azam, Jean-Paul, and Christian Morrisson (1999) *Conflict and Growth in Africa, Vol. 1: The Sahel*, Paris: Development Centre of the Organization for Economic Co-operation and Development.

Ba, Ahmed Tidjani (1989) "Le régime disciplinaire des agents publics du Burkina Faso," *Revue burkinabè de droit*, No. 16, July, pp. 201–230, and No. 18, July 1990, pp. 285–317.

Balima, Salfo-Albert (1960) "Notes on the Social and Labour Situation in the Republic of Upper Volta," *International Labour Review*, Vol. 82, No. 4, October, pp. 358–362.

Balima, Salfo-Albert (1996) *Légendes et histoire des peuples du Burkina Faso*, Paris: J.A. Conseil.

Banégas, Richard (1993) *Insoumissions populaires et révolution au Burkina Faso*, Bourdeaux: Centre d'étude d'Afrique noire.

Banégas, Richard, and René Otayek (2003) "Le Burkina Faso dans la crise ivoirienne: effets d'aubaine et incertitudes politiques," *Politique africaine*, No. 89, pp. 71–87.

Bantenga, Moussa Willy, ed. [2015] *Burkina Faso: 30 et 31 octobre 2014. Au coeur de l'insurrection populaire*, Ouagadougou: Presses universitaires de Ouagadougou.

Bayart, Jean-François (1979) *L'Etat au Cameroun*, Paris: Presses de la fondation nationale des sciences politiques.

Bayart, Jean-François (1993) *The State in Africa: The Politics of the Belly*, London: Longman.

Beucher, Benoît (2009), "La naissance de la communauté nationale burkinabè, ou comment le Voltaïque devient un 'Homme intègre'," *Sociétés politiques comparées*, No. 3, March.

Beucher, Benoît (2010) "Le mythe de l'«Empire mossi»: l'affirmation des royautés comme force d'accompagnement ou de rejet des nouveaux pouvoirs centraux, 1897–1991," in Mathieu Hilgers and Jacinthe Mazzocchetti, eds., *Révoltes et oppositions dans un régime semi-autoritaire: le cas du Burkina Faso*, Paris: Karthala, pp. 25–50.

Biehler, Alexandra (2006) "Renouveau urbain et marginalisation: le cas d'habitants du centre-ville de Ouagadougou—Burkina Faso," *Revue Tiers Monde*, No. 185, pp. 57–78.

Bieri, Arnaud, and Sylvain Froidevaux (2010), "Dieu, le président et le wak: a propos de certains phénomènes 'magico-religieux' au Burkina Faso," in Mathieu Hilgers and Jacinthe Mazzocchetti, eds., *Révoltes et oppositions dans un régime semi-autoritaire: le cas du Burkina Faso*, Paris: Karthala, pp. 67–83.

Bohmer, Carol (1978) "Community Values, Domestic Tranquility, and Customary Law in Upper Volta," *Journal of Modern African Studies*, Vol. 16, No. 2, June, pp. 295–310.

Bonnafé, Pierre, Michèle Fiéloux, and Jeanne-Marie Kambou (1982) "Un vent de folie? Le conflit armé dans une population sans Etat: les Lobi de Haute-Volta," in Jean Bazin and Emmanuel Terray, eds., *Guerres de lignages et guerres d'Etats en Afrique*, Paris: Editions des archives contemporaines, pp. 73–141.

Boone, Catherine (1992) *Merchant Capital and the Roots of State Power in Senegal, 1930–1985*, Cambridge: Cambridge University Press.

Boutillier, J.L. (1963) *Land Tenure and Economic Development in Upper Volta*, New York: UN Economic and Social Council, E/CN.14/SDP/5.

Bovin, Mette (1990) "Nomads of the Drought: Fulbe and Wodabee Nomads Between Power and Marginalization in the Sahel of Burkina Faso and Niger Republic," in Mette Bovin and Leif Manger, eds., *Adaptive Strategies in African Arid Lands*, Uppsala: Scandinavian Institute of African Studies, pp. 29–57.

Bratton, Michael, and Nicolas van de Walle (1997) *Democratic Experiments in Africa: Regime Transitions in Comparative Perspective*, Cambridge: Cambridge University Press.

Bretout, Françoise (1976) *Mogho Naba Wobgho: la résistance du royaume mossi de Ouagadougou*, Paris: ABC.

Cabanis, André, and Michel L. Martin (1987) "L'Administration locale en Haute-Volta de 1962 à 1983," in Ecole nationale d'administration et de magistrature, *Administration et développement au Burkina Faso*, Toulouse: Presses de l'institut d'études politiques de Toulouse, pp. 15–34.

Cadenat, Patrick (1978) "La constitution voltaïque du 27 novembre 1977," *Revue juridique et politique, indépendance et coopération*, Vol. 32, No. 4, October–December, pp. 973–1088.

Callaghy, Thomas M. (1984) *The State–Society Struggle: Zaire in Comparative Perspective*, New York: Columbia University Press.

Central Intelligence Agency (2006) World Factbook, Washington, DC, www.cia.gov/library/publications/the-world-factbook/geos/uv.html, accessed 12 September 2016.

Centre national de press Norbert Zongo (1999) "La mort du journaliste Norbert Zongo vient allonger la longue liste des meutres non elucidés," information note, Ouagadougou.

Centre pour la governance démocratique (2009) *La gouvernance locale au Burkina Faso: perceptions globales des Burkinabès et expérience concrète dans la commune urbaine de Pô*, Ouagadougou.

Centre pour la governance démocratique (2012) *Summary of Results: Afrobarometer Round 5 Survey in Burkina Faso*, Ouagadougou.

"Charte de transition" (2014) Ouagadougou, 13 November, http://archives.assembleenationale.bf/, accessed 12 July 2016.

Cheru, Fantu (2002) *African Renaissance: Roadmaps to the Challenge of Globalization*, London and New York: Zed Books.

Chouli, Lila (2012) *Burkina Faso 2011: chronique d'un mouvement social*, Lyon: Tahin Party.

Collectif d'organisations démocratiques de masse et de partis politiques (1999) "Plateforme d'action: plus de transparence et de libertés," Ouagadougou, January.

Collège de sages (1999) *Rapport intégral du collège de sages*, Ouagadougou, 30 July.

Comité information Sahel (1974) *Qui se nourrit de la famine en Afrique? Le dossier politique de la faim au Sahel*, Paris: François Maspero.

Commission d'enquête indépendante (1999) *Rapport sur la cause de la mort des occupants du véhicule de marque Toyota Land Cruiser de type 4 X 4 immatriculé 11 J 6485 BF, survenue le 13 décembre 1998 sur l'axe routier Ouagadougou (province du Kadiogo)—Sapouy (province du Ziro), dont le journaliste Norbert Zongo*, 6 May.

Commission de la réconciliation nationale et des reformes (2015) *Rapport général: Les voies du renouveau*, Ouagadougou, September.

Commission électorale nationale indépendante (2012) *Résultats provisoires elections municipales du 2 décembre 2012*, www.ceni.bf, accessed 23 December 2015.

Compaoré, Blaise (1990) *Discours d'ouverture au 1er congrès du Front populaire*, Ouagadougou: INC, 1 March.

Compaoré, Blaise (1999) "Décret portant création, composition et missions du collège des sages," 1 June.

Conseil constitutionnel (2015) "Extrait des minutes du greffe du Conseil constitutionnel, Décision n° 2015-012/CC/EL sur le recours...," Ouagadougou, Constitutional Court, 25 August.

Conseil des ministres (2015) *Compte rendu du Conseil des ministres du vendredi 14 août 2015*, Ouagadougou: Service d'information du Gouvernement.

Conseil national de la révolution (1984) *Statut général des comités de défense de la révolution*, Ouagadougou: Imprimerie des Forces armées nationales.

Conseil national de la révolution (1985a) "Kiti N° 85-108/CNR PRES portant organisation des structures dirigeants de l'exécutif révolutionnaire au Burkina Faso," Ouagadougou, 2 November.

Conseil national de la révolution (1985b) *Directives du Conseil national de la révolution pour l'élaboration du premier plan quiquennal de développement populaire, 1986–1990*, Ouadagougou.

Conseil national de la révolution (1985c) Ministère de la planification et du développement populaire, *Premier plan quinquennal de développement populaire, 1986–1990: rapport général de synthèse*, Ouagadougou.

Conseil national de la révolution (1986) *La Justice populaire au Burkina Faso*, 2nd edition, Ouagadougou, Ministère de la justice.

Conseil national de la transition (2015a) "Procès-verbal de la séance plenière du vendredi 05 juin 2015 (matin)," Ouagadougou.

Conseil national de la révolution (2015b) "Procès-verbal de la séance plenière du mardi 27 octobre 2015," Ouagadougou.

Conseil national de la révolution (2015c) "Procès-verbal de la séance plenière du jeudi 05 novembre 2015," Ouagadougou.

Cooper, Frederick (2014) *Citizenship between Empire and Nation: Remaking France and French Africa, 1945–1960*, Princeton, NJ and Oxford: Princeton University Press.

Cross, Nigel, and Rhiannon Barker, eds. (n.d.) *At the Desert's Edge: Oral Histories from the Sahel*, London: Panos Publications.

Cuomo, Anna (2015) "Des artistes engagés au Burkina Faso: rappeurs burkinabè, trajectoires artistiques et contournements identitaires," *Afrique contemporaine*, No. 254, pp. 89–103.

Curtin, Philip D. (1984) *Cross-Cultural Trade in World History*, Cambridge: Cambridge University Press.

Damiba, Aimé (1970) "La Nouvelle constitution de la Haute-Volta (14 juin 1970)," *Revue juridique et politique, indépendance et coopération*, Vol. 25, No. 2, April–June, pp. 151–178.

Delavignette, Robert (1946) *Service africain*, Paris: Gallimard.

Delmond, Paul (1953) *Dans la boucle du Niger: Dori, ville peule*, Dakar: Institut français d'Afrique noire.

Delouvroy, Jacques (1987) "Le développement du droit judiciare au Burkina Faso," *Revue juridique et politique, indépendance et coopération*, Vol. 41, No. 3, July–September, pp. 228–244.

Diabré, Zéphirin (1998) "The Political Economy of Adjustment in Burkina Faso," Harvard Institute for International Development, CAER II Discussion Paper 28, August.

Diané, Charles (1990) *La FEANF et les grandes heures du mouvement syndical étudiant noir*, Paris: Editions Chaka.

Diawara, Mahamadou (1996) "Mouvement associatif et transformations du champ politique," in René Otayek, Filiga Michel Sawadogo, and Jean-Pierre Guingané, eds., *Le Burkina entre révolution et démocratie (1983–1993)*, Paris: Karthala, pp. 229–246.

Dicko, Ahmadou A. (1992) *Journal d'une défaite autour du référendum du 28 septembre 1958 en Afrique noire*, Paris: L'Harmattan.

Dubus, Jack (2006) "L'élection présidentielle de 2005 depuis un village Sénoufo," *Politique africaine*, No. 101, March–April, pp. 102–110.

Dumont, René (1978) *Paysans écracés, terres massacrées: Equator, Inde, Bengladesh, Thailande, Haute-Volta*, Paris: Editions Robert Laffont.

Dumont, René (1986) *Pour l'Afrique j'accuse*, Paris: Plon.

Duperray, Anne-Marie (1984) *Les Gourounsi de Haute-Volta: conquête et colonisation 1896–1933*, Stuttgart: Franz Steiner Verlag Wiesbaden.

Ecole nationale d'administration et de magistrature (1987) *Administration et développement au Burkina Faso*, Toulouse: Presses de l'institut d'études politiques de Toulouse.

Ellis, Stephen (2001) *The Mask of Anarchy: The Destruction of Liberia and the Religious Dimension of an African Civil War*, New York: NYU Press.

Ellis, Stephen, and Ineke van Kessel (2009) "Introduction: African Social Movements or Social Movements in Africa?," in Stephen Ellis and Ineke van Kessel, eds., *Movers and Shakers: Social Movements in Africa*, Leiden: Brill, pp. 1–16.

Engels, Bettina (2015) "Contentious Politics of Scale: The Global Food Price Crisis and Local Protest in Burkina Faso," *Social Movement Studies*, Vol. 14, No. 2, pp. 180–194.

Englebert, Pierre (1986) *La révolution burkinabè*, Paris: L'Harmattan.

Englebert, Pierre (1995) "Burkina Faso: Towards a Constitution and Economic Adjustment," in Marion E. Doro, ed., *Africa Contemporary Record*, Vol. 22, 1989–1990, New York: Africana Publishing Company, pp. B9–B19.

Englebert, Pierre (1996) *Burkina Faso: Unsteady Statehood in West Africa*, Boulder, CO: Westview Press.

Englebert, Pierre (1998) "Burkina Faso: Uneasy Transition into the Fourth Republic, 1990–1992," in Colin Legum, ed., *Africa Contemporary Record*, Vol. 23, 1990–92, New York: Africana Publishing Company, pp. B12–B21.

Etats généraux de la justice (2015) "Pacte national pour le renouveau de la justice," Ouagadougou, 28 March.

Faure, Armelle (1991) "'La panthère est l'enfant d'un génie', réflexions sur le traitement d'une crise villageoise pendant la révolution burkinabè," *Politique africaine*, No. 44, December, pp. 102–109.

Foran, John (2005) *Taking Power: The Origins of Third World Revolutions*, New York: Cambridge University Press.

Front populaire (1988a) *Statuts et Programme d'action*, Ouagadougou: Imprimerie nationale.

Front populaire (1988b) *Assises nationales sur le bilan des 4 années de révolution. Documents finaux*, Ouagadougou: Imprimerie de Forces armées populaires.

Front populaire (1989) *Statut générale des Comités révolutionnaires*, Ouagadougou: Imprimerie nationale.

Ganne, Bernard, and Moussa Ouédraogo (1994) "Sentiers inédits et voies fragiles au Burkina Faso: du commerce à industries?," *Politique africaine*, No. 56, December, pp. 55–65.

Gervais, Raymond (1987) "Creating Hunger: Labor and Agricultural Policies in Southern Mosi, 1919–1940," in Dennis D. Cordell and Joel W. Gregory, eds., *African Population and Capitalism: Historical Perspectives*, Boulder, CO: Westview Press, pp. 109–121.

Gnimien, Gaston (2016) "La révolt Bwa de 1915–16," *Le Pays*, 7–9 October.

Goody, Jack (1964) "Reflections on the Early History of the Mossi-Dagomba Group of States," in J. Vansina, R. Mauny, and L.V. Thomas, eds., *The Historian in Tropical Africa*, London: Oxford University Press, pp. 177–189.

Goody, Jack (1967) *The Social Organisation of the LoWiili*, Oxford: Oxford University Press.

Gosselin, Louis Audet, and Muriel Gomez-Perez (2011) "L'Opposition au projet ZACA à Ouagadougou (2001–03): feu de paille ou mutations profondes de l'islam burkinabè?," *Canadian Journal of African Studies*, Vol. 45, No. 2, pp. 273–309.

Guion, Jean R. (1991) *Blaise Compaoré: réalisme et intégrité*, Paris: Berger-Levrault International.

Guirma, Frédéric (1991) *Comment perdre le pouvoir? Le cas de Maurice Yaméogo*, Paris: Editions Chaka.

Guissou, Basile (1995a) *Burkina Faso: un espoir en Afrique*, Paris: L'Harmattan.

Guissou, Basile (1995b) "Militaires et militarisme en Afrique: cas du Burkina Faso," *Afrique et développement/Africa Development*, Vol. 20, No. 2, pp. 55–75.

Gurr, Ted (1968) "Psychological Factors in Civil Violence," *World Politics*, Vol. 20, No. 2, January, pp. 245–278.

Gurr, Ted (1970) *Why Men Rebel*, Princeton, NJ: Princeton University Press.

Hagberg, Sten (2002) "'Enough Is Enough': An Ethnography of the Struggle Against Impunity in Burkina Faso," *Journal of Modern African Studies*, Vol. 40, No. 2, pp. 217–246.

Hannequin, Brigitte (1990) "Etat, patriarcat et développement: le cas d'un village mossi du Burkina Faso," *Canadian Journal of African Studies*, Vol. 24, No. 1, pp. 36–49.

Harrison, Paul (1987) *The Greening of Africa*, Harmondsworth: Penguin.

Harsch, Ernest (1987a) "Burkina Faso: Literacy and Freedom," *West Africa*, 1 June.

Harsch, Ernest (1987b) "Burkina: 'Sankara or No One'," *West Africa*, 2 November.

Harsch, Ernest (1989) "Burkina Faso: How Popular Is the Front?," *Africa Report*, Vol. 34, No. 1, January–February, pp. 56–61.

Harsch, Ernest (1991) "Burkina Secures Adjustment Deal," *Africa Recovery* (United Nations), Vol. 5, No. 1, pp. 18–19.

Harsch, Ernest (1998) "Burkina Faso in the Winds of Liberalisation," *Review of African Political Economy*, Vol. 25, No. 78, December, pp. 639–640.

Harsch, Ernest (1999) "Trop, c'est trop!: Civil Insurgence in Burkina Faso, 1998–99," *Review of African Political Economy*, Vol. 26, No. 81, pp. 395–406.

Harsch, Ernest (2012) "An African Spring in the Making: Protest and Voice Across a Continent," *Whitehead Journal of Diplomacy and International Relations*, Vol. 13, No. 1, Winter/Spring, pp. 45–61.

Harsch, Ernest (2013) "The Legacies of Thomas Sankara: A Revolutionary Experience in Retrospect," *Review of African Political Economy*, Vol. 40, No. 137, pp. 358–374.

Harsch, Ernest (2014) *Thomas Sankara: An African Revolutionary*, Athens, OH: Ohio University Press.

Harsch, Ernest (2016) "Blowing the Same Trumpet? Pluralist Protest in Burkina Faso," *Social Movement Studies*, Vol. 15, No. 2, pp. 231–238.

Harsch, Ernest (2017) "Burkina Faso Looks to Its Neighbors for Help in Battling a Domestic Jihadi Threat," *World Politics Review*, 1 March.

"Haute-Volta: le coup d'état du 7 novembre 1982" (1982) *Afrique contemporaine*, Vol. 21, No. 124, November–December, pp. 23–24.

"Haute-Volta: les raisons sociales d'un coup d'état" (1983) *Politique africaine*, No. 9, March, pp. 85–90.

Hilgers, Mathieu (2006) "Voter à Koudougou: la soumission d'une ville rebelle?," *Politique africaine*, No. 101, March–April, pp. 42–62.

Hilgers, Mathieu (2008) "Politiques urbaines, contestation et décentralisation: lotissement et représentations sociales au Burkina Faso," *Autrepart*, Vol. 3, No. 47, pp. 209–226.

Hilgers, Mathieu, and Augustin Loada (2013) "Tensions et protestations dans un régime semi-autoritaire: croissances des révolts populaires et maintien du pouvoir au Burkina Faso," *Politique africaine*, No. 131, pp. 187–208.

Hilgers, Mathieu, and Jacinthe Mazzocchetti (2006) "L'après-Zongo: entre ouverture politique et fermeture des possibles," *Politique africaine*, No. 101, March–April, pp. 5–18.

Hilgers, Mathieu, and Jacinthe Mazzocchetti, eds. (2010) *Révoltes et oppositions dans un régime semi-autoritaire: le cas du Burkina Faso*, Paris: Karthala.

Hodgkin, Thomas (1957) *Nationalism in Colonial Africa*, New York: New York University Press.

Holston, James (2008) *Insurgent Citizenship: Disjunctions of Democracy and Modernity in Brazil*, Princeton, NJ: Princeton University Press.

International Court of Justice (1986) *Case Concerning the Frontier Dispute (Burkina Faso/Republic of Mali)*, The Hague: 22 December.

International Crisis Group (2013) *Burkina Faso: With or Without Compaoré, Times of Uncertainty*, Brussels: Africa Report No. 205.

International Crisis Group (2016) *Burkina Faso: Preserving the Religious Balance*, Brussels: Africa Report No. 240.

International Monetary Fund (1992) *Government Finance Statistics Yearbook*, Washington, DC.

International Monetary Fund (2014a) *Burkina Faso: Country Report*, No. 14/215, July.

International Monetary Fund (2014b) *Burkina Faso: Selected Issues*, County Report No. 14/230, July.

International Monetary Fund (2015) "Second and Third Reviews under the Extended Credit Arrangement," *Burkina Faso Country Report*, No. 15/202, July.

International Telecommunications Union (2013) "Percentage of Individuals using the Internet 2000–2012," Geneva, June.

Irwin, Paul (1981) *Liptako Speaks: History from Oral Tradition in Africa*, Princeton, NJ: Princeton University Press.

Izard, Michel (1984) "The Peoples and Kingdoms of the Niger Bend and the Volta Basin from the 12th to the 16th Century," in D.T. Niane, ed., *General History of Africa, Vol. IV: Africa from the Twelfth to the Sixteenth Century*, Paris: UNESCO; Berkeley: University of California Press, pp. 211–237.

Izard, Michel (1985a) *Gens du pouvoir, gens de la terre: les institutions politiques de l'ancien royaume du Yatenga (Bassin de la Volta Blanche)*, Cambridge: Cambridge University Press; Paris: Editions de la maison des sciences de l'homme.

Izard, Michel (1985b) *Le Yatenga précolonial: un ancien royaume du Burkina*, Paris: Karthala.

Jacob, Jean-Pierre (2001) "Introduction à la thématique des rapports entre corruption et sociétés anciennes," in Alain Sanou, Pierre Bouda, Lazare K-Zerbo, and Jean-Pierre Jacob, *Morale et corruption dans des sociétés anciennes du Burkina*, Ouagadougou: Réseau national de lutte anti-corruption, pp. 6–24.

Jaffré, Bruno (1989) *Burkina Faso: les années Sankara, de la révolution à la rectification*, Paris: Editions L'Harmattan.

Jaffré, Bruno (2007) *Biographie de Thomas Sankara: la patrie ou la mort...*, 2nd edition, Paris: L'Harmattan.

Jaffré, Bruno (2009) "Que sait-on sur l'assassinat de Sankara?," http://thomassankara.net.

Jaffré, Bruno (2015) "Burkina: 'Allons seulement' aux élections," 27 November, https://blogs.mediapart.fr/bruno-jaffre/blog,

Jaglin, Sylvy (1995) *Gestion urbaine partagée à Ouagadougou: pouvoirs et périphéries (1983–1991)*, Paris: Editions Karthala and Editions de l'ORSTOM.

Jaglin, Sylvy (1996) "De la défense révolutionnaire à la gestion urbaine: 'le cercle des CR disparus'," in René Otayek, Filiga Michel Sawadogo, and Jean-Pierre Guingané, eds., *Le Burkina entre révolution et démocratie (1983–1993)*, Paris: Karthala, pp. 247–274.

Johnston, Hank (2011) *States and Social Movements*, Cambridge: Polity Press.

Joseph, Richard (1987) *Democracy and Prebendal Politics in Nigeria: The Rise and Fall of the Second Republic*, Cambridge: Cambridge University Press.

Kambou, G. Benoît (1988) "Le decentralisation au Burkina Faso: mythe ou realité?," *Revue burkinabè de droit*, No. 14, July, pp. 379–389.

Kambou-Ferrand, Jeanne-Marie (1993) *Peuples voltaïques et conquête coloniale, 1885–1914, Burkina Faso*, Paris: Editions l'Harmattan.

Kanse, Mathias S. (1989) "Le CNR et les femmes: de la difficulté de liberer la 'moitié du ciel'," *Politique africaine*, No. 33, March, pp. 66–72.

Kevane, Michael (2014) *Women and Development in Africa: How Gender Works*, Boulder, CO: Lynne Rienner Publishers.

Ki-Zerbo, Joseph (1972) *Histoire de l'Afrique*, Paris: Hatier.

Kiemde, Paul (1996) "Réflexions sur le référendum constitutionnel et les élections présidentielle et législatives de 1991 et 1992," in René Otayek, Filiga Michel Sawadogo, and Jean-Pierre Guingané, eds., *Le Burkina entre révolution et démocratie (1983–1993)*, Paris: Karthala, pp. 353–369.

Klitgaard, Robert (1988) *Controlling Corruption*, Berkeley: University of California Press.

Kohler, Jean-Marie (1971) *Activités agricoles et changements sociaux dans l'ouest-Mossi*, Paris: ORSTOM.

Koumba, Barry (1990) "Popular Participation in Burkina Faso: Contribution of the Peasant Society," Addis Ababa: UN Economic Commission for Africa, E/ECA/ICPP/90/27.

Labazée, Pascal (1985) "Réorganisation économique et résistances sociales: la question des alliances au Burkina," *Politique africaine*, No. 20, December, pp. 10–28.

Labazée, Pascal (1986) "Une nouvelle phase de la révolution au Burkina Faso," *Politique africaine*, No. 24, December, pp. 114–120.

Labazée, Pascal (1988) *Entreprises et entrepreneurs du Burkina Faso*, Paris: Karthala.

Lampué, Pierre (1979) "Droit écrit et droit coutumier en Afrique francophone," *Penant*, Vol. 89, No. 765, July–September, pp. 245–287.

Lamy, E. (1989) "Droit coutumier—droit positif: intégration ou rupture," *Revue burkinabè de droit*, No. 15, January, pp. 71–87.

Lecaillon, Jacques, and Christian Morrisson (1985) *Economic Policies and Agricultural Performance: The Case of Burkina Faso*, Paris: Development Centre of the Organization for Economic Co-operation and Development.

Lemarchand, René (1988) "The State, the Parallel Economy, and the Changing Structure of Patronage Systems," in Donald Rothchild and Naomi Chazan, eds., *The Precarious Balance: State & Society in Africa*, Boulder, CO and London: Westview Press, pp. 149–170.

Le Moal, Guy, ed. (1967) *Colloque sue les cultures voltaïque*, Paris: Centre national de la recherche scientifique; Ouagadougou: Centre voltaïque de la recherche scientifique.

Lippens, Philippe (1972) *La République de Haute-Volta*, Paris: Editions Berger-Levrault.

Loada, Augustin (1996) "Blaise Compaoré ou l'architecte d'un nouvel order politique," in René Otayek, Filiga Michel Sawadogo, and Jean-Pierre Guingané, eds., *Le Burkina entre révolution et démocratie (1983–1993)*, Paris: Karthala, pp. 277–297.

Loada, Augustin (1998) "Les élections législatives burkinabè du 11 mai 1997: des 'élections pas comme les autres'?," *Politique africaine*, No. 69, March, pp. 62–74.

Loada, Augustin (1999) "Réflexion sur la société civile en Afrique: le Burkina de l'après-Zongo," *Politique africaine*, No. 76, pp. 136–150.

Loada, Augustin (2006) "L'élection présidentielle du 13 novembre 2005: un plébiscite par défaut," *Politique africaine*, No. 101, March–April, pp. 19–41.

Loada, Augustin (2010) "Contrôler l'opposition dans un régime semi-autoritaire: le cas du Burkina Faso de Blaise Compaoré," in Mathieu Hilgers and Jacinthe Mazzocchetti, eds., *Révoltes et oppositions dans un régime semi-autoritaire: le cas du Burkina Faso*, Paris: Karthala, pp. 269–294.

Lompo, Myemba Benoît (1995) *Les Tribunaux départementaux et les Tribunaux d'arrondissements au Burkina Faso*, Ouagadougou: Sankofa Editions.

McAdam, Doug, John D. McCarthy, and Mayer Zald, eds. (1996) *Comparative Perspectives on Social Movements: Political Opportunities, Mobilizing Structures and Cultural Framings*, Cambridge: Cambridge University Press.

McAdam, Doug, Sidney Tarrow, and Charles Tilly (2001) *Dynamics of Contention*, Cambridge: Cambridge University Press.

Mamdani, Mahmood (1996) *Citizen and Subject: Contemporary Africa and the Legacy of Late Colonialism*, Princeton, NJ: Princeton University Press.

Marçais, Marcel (1964) "L'Ecole national d'administration de la République de Haute Volta," *Penant*, Vol. 74, No. 702, July–September, pp. 321–329.

Marchal, Jean-Yves, ed., (1980) *Chroniques d'un cercle de l'A.O.F.: recueil d'archives du poste de Ouahigouya (Haute Volta), 1908–1941*, Paris: ORSTOM.

Martens, Ludo (1989) *Sankara, Compaoré et la révolution burkinabè*, Anvers, Belgium: Editions EPO.

Massa, Gabriel, and Y. George Madiéga, eds. (1995) *La Haute-Volta coloniale: témoignages, recherches, regards*, Paris: Editions Karthala.

Mazzocchetti, Jacinthe (2006) "'Quand les poussins se réunissent, ils font peur à l'épervier...': les étudiants burkinabè en politique," *Politique africaine*, No. 101, March–April, pp. 83–101.

Mazzocchetti, Jacinthe (2010) "Entre espoirs et désillusions: représentations politiques des étudiants burkinabè," in Mathieu Hilgers and Jacinthe Mazzocchetti, eds., *Révoltes et oppositions dans un régime semi-autoritaire: le cas du Burkina Faso*, Paris: Karthala, pp. 205–222.

Meerpoel, A. (1988) "Rapport général," *Revue burkinabè de droit*, No. 13, January, pp. 298–310.

Meyer, Pierre (1988) "L'évolution du dualisme des juridictions," *Revue burkinabè de droit*, No. 13, January, pp. 39-68.

Meyer, Pierre, and Filiga Michel Sawadogo (1986) "Le nouveau code des investissement au Burkina: changement ou continuité?," *Revue burkinabè de droit*, No. 9, January, pp. 35–62.

Migdal, Joel S. (1988) *Strong Societies and Weak States: State–Society Relations and State Capabilities in the Third World*, Princeton, NJ: Princeton University Press.

Migdal, Joel S., Atul Kohli, and Vivienne Shue, eds. (1994) *State Power and Social Forces: Domination and Transformation in the Third World*, Cambridge: Cambridge University Press.

Ministry of Economy and Development (2002) *Poverty Reduction Strategy Paper: Progress Report 2001*, September.

Ministry of Economy and Development (2006) *Priority Action Programme for PRSP Implementation: 2005 Implementation Report*, Ouagadougou, April.

Ministry of Health and UNICEF (1985) "Vaccination Commando in Burkina Faso: The

Spearhead for Accelerated EPI and PHC," *Assignment Children*, Vol. 69, No. 72, pp. 301–327.

Ministry of Justice (2001) "Strategie et plan d'action national pour la reforme de la justice au Burkina Faso, 2002–2006," Ouagadougou.

Mitterrand, François (1990) "Allocution prononcée par M. François Mitterrand, Président de la République, a l'occasion de la séance solennelle d'ouverture de la 16ème conference des chefs d'Etats de France et d'Afrique," La Baule, France, 20 June.

Mkandawire, Thandika, and Charles C. Soludo (1999) *Our Continent, Our Future: African Perspectives on Structural Adjustment*, Trenton, NJ: Africa World Press.

Mouvement des démocrates progressistes [1988] *Declaration de soutien au Front populaire (F.P.)*, Ouagadougou: Executive Bureau of the MDP.

Muase, Charles Kabeya (1989a) *Syndicalisme et démocratie en Afrique noire: L'expérience du Burkina Faso (1936–1988)*, Paris: Editions Karthala; Abidjan: INADES Edition.

Muase, Charles Kabeya (1989b) "Un pouvoir des travailleurs peut-il être contre les syndicats," *Politique africaine*, No. 33, March, pp. 50–58.

Natielsé, Julien K. (2009) *The APRM Process in Burkina Faso*, Dakar: Open Society Initiative for West Africa.

Nikiema, Aimé (1983) "Une fonction publique de développement?," *Revue burkinabè de droit*, No. 15, January, pp. 121–129.

Novicki, Margaret A. (1986) "Burkina Faso: Transforming the Statistics," *Africa Report*, Vol. 31, No. 3, May–June, pp. 68–72.

Olukoshi, Adebayo O. (2003) "The Elusive Prince of Denmark: Structural Adjustment and the Crisis of Governance in Africa," in Thandika Mkandawire and Charles C. Soludo, eds., *African Voices on Structural Adjustment*, Trenton, NJ: Africa World Press, pp. 229–273.

Olukoshi, Adebayo O., and Liisa Laakso, eds. (1996) *Challenges to the Nation-State in Africa*, Uppsala: Nordiska Afrikainstitutet.

Otayek, René (1985) "The Revolutionary Process in Burkina Faso: Breaks and Continuities," *Journal of Communist Studies*, Vol. 1, Nos. 3–4, September–December, pp. 82–100.

Otayek, René (1989) "Rectification," *Politique africaine*, No. 33, March, pp. 2–10.

Otayek, René, Filiga Michel Sawadogo, and Jean-Pierre Guingané, eds. (1996) *Le Burkina entre révolution et démocratie (1983–1993)*, Paris: Karthala.

Ouattara, Soungalo (2007) *Governance et libertés locales: pour une renaissance de l'Afrique*, Paris: Editions Karthala.

Ouattara, Vincent (2004) *Procès des putschistes à Ouagadougou*, Ouagadougou: Imprimerie du progrès.

Ouédraogo, Bernard Lédéa (1990) *Entraide villageoise et développement: groupements paysans au Burkina Faso*, Paris: L'Harmattan.

Ouédraogo, Emile (2014) *Advancing Military Professionalism in Africa*, Washington, DC: Africa Center for Strategic Studies, Research Paper No. 6, July.

Ouédraogo, Tidiane, and Martine Yabré (2015) *Analyse genre des acteurs de l'insurrection des 30 et 31 octobre 2014 au Burkina Faso: Rapport final*, Ouagadougou: Association d'appui et d'eveil Pugsada.

Owona, Joseph (1979) "La constitution de la III[e] république voltaïque du 21 Octobre 1977: retour au parlementarisme rationnalisé et au multipartisme limité," *Penant*, Vol. 88, No. 765, July–September, pp. 309–328.

Pacere, Titinga Frédéric (1981) *Ainsi on a assassiné tous les Mossé*, Sherbrooke, Quebec: Editions Naaman.

"Permanences: Mardi 5 janvier 1999" (1999) *Politique africaine*, No. 74, p. 180.

Queneudec, Jean-Pierre (1988) "Le régelement du différend frontalier Burkina Faso/Mali par la Cour internationale de justice," *Revue juridique et politique, indépendance et coopération*, Vol. 42, No. 1, January–February, pp. 29–41.

Ren-Lac (2000–2012) *Etat de la corruption au Burkina Faso*, annual reports, Réseau national de lutte anti-corruption, Ouagadougou.

Roussillon, Henry (1987) "Brèves remarques sur un couple contesté, 'décentralisation et développment,' l'exemple du Burkina Faso," in Ecole nationale d'administration et de magistrature, *Administration et développement au Burkina Faso*, Toulouse: Presses de l'institut d'études politiques de Toulouse, pp. 185–193.

Saint-Girons, Bernard (1987) "A propos de la notion d'etablissement public en droit burkinabè," in Ecole nationale d'administration et de magistrature, *Administration et développement au Burkina Faso*, Toulouse: Presses de l'institut d'études politiques de Toulouse, pp. 195–203.

Sankara, Thomas (1983) "Discours prononcé par le capitaine Thomas Sankara, nommé ultérieurement Premier ministre de Haute-Volta, devant le congrès du SUVESS," *Politique africaine*, No. 9, March, pp. 90–92.

Sankara, Thomas (1991) *Oser inventer l'avenir: la parole de Sankara*, Paris: Pathfinder and L'Harmattan.

Sankara, Thomas (2007) *Thomas Sankara Speaks: The Burkina Faso Revolution, 1983–87*, 2nd edition, New York: Pathfinder Press.

Sanou, Alain (2010) "La révolte des autochtones bobo contre les autorité municipales," in Mathieu Hilgers and Jacinthe Mazzocchetti, eds., *Révoltes et oppositions dans un régime semi-autoritaire: le cas du Burkina Faso*, Paris: Karthala, pp. 119–132.

Saul, Mahir (1987) "The Organization of a West Africa Grain Market," *American Anthropologist*, Vol. 89, No. 1, March, pp. 74–95.

Saul, Mahir, and Patrick Royer (2001) West African Challenge to the Empire: Culture and History in the Volta-Bani Anticolonial War, Athens, OH: Ohio University Press; Oxford: and James Currey.

Savadogo, Kimseyinga, and Claude Wetta (1992) "The Impact of Self-imposed Adjustment: The Case of Burkina Faso, 1983–9," in Giovanni Andrea Cornia, Rolph van der Hoeven, and Thandika Mkandawire, eds., *Africa's Recovery in the 1990s: From Stagnation and Adjustment to Human Development*, New York: St. Martin's Press, pp. 53–71.

Savonnet, Georges (1976) *Les Birifor de Diépla et sa region insulaires du rameau lobi (Haute-Volta)*, Paris: ORSTOM.

Savonnet-Guyot, Claudette (1986) *Etat et sociétés au Burkina: essai sur le politique africain*, Karthala: Paris.

Sawadogo, Filiga Michel (1996) "L'élaboration de la Constitution de la Quatrième République," in René Otayek, Filiga Michel Sawadogo, and Jean-Pierre Guingané, eds., *Le Burkina entre révolution et démocratie (1983–1993)*, Paris: Karthala pp. 311–323.

Sawadogo, Raogo Antoine (2001) *L'Etat africain face à la décentralisation*, Paris: Editions Karthala and Club du Sahel et de l'Afrique de l'Ouest.

Secrétariat général national des CDR (1986) *Première conférence nationale des Comités de défense de la révolution: documents finaux*, Ouagadougou: Imprimerie presses africaines.

Schmidt, Steffen W., Laura Guasti, Carl H. Landé, and James C. Scott, eds. (1977) *Friends, Followers, and Factions: A Reader in Political Clientelism*, Berkeley: University of California Press.

Sierra Leone (2004), *Truth and Reconciliation Commission's Report*, Freetown: October.

Six S (1987) *De la pratique communautaire à la gestion cooperative réelle: rapport d'étude*, Milan: FOCSIV.

Skinner, Elliott P. (1964) *The Mossi of the Upper Volta: The Political Development of a Sudanese People*, Stanford, CA: Stanford University Press.

Skurnik, W.A.E. (1970) "The Military and Politics: Dahomey and Upper Volta," in Claude E. Welch, Jr., ed., *Soldier and State in Africa: A Comparative Analysis of Military Intervention and Political Change*, Evanston, IL: Northwestern University Press, pp. 62–121.

Sneyd, Adam (2015) "The Poverty of 'Poverty Reduction': The Case of African Cotton," *Third World Quarterly*, Vol. 36, No. 1, pp. 55–74.

Somda, Ernest (1987) *Dissin: marche des paysans vers l'autonomie*, Milan: FOCSIV.

Somé, Valère D. (1990) *Thomas Sankara: l'espoir assassiné*, Paris: L'Harmattan.

Somé, Valère D. [2015] *Les nuits froids de décembre (l'exil ou… la mort)*, Ouagadougou: Editions du millennium.

Somé, Valère D. (2016) *Recueil de textes politiques*, Ouagadougou: Editions du millennium.

South African Broadcasting Corporation (2015) "Question Time," Interview with Issaka Traoré, 1 April.

Sy, Chériff (2015a) "L'appel de la Patrie du Président du CNT," Ouagadougou: Conseil national de la transition, 16 September.

Sy, Chériff (2015b) "Discours du PCNT à la cérémonie de clôture de la session parlementaire unique du Conseil National de la Transition, Ouagadougou, le lundi 28 décembre 2015," Ouagadougou: Conseil national de la transition.

Syndicat autonome des magistrats burkinabè (1984) *Le Journal du Syndicat autonome des magistrats burkinabè*, Ouagadougou, No. 2.

Tallet, Bernard (1985) "Espaces ethniques et migrations: comment gérer le mouvement?," *Politique africaine*, No. 20, December, pp. 65–77.

Tarrow, Sidney (1998) *Power in Movement: Social Movements and Contentious Politics*, 2nd edition, Cambridge: Cambridge University Press.

Theobald, Robin (1990) *Corruption, Development and Underdevelopment*, London: MacMillan.

Thompson, Virginia, and Richard Adloff (1969) *French West Africa*, New York: Greenwood Press.

Tilly, Charles (1978) *From Mobilization to Revolution*, New York: Random House.

Tilly, Charles (1992) *Coercion, Capital, and European States, AD 990–1992*, Cambridge, MA: Blackwell Publishers.

Tilly, Charles (1995a) *European Revolutions, 1492–1992*, Oxford: Blackwell Publishers.

Tilly, Charles (1995b) *Popular Contention in Great Britain, 1758–1834*, Cambridge, MA: Harvard University Press.

Tilly, Charles, and Sidney Tarrow (2007) *Contentious Politics*, Boulder, CO: Paradigm Publishers.

United Nations (2000a) *Report of the Panel of Experts on Violations of Security Council Sanctions Against UNITA*, S/2000/203, 10 March.

United Nations (2000b) *Report of the Panel of Experts Appointed Pursuant to UN Security Council Resolution 1306 (2000), Paragraph 19 in Relation to Sierra Leone*, S/2000/1195, 20 December.

United Nations (2009), *Final Report of the Group of Experts on Côte d'Ivoire pursuant to paragraph 11 of Security Council resolution 1842 (2008)*, S/2009/521, 9 October.

United Nations Development Programme (1997) *Rapport sur le développement humain durable: Burkina Faso*, Ouagadougou.

United Nations Development Programme (2007) *Rapport sur le développement humain durable: Burkina Faso*, Ouagadougou.

United States (2005–2012) *Foreign Military Training, Joint Report to Congress*, Departments of Defense and State, fiscal years 2005–06 to 2012–13.

Vaast, Marion (2010) "Le recours à la chefferie moaga dans la commune de Kaya: stratégies personnelles ou opposition populaire?," in Mathieu Hilgers and Jacinthe Mazzocchetti, eds., *Révoltes et oppositions dans un régime semi-autoritaire: le cas du Burkina Faso*, Paris: Karthala, pp. 51–65.

Weber, Max (1978) *Economy and Society*, Vol. 1, Berkeley, CA: University of California Press.

Wise, Christopher (1998) "Chronicle of a Student Strike in Africa: The Case of Burkina Faso, 1996–1997," *African Studies Review*, Vol. 41, No. 2, September, pp. 19–32.

World Bank (1995) *African Development Indicators, 1994–95*, Washington.

World Bank (2000) *World Development Indicators 2000*, Washington, CD ROM version.

Yarba, Larba (1980) "Le Tripartisme dans le droit public voltaïque," *Le Mois en Afrique*, Vol. 15, No. 174–175, June–July, pp. 114–129.

Yé, Bongnessan Arsène (1995) *Burkina Faso: les fondements politiques de la IV*[e] République, Ouagadougou: Presses universitaires de Ouagadougou.

Yonaba, Salif (1986) "La procedure sous le Conseil national de la révolution: tradition ou innovation?," *Revue burkinabè de droit*, No. 10, June, pp. 159–162.

Yonaba, Salif (1988) "L'apport de la zatu N° AN-IV-021/CNR-BUD/REFI du 1er janvier 1987 portant zatu de finances pour l'exercice du budget de l'état—exercice 1987—à la définition du détournement de deniers publics en droit financier burkinabè," *Revue burkinabè de droit*, No. 14, July, pp. 365–374.

Young, Crawford (1991) "Democratization in Africa: Contradictions of a Political Imperative," paper presented to the Annual Meeting of the African Studies Association, St. Louis, Missouri, 23–26 November.

Zagré, Pascal (1994) *Les politiques économiques du Burkina Faso: une tradition d'ajustement structurel*, Paris: Karthala.

Zahan, Dominique (1967) "The Mossi Kingdoms," in Daryll Forde and P.M. Kaberry, eds., *West African Kingdoms in the Nineteenth Century*, London: Oxford University Press, pp. 152–178.

Zaum, Dominik (2012) "Statebuilding and Governance: The Conundrums of Legitimacy and Local Ownership," in Devon Curtis and Gwinyayi Dzinesa, eds, *Peace, Power, and Politics in Africa*, Athens: Ohio University Press, pp. 47–62.

Zongo, G. Jean Luc (2011) "Sciences et politiques institutionnelles au Burkina Faso: élaboration et réformes de la Constitution de la IVème République," Master of Advanced Study (DEA), University of Ouagadougou.

## SELECTED PERIODICALS, NEWS SOURCES

AFP (Agence France-Presse, Paris, www.afp.com)
AIB (Agence d'information du Burkina, Ouagadougou, www.aib.bf)
*Bayiri* (Ouagadougou, www.bayiri.com)
*Bendré* (Ouagadougou)
*Burkina 24* (Ouagadougou, www.burkina24.com)
*Carrefour africain* (Ouagadougou)
EIU (Economist Intelligence Unit, London, www.eiu.com)
FBIS (Foreign Broadcast Information Service, Washington, DC)
*Jeune Afrique* (Paris, www.jeuneafrique.com)
*Journal du jeudi* (Ouagadougou, www.journaldujeudi.com)
*Journal du soir* (Ouagadougou)
*La lettre du continent* (Paris, www.africaintelligence.fr)
*Le Faso.net* (Ouagadougou, www.lefaso.net)
*Les echos du Faso* (Ouagadougou, www.lesechosdufaso.net)
*L'Evénement* (Ouagadougou, www.evenement-bf.net)
*L'Indépendant* (Ouagadougou)
*L'Intrus* (Ouagadougou)
*L'Observateur/L'Observateur Paalga* (Ouagadougou, www.lobservateur.bf)
*Le Monde* (Paris, www.lemonde.fr)

*Le Pays* (Ouagadougou, www.lepays.bf)
*Le Reporter* (Ouagadougou, www.reporterbf.net)
*L'Unité* (Ouagadougou)
*Lolowulen* (Ouagadougou)
*Marchés tropicaux et méditerranéens* (Paris)
*Mutations* (Ouagadougou, www.mutationsbf.net)
RTB (Radiodiffusion télévision du Burkina, Ouagadougou, www.rtb.bf)
*San Finna* (Ouagadougou)
*Sidwaya* (Ouagadougou, www.sidwaya.bf)

## AUTHOR'S INTERVIEWS

Bambara, Serge ("Smockey"), Balai citoyen leader, by email, 28 April 2016.
Bazié, Bassolma, CGTB general secretary, Ouagadougou, 24 February 2016.
Compaoré, Aristide, CDR leader, Ouagadougou, 14 March 1985.
Compaoré, Léonard, CNR minister of peasant affairs, Ouagadougou, 5 March 1987.
Coulibaly, Siaka, political analyst, Ouagadougou, 16 February 2016.
Diallo, Ismael, FRC spokesperson, Ouagadougou, 11 February 2016.
Guissou, Basile, CNR foreign minister, Ouagadougou, 12 March 1985.
Kyélem de Tambèla, Apollinaire J., lawyer, Ouagadougou, 12 February 2016.
Monné, Laurent, CAR secretary-general, Ouagadougou, 17 February 2016.
Natama, Jean Baptiste, CDR leader, Pô, 16 March 1985.
Ouali, Louis Armand, UPC leader, Ouagadougou, 18 February 2016.
Ouédraogo, Ernest Nongma, former CNR interior minister, Ouagadougou, 4 March 1999.
Ouédraogo, Fousséni, MBDC president, Ouagadougou, 23 February 2016.
Ouédraogo, Halidou, MBDHP president, Ouagadougou, 26 February 1999.
Ouédraogo, Pierre, CDR secretary-general, Ouagadougou, 15 March 1985; 12 March 1987.
Ouédraogo, Youssouf, CNR minister of planning, Ouagadougou, 15 March 1985.
Ouattara, Charles Lona, UPC leader, Ouagadougou, 27 February 2016.
Ouattara, Hervé, CAR president, Ouagdougou, 10 February 2016.
Sana, Aziz, Mouvement ça suffit coordinator-general, Ouagadougou, 9 February 2016.
Sankara, Bénéwendé, UNIR/PS president, Ouagadougou, 22 February 2016.
Sankara, Thomas, CNR president, New York, 2 October 1984; Ouagadougou, 17 March 1985.
Sanogo, Guézuma, AJB president, Ouagadougou, 18 February 2016.
Sawadogo, Lookman, SEP president, Ouagadougou, 27 February 2016.
Somda, Marie Madeleine, Cofedec leader, Ouagadougou, 17 February 2016.
Tankoano, Marcel, M21 president, Ouagadougou, 11 February 2016.
Traoré, Fayçal, MBDC project coordinator, Ouagadougou, 23 February 2016.
Wetta, Claude, Ren-lac executive secretary, Ouagadougou, 23 February 2016.

# INDEX